THE
TRADING GAME

THE
TRADING
GAME

A Confession

GARY STEVENSON

**CROWN
CURRENCY**
New York

Published in the United States by Crown Currency, an imprint of
the Crown Publishing Group, a division of Penguin Random House LLC,
New York.

CROWN is a registered trademark and CROWN CURRENCY and
colophon are trademarks of Penguin Random House LLC.

Simultaneously published in Great Britain by Allen Lane,
an imprint of Penguin Random House Ltd., London.

Hardback ISBN 978-0-593-72721-8
Ebook ISBN 978-0-593-72722-5

Printed in the United States of America on acid-free paper

currencybooks.com

9 8 7 6 5 4 3 2 1

FIRST U.S. EDITION

Book design by Ralph Fowler

For all the cold kids and the hungry kids,
who dream of being millionaires.
I did it for me so I did it for you.

Contents

Prologue xi

One
GOING UP 1

Two
YOU WANT SOME? 47

Three
GO HOME AND ASK YOUR MUM 135

Four
THERMOSTAT 173

Five
GOING DOWN 239

Postscript 331
Acknowledgments 333

"In a mad world, only the mad are sane."
—Akira Kurosawa

"Life is life, game is a game."
—Anish's grandad

Prologue

"I WANT TO TELL YOU A STORY."

Caleb's oversized face loomed over the table. Beneath it sat two ramen bowls. One empty, one full. A few stray wisps of steam floated upward, where they danced with his beaming white smile. From where I was sitting, slumped down low in my chair, the two chopsticks jutting upward from my bowl seemed to reach nearly up to his chin. His smile grew.

"I used to know a really good trader. A really, really good trader. He used to work for Deutsche Bank. Smart guy. Young. Just like you."

Caleb's thick forearms were wrapped around his warm, empty bowl, and they pushed down, hard, into the table. His hands were not far from my face now, clasped tightly together. I've never forgotten how those fingers looked. Thick, round and pink, like raw sausages. They looked ready to burst.

"You know, he was a really good trader, this guy. Made a lot of money. Made a lot of money for himself, made a lot of money for Deutsche Bank. He had a good career ahead of him."

The hubbub of the restaurant filled the space around us. It wasn't one of those rustic, hole-in-the-wall ramen joints that seem to birth themselves in the back alleys of Japan's big cities. This was a big, sprawling, corporate restaurant on the sixth floor of a big, sprawling, corporate skyscraper. Loose-tied businessmen clinked beer glasses with their bosses, laughing at their jokes. A few American bankers mixed in with the Japanese salaryman types, talking too much and too loudly. I wasn't talking at all. I was watching that oversized face float through the darkness, across the table, toward me.

"But you know, this guy, this young trader. Even though he was a good trader, he had one really serious problem. One fatal flaw, you could say . . . You see, this guy, he thought he could walk away. He thought he could leave. Do you know what I mean?"

Caleb was a big guy. I've probably made that clear by now, but it wasn't just his face and his fingers that were big. Everything about him seemed about two sizes bigger than it should have been. His eyebrows were big, his chin was big. Somehow, the hair on his head was too big, too thick, and too dark. More than all of that, his smile was enormous. Huge, white and pearly. Right now it seemed to me to stretch wider than his face. Like the Tuesday night Cheshire cat of the ramen-ya, that smile seemed to shine through the dark of the room.

"So this guy, he decided he was going to take the money and walk away. Leave the industry, you know? Nice idea. Have a family somewhere. Sweet. You see, the thing is, this guy though, he just didn't really understand how this industry works. Deutsche didn't really want to see him leave. You know?"

It didn't take a genius to tell where this conversation was going, and I felt my stomach starting to sink. I began to feel a bit sick, and I could taste or smell something in my mouth. Was it blood? I sat deep in my chair and I watched. Caleb was still smiling. That smile seemed to grow bigger by the minute.

"Anyway, Deutsche Bank went back and had a look, at all of his trades, you know? All of his chat history, all of his emails. He had been working there for a long time, you know, he'd done a lot of trades. And they managed to find some stuff in there that wasn't good stuff. Do you know what I'm talking about? Stuff he shouldn't have done."

I could start to feel fire in my legs now. In my feet. A hot, growing, itchy feeling. A burning. But I didn't move.

"So you know, it wasn't the right thing to do, but Deutsche actually took that trader to court for a few things. He hadn't really done anything that bad, to be honest, but they managed to put something together. The case rumbled through the courts for years and years. Do you know what I mean? In and out of court, in and out of court. Real nightmare. That trader, great young trader, he never really got to leave, you see. Never got to have that family. Just courtrooms. Best years of his life. Can you imagine that, Gary? Can you imagine? The case never went anywhere, but he lost all of his money anyway, in the end. Lawyers' fees. All of his money, and much more besides. In the end, he was bankrupt. In the end, that guy lost everything."

The fire was everywhere now, so was the sickness, and that blood taste. I still didn't move though. I looked up at his face.

"Gary, are you listening to me? Do you understand what I'm saying here?"

That big round face loomed closer still.

"Gary. I like you. I think you're a good person. But sometimes, bad things happen to good people. You are going to learn that. We can make life very difficult for you."

In that moment, a lot of memories came flooding back. Memories that carried me thousands of miles. Away from Tokyo and back to Ilford, East London. I was eighteen and sitting on a football, in a dead cul-de-sac next to the railway, as Harry told me that his mum had cancer. I hadn't known what to say, at the time: "Do you wanna play football?" I remembered being stood up against the wall of an alleyway on a dark night and watching Saravan as he threatened to stab me. His hands were in his pockets. Did he have a knife? I didn't know. I remembered being chased down streets of terraced houses and jumping over garden fences and that time that Brathap got run over and the way that his body shook as it lay on the ground. I remembered all the stupid violence and the blood and the nonsense so much nonsense of the kids on the street and all the promises that I'd made and the people I'd known. I remembered sitting with Jamie on the top of the multistory carpark in the nighttime, watching the new skyscrapers go up around us in our city and telling him that I was gonna be somebody, someday. Promising him that I'd do it. He'd laughed at me, smoking into the moonlight. But he knew that I would though. So did I.

No, I thought. It doesn't end here.

Not here in this cold, corporate restaurant. Not buried down by the weight of that smile.

Part One

GOING UP

1

IN SOME WAYS, I WAS BORN TO BE A TRADER.

At the end of the street I grew up on, in front of the tall, concave wall of a recycling center, a lamp post and a telegraph pole stand four meters apart from one another, forming the perfect set of impromptu goalposts.

If you stand between those two posts, take ten big steps backward and stare upward and between them, into the far distance, the light of the tallest Canary Wharf skyscraper will peek over that high wall, and wink at you.

After school, as a child, I would spend long evenings kicking battered foam footballs in and around those goalposts, wearing battered school shoes and my brother's school uniform. When my mum would come and call me home for dinner, I'd look back and watch that skyscraper wink at me. It seemed to mean some sort of new life.

It wasn't just the streets of East London I shared with those gleaming, towering temples of capitalism. There was something else too, some kind of shared belief. Something about money. Something about want.

The importance of money, and the knowledge that we didn't have much of it, was something I always felt deeply. In one of my earliest memories, my parents gave me a pound coin, and sent me to the Esso garage to buy lemonade. At some point in the trip, I dropped that pound coin, and lost it. In my memory, I searched for that pound coin for what seemed like hours—crawling under cars, scrabbling in the drains— before returning home, empty-handed, and in floods of tears. In reality, it was probably only thirty minutes. But thirty minutes is a long time when you're a child, I guess, and one pound was a lot of money.

I don't know if I ever really lost that love for money. Although, now, when I look back and think about it, I'm not sure that love is the right word. Perhaps, especially when I was a kid, I think it might have been more of a fear. But whether it was fear, or a love, or a hunger, it only got stronger as I started to grow, and I was always chasing those pounds I didn't have. At twelve, I started selling penny sweets in school; at thirteen, I started delivering papers, 364 days a year, for £13 a week. By sixteen, my high school sales business had become considerably more adventurous, more profitable, and more illicit. But those small kills were never really the end game, and every evening, after the sun went down, I'd always look up at those skyscrapers, winking down at me from the end of the street.

But there were many other ways in which I was not born to be a trader, and those ways were and are, very important.

Because there are many, many, young, hungry, ambitious boys kicking broken footballs around lamp posts and cars in the shadows of East London's skyscrapers. Many of them are smart, many of them are committed, almost all of them would make all kinds of sacrifices to put on a tie and some cufflinks and go walk into those tall, shiny towers of money. But if you step onto those trading floors, which take pride of place in those glimmering skyscrapers where young men earn millions of pounds every year in the heart of what was once East London's docklands, you will not hear the proud accents of Millwall and Bow, of Stepney and Mile End and Shadwell and Poplar. I know, because I worked on one of those trading floors. Someone once asked me where my accent was from. He'd just graduated from Oxford.

The Citibank Tower in Canary Wharf has forty-two floors. In 2006, which was the year I first entered that building, it was the joint second-tallest building in the UK. One day, in 2007, I decided to go up to the top floor of the building, to see what the view was like, and to see if I could see my home.

The top floor of the Citibank Center was used only for conferences and events. This meant that, when it was not in use, the entire space sat totally empty. A vast, uninterrupted country of lush blue carpet, bordered on all sides by thick glass windows. I floated across the soundless carpet to the window, but I couldn't see the place where I lived. From the 42nd floor of the Citibank Center, you cannot see East London. You can only see the 42nd floor of the HSBC Tower. The ambitious young children of East London look up to the skyscrapers that cast shadows on their houses, but the skyscrapers don't look back. They look at each other.

This is the story of how I, of all the kids playing football and selling sweets in those shadows, got a job on the Citibank trading floor. It's a story of how I became Citibank's most profitable trader, in the whole world, and it's a story about why, after all of that, I quit.

These were the years when the global economy started to slip off the precipice from which it's still falling. At times, my sanity slipped with it. At times it still does. God knows, I didn't treat everyone the best. Harry, Wizard, JB, myself. All the others who really should have had names. I hope you can forgive me for telling your stories. They're all part of my story, you know?

I'll dedicate it to Anish's grandad, who, when we were drunken teenagers, and he was a drunken old man, would mutter to us endlessly the only sentence that he knew well in English.

"Life is life. Game is a game."

We never really figured out what it meant. I still hope that one day we will.

2

MY PATH TO THE TRADING FLOOR BEGAN AT THE LONDON SCHOOL of Economics.

The London School of Economics is not really a normal university. With no grand, leafy campus, the university buildings camouflage themselves as a cluster of innocuous offices, and secrete themselves down a side alley of London's West End.

In spite of these relatively innocuous surroundings, the global elite funnel their children into the university with astonishing enthusiasm. It seemed that no Russian oligarch, no Pakistani Air Force Commander, and no Chinese Politburo member had missed the opportunity to send an ambitious son, daughter, nephew or niece over to this unremarkable corner of central London to study simultaneous equations for a few years, before flying home to take over the running of the mother country, perhaps with a few years working at Goldman Sachs or Deloitte in between.

In 2005, when I arrived at the university to study Maths and Economics, I was not a typical LSE student. Three years earlier, I had been expelled from my high school for selling exactly £3-worth of cannabis. Before that, I had tried to start a grime music collective; I had had a hoodie custom-made with "MC Gaz" on the front and "Cadaverous Crew" in big, stylized letters on the back. I turned up for my first day of lectures in an Ecko tracksuit of matching blue and white hoodie and jogging bottoms. The white hoodie had a big navy blue rhino emblazoned on the front. I didn't really have much idea, before I got there, of anything about the university. But a kid at school had told me that a degree from the LSE was a one-way ticket to a big-money job in the City, and that had been good enough for me.

Unsurprisingly, I didn't really fit in. The Russian oligarchs didn't eat at halal fried chicken shops. The Singaporeans didn't understand my accent. To save money, I was living with my parents, in Ilford, ten miles east of the university. I had just gotten my first proper girlfriend, who was also from Ilford, and I spent the majority of my first year drinking with her on park benches, sneaking her out of my bedroom window and over the railway tracks when my mum came home from work, and only really going to university for lectures and classes.

Despite that, I was committed to doing well at the LSE. I didn't have any family connections, or any knowledge of the City. I wasn't tall or handsome and I didn't have a nice suit or smooth networking skills. The most impressive extracurriculars on my CV were an extremely uninspired career as a fast-rapping grime MC and two years fluffing pillows at the DFS sofa store in Beckton. But maths had always come naturally to me, so, the way I saw it, there was only one path for me into the City—beat all the Arab billionaires and Chinese industrialists to a top first class degree, and just pray to God that Goldman Sachs noticed.

My plan to achieve this was relatively simple: sit at the front of every lecture and class, and make sure I understood everything that every professor and class teacher said.

The strategy worked pretty effectively, and I finished the first year of the course with a decently high first. If I'm being totally honest, I'd found it pretty easy. I went away for the summer feeling as though my plan might just work.

But when I returned to the LSE for my second year, a couple of things had markedly changed.

Firstly, suddenly, unprecedentedly, and seemingly apropos of nothing, nearly every student in the entire year group had become an intensely studied junior banker. I don't mean to say that everyone had actually secured jobs in the glittering skyscrapers of Canary Wharf or the City, but everyone, totally unexpectedly, to me at least, began to behave as if they had. People started attending Finance Society events on Wednesdays and Fridays, and networking events with the Investment Society on Mondays as well. They began to use sentences consisting almost entirely of three-letter acronyms—ABS, IBD, CDS, CDO, M&A—and talked about "Sales and Trading" and "Securitization." For some inexplicable reason, a large number of people started to attend lectures wearing full business suits. Rumors began to abound that various students, inevitably the tall, broad-chested, finely coiffed, suit-wearing contingent of nationally-ambiguous-clearly-wealthy origin, had already secured illustrious internships at Goldman Sachs, Deutsche Bank, JPMorgan or Lehman Brothers. Some were even rumored to have gotten full-time jobs.

All students started to apply for internships. Not just one or two internships, but fifteen or twenty, sometimes more. Theoretical interview questions began to circulate among the student community, on the alleged basis of having been put to a mythical student from the Statistics or International Relations departments. It became generally accepted knowledge that an interview candidate was likely to be asked how many bald people there were in the state of Virginia. One student was allegedly given five seconds to provide the answer to 49 times 49. All students diligently recorded that it was, of course, 2,401. Inexplicably long queues began to form spontaneously in unpredictable areas of the campus. Usually, most of the queueing students would not be quite certain, when asked, what the queue was actually for. But maybe, at the end of it, someone would get an internship. Maybe there would be a networking opportunity. Large clusters of twenty or so calculator-wielding students began to appear surrounding computers in the library, barking out numbers and letters, communally tackling Morgan Stanley's online numerical tests as a group.

I had no idea how to react to this complete change in the attitude, approach and priorities of the students surrounding me. Many had stopped attending lectures altogether, so as to allow their time and energies to be devoted more completely to the arts of networking, applying for jobs, and learning the language and acronyms of the world of finance. My hitherto successful-seeming strategy of simply turning up for lectures and classes, and fully understanding the course material, began to feel painfully insufficient and naive.

Perplexed, I turned to one of the few good friends that I had gathered in my first year of university: a tall, handsome, British-raised Slovenian boy named Matic, who studied alongside me in the maths department. Whilst Matic had not gone "full business suit," like many of the other students, his manner of dress had notably sharpened. He was a member of the finance societies. He used acronyms. He made applications. He went for interviews. He attended events.

I asked Matic what on earth could possibly have happened over the summer to have wrought such a world-bending change in the student community.

"What do you mean Gary? Don't you know? Second year is internship year!"

So here's how it works. Or, at least, I'll tell you now what Matic told me then.

Everyone at LSE wants to work for Goldman Sachs. Or Deutsche Bank. Or Morgan Stanley. Or JPMorgan. Or UBS.

Not just everyone at LSE, but everyone at Imperial. Also everybody at Warwick. Of course everyone at Nottingham and Durham and Bath. And also the people at Manchester and Birmingham want to work at those places, but they have got no chance, well, unless they know someone in the industry, of course. The people at Oxford and Cambridge want to work there too, at least the ones who aren't rich enough to never have to work.

There are not enough jobs for all of these people. Not even nearly enough. Not only that, but not all jobs are made equal. The best job is "Sales and Trading." That job has the best hours (you only have to work twelve hours a day, plus you get weekends off), and also you can make the money in the quickest time, so long as you're good. If you don't get Sales and Trading, you have to work in IBD or M&A or something working hundred-hour weeks until your soul dies and then longer still. If you don't make that you'll have to work in *"Consulting."*

I had literally no idea what consulting was. From the way that Matic said the word, it might have been cleaning toilets.

There is no way to get a job without an internship, unless you've got contacts, and the only time to get an internship is *now.* If you don't get an internship after second year, you'll have to get an internship after third year. After your internship, 50 percent of interns will get an offer of a full-time job a full year later, so if you interned after third year, you'd be facing a full year of unemployment. But really, that's just theoretical, because no investment bank is going to hire an intern at the end of their third year—they'll know everyone rejected you in second year, and nobody's going to want a rejected intern.

"So that's it. It's make or break. It's do or die. Your future will be decided now. Forget about your "Maths and Economics." You need to know what a CDS is. What's M&A? What's IBD? How can you not know Gary? Everyone knows! And you need to send applications. These internships are ridiculously overapplied, and you don't have any connections. Your only hope of getting one is to apply to at least thirty banks. How many have you applied to so far? None!?!"

None was the answer. I was lost.

I could do maths. I could do economics. But in this new world of acronyms, I had nothing. I'd believed it when the teachers back at school had told me: study hard and do well in your exams and you will get a good job. I had been an idiot. I had been a fool.

Matic was a kindly guy, if a little intense, and he took pity on me. He took me along to a finance society event titled "How to Get a Job at an Investment Bank."

The event, held in one of LSE's grander, older, brighter lecture theaters, was well attended. We were there for a talk given by a former investment banker who looked as if he was taking time off from being an extra in a Hollywood movie about Wall Street. All pinstripes and slicked-back hair and height.

The talk seemed to me a stream-of-consciousness monologue on the theme of hard work, with each sentence pockmarked by those words and acronyms that by now I was *sure* I had heard somewhere, but still didn't quite know the meaning of, as if it was being delivered in a language that I had half-studied at high school and never quite fully learned. The speaker moved constantly and rapidly across the stage and spoke with an unbelievable intensity. The message I came away with was a pretty straightforward one: read everything, know all of these acronyms and their meanings, network everyone, apply everywhere, work always, don't sleep. I'm not sure if that had been exactly the message intended. I left the talk thoroughly depressed.

To Matic's disappointment, and to some extent, my own I think, I gave up on applying for internships. I couldn't do it. I've never been good at memorizing acronyms. It weighed just too much on my soul. Besides, the first stage of the application process was CV and cover letter. Everyone else had been prepping for this since they were about four. They all seemed to have trekked the Sahara, or led the Junior United Nations, or played the fucking oboe at the Royal Albert Hall or some shit. My CV had six years of delivering newspapers, one year as a failed grime rapper, and two years fluffing pillows at a sofa shop next to a sewage works in Beckton. What was the point?

What saved me was the second change in my university experience, which was equally unexpected and inexplicable. When I returned to uni for my second year, people suddenly knew who I was. Students who I had never seen before in my life, even sometimes from the clan of suit-wearers, would approach me in the library and start talking to me. Once, a Chinese student stopped me physically in a corridor, looked me up and down, angrily, wordlessly, for approximately ten seconds, then said nothing, and just walked away. Another time a tall European girl with an ambiguous accent and fantastic hair asked to study with me. None of it made any sense.

In my confusion, I raised this mystery with my friend and fellow student Sagar Malde, a tall, wiry Kenyan Indian boy with a wonderfully florid accent, whose father owned the entire East African soap industry.

"Of course they know!" cried Sagar, as if it was obvious. "They know how you did in your exams."

This answer didn't quite explain the mystery. My results had been good, but, as far as I was aware, they hadn't been public, and besides, they were far from the best in the university. Sagar himself, for example, had done significantly better than me.

"Of course, Gary," he said kindly, when I put that to him, "but no one expects that from you."

Sagar was a lovely boy, we're still good friends. But in that moment I was genuinely shocked. I've always been good at maths, very good, since as far back as I can remember. Everyone in my primary school knew I was good at maths, everyone in my high school knew. I used to enter competitions every now and again, and usually, I'd win. Teachers, family, friends all expected it of me. I had always expected it of myself. Some people might have been jealous of me, but no one had ever been surprised.

Sagar's offhand comment, though, made me realize something for the first time, something which had never even occurred to me before: a lot of rich people expect poor people to be stupid. The LSE first-year economics lectures are enormous, with attendances of over a thousand students. By sitting in the front row during those lectures, wearing a tracksuit and carrying a Nike string backpack, and asking questions in a distinctively East London accent, I had apparently advertised myself to those other, generally wealthier students as a bit of fun, but not really a threat. My first-year results had turned things on their head.

I rolled it around in my head a bit, and I asked myself what should I do. I decided, right then, that I'd show 'em: we're not all stupid, us kids in tracksuits. Yeah, I didn't know what a CDS was, but I could do some maths if I had to. We'll show 'em, yeah we're gonna show 'em. We'll show those guys what we can do.

So while everyone else was applying to thirty-seven investment banks, I set about rather extravagantly showing everyone who would listen how good I was at economics and, particularly, maths. For the first time in my life, I started to study in my spare time. I asked even more questions of the lecturers. I started to challenge them when they made mistakes. I didn't really have any idea if or how it would ever lead me to a career, to be honest, but I wasn't really thinking too much about that, anymore. I just wanted them to know they weren't better than us. Because they're not.

Anyway, one day this kind of strange thing happened. A gangly northern kid from Grimsby, looking about six inches too tall with a thick mop of black hair and a mussed-up business suit, wandered over to me in the library. His name was Luke Blackwood, a fellow Maths student from the year above me.

"Are you Gary?" he asked me, and I told him I was.

"Listen, Citibank have an event next week. It's called "The Trading Game," but it's basically a maths game. If you win it, you can get invited to the national final, and if you win that you get an internship. I heard you're pretty good at maths. You should go."

I had never met Luke before, but he sat down next to me, told me the date and time of the competition, and briefly explained to me the rules of the game. I didn't know anything about trading, but, as Luke said, I didn't have to: it was essentially a relatively simple maths game. After showing me how it worked, Luke got up, and simply walked off, leaving me sitting in front of a blinking computer and a few half-finished A4 pages of maths homework.

I don't know why, maybe I was just cocky and overconfident, but I was immediately pretty sure I was going to win that game. I might not have known anything about CDSs or CDOs or Asset Backed Securities, but I knew about games, and I knew about maths. Here, it seemed to me, was finally a path into the City that didn't require me to have played the fucking oboe. Here, finally, was a level playing field, a real competition. And I knew it was one I could win. I put away my textbooks and closed down my maths homework. I opened up a spreadsheet and set about working out all of the maths of the game.

The first round of the Trading Game event was only a few days after my conversation with Luke. It was only the second finance event that I'd ever attended. It was a warm autumn evening and, although the game hadn't been advertised (or not that I'd seen anyway), a medium-sized queue snaked out of one of LSE's large office block buildings. The usual LSE-finance-society type of queue: an international potpourri of Chinese, Russians and Pakistanis alongside plenty more whose accents and outfits spoke more of trust funds than any particular nationality.

I had an advantage over these people, and I knew it. I'd had the rules of the game previously explained to me, and they hadn't. That wasn't fair, but life isn't fair. God knows these guys had had plenty of rules explained to them in their lives that I was never going to know. It felt like the first advantage I'd ever had. I enjoyed that feeling as the queue filtered in, a vibration in my fingers and toes.

The queue of hungry, young aspiring traders filtered into a large, high-ceilinged, windowless room, a lecture theater somewhere in the bowels of the building, albeit one that I'd never seen before. We were split up into groups of five and placed onto separate tables. A huge man stood, gleaming, in front of a large flip chart at the front of the room. This was the first trader I had seen in my life. That's what a trader must look like then, I thought.

Once we were seated the trader explained the rules of the game. I, of course, already knew the rules, so I had time to watch him as he spoke. He moved around the room with a slow, decisive heaviness. He smiled unerringly and scanned across the crowd with bright eyes, looking into each student one at a time. A confidence seemed to snake off of him, like smoke from a candle, flowing into the room. There was a kind of thick, sticky darkness to it, but also a sharp, shiny brightness, like treacle inside a glass jar, and alongside it that huge, never-ending, pearly white smile. Something about that dark, sticky confidence transported me back home again, to Ilford. To the cool kids at school turned drug dealers making £10 into £100 by selling bags. But there was a depth there that I'd not seen in Ilford. Something that I'd started to see at LSE. The confidence of a man who wins, not just today, but tomorrow. That of a man who knows that he can't lose. Somehow, even at that early stage when I knew nothing of anything of trading, I felt it was destined for me.

But still there's a job to be done first. I had a competition to win.

And how was I going to do that? Well, first you need to understand the game.

The trading game was supposed to be a simulation of trading, but actually, it was just a numbers game.

It ran using a special deck of seventeen numbered cards: some higher, some lower. In case you ever want to play it yourself, the full deck of cards was a -10, a 20, and all the numbers 1 through 15. Each player is dealt their own card, which they could look at, and then another three cards are placed, face down, in the center of the table. The game works by players essentially making bets against each other on what will be the total numerical value of the eight cards in the game (each of five players has one card, plus the three in the middle).

Conceptually, you can think of it like this: you are all buying and selling some asset and the total value of that asset is the sum of the cards in the game. You only have certain information (your own card); more information (the cards in the middle) is revealed as the game goes on. If you have a high card, say the 15, or the 20, then that gives you inside information that the total will probably be quite high, so you want to make "buy" bets that it's a high total. If you have a low card like the -10 you probably want to make "sell" bets that the total is low. If you get a middle card like a 6 or a 7, then I guess you'll have to make something up.

The betting system is mainly what made the game a "trading game," because it was designed to mimic the way that traders make bets in the markets: "price-making" and "price-taking" using "two-way markets."

Let me quickly outline how trading happens in financial markets. A big customer—like a pension fund or a hedge fund or a big corporation—wants to buy, or sell, something. It could be anything really, but in this example let's assume they want to buy ten million British pounds in exchange for US dollars. In general, they do not call up a bank and say, "Hi there, I want to buy ten million British pounds in exchange for USD." They don't do this for two reasons:

1. If the trader knows you want to buy British pounds, he's probably going to try and push the price of pounds up.

2. If the trader knows you want to buy British pounds, he could even go out into the market and quickly buy loads of pounds, in the hope of pushing the market price up before selling them to you at that higher price. This is called "frontrunning" and is, in many cases, illegal, but it happens a lot.

To be clear, if you are a customer, you don't want to tell the trader that you want to buy before you actually get the chance to buy. To avoid this, you say "Hi, give me a price on ten million pounds."

When you say this, the trader (in theory) won't know whether you want to buy or sell. The convention then is that he has to give you *two* prices—one at which you can buy and one at which you can sell. This is known as a "two-way price" and is the way that almost all large financial markets work. If you think about it, you see something similar when you approach the foreign exchange counter at an airport: it will have one price at which they *buy* pounds in exchange for dollars, and another price at which they *sell* pounds in exchange for dollars. The price at which they buy is, of course, always much lower than the price at which they are selling. That is how foreign exchange counters make their money. Traders do exactly the same thing.

Citibank's Trading Game functioned in the same way. Any player could ask any other player at any time "what's your price?"; the other player would have to provide a two-way price with a spread (between the buy price and the sell price) of 2.

So, say you're a young, money-hungry, wannabe trader, an LSE student playing this game. You sit down at a table, wearing an expensive suit that your dad, who is a member of the Chinese Politburo, bought you at great expense from the finest tailor in London. A large and extremely confident-looking man explains to you briefly the rules of what appears a pretty straightforward maths game, and then suddenly a small, aggressive-looking boy with an almost incomprehensible accent and a white hoodie with a blue rhino on it turns to you and asks, "What's your price?"

What do you do?

For most LSE students, well trained in economics, mathematics and statistics, the answer is obvious. You look at the card in your hand, you look at the possible cards in the deck, and you do a simple statistical calculation to work out the "expected value" of the total sum of the cards. This is not a difficult mathematical calculation. The average value of a card in the deck is 7.65. There are eight cards in the game, so the average total should be 61.2. You already know one of the cards, so, if your card is particularly high or low you will shift that total up or down accordingly. If you have a 20, your expected value is 68. You might have expected that to be something like 73, since 20 is 12 more than 7.65, but you having the 20 means no one else has the 20, so it only brings up the expectation by 7. If you have a -10, your expected value is 51.2.

This is all simple maths, and it's not difficult to do. Everyone at the table was able to do it.

But it's stupid. And I'll explain to you why.

I had been studying with LSE maths and economics and finance types for a year by this point. I knew how they thought, and I figured that this is what they were going to do. Because imagine you are playing this game. Imagine one guy on your table has the 20, and he starts right away quoting 67–69 (remember, his expectation is 68). Another guy has the -10, and he starts quoting 50–52. What do you do?

Well first of all, you know right away that one guy has the -10 and another guy has the 20. They've revealed to you exactly their cards with the first words that they've spoken. But that isn't even the point here. The point is, that you can go to the 50–52 guy, and bet that the total will be higher than 52. Then you can turn to the 67–69 guy, and bet that the total will be lower than 67. Buy at 52; sell at 67. Those two bets cancel out immediately, and you make a profit of 15. That happens regardless of what the actual total of the game is, a completely risk-free profit of 15. Then you do it again.

Now if the other players in the game are smart, they will realize that you've made a quick profit. They will realize that it's stupid to offer to sell something at 52 when another gentleman is offering to buy it at 67. If the other players are smart, they will realize that the small boy with the rhino hoodie has asked for 15 prices in the first minute, and has already made a guaranteed profit of 100. They will realize that perhaps he knows what he's doing. They will think, perhaps, they should adjust.

But the kind of person who studies Economics at LSE and attends Finance Society events is not smart. Or rather, they're a different kind of smart. They are smart with a calculator, and they are good with a spreadsheet. Give them a nice tie and a glass of wine and put them in a room with a Deutsche Bank recruiter, and they may well make sparkling conversation. Make them play a card game with a quick-talking boy from East London who has already had three days to figure the game out, and they probably won't realize that they are losing the game until it's about an hour too late.

Just like that, I won the whole competition. Buy low, sell high, buy low, sell high, buy low and sell high again. It was ridiculous. The other players barely looked up from their calculators. While they were working out their expected values, I was just chucking points into the bag.

Now this game was only a maths game, but it does tell you a few things about markets:

1. Individual traders don't set the price. Just because you think something is worth 60, you don't offer to buy it at 59 if everyone else is selling it at 50. If other people are selling it at 50, the highest you should possibly quote is 50–52. There is no point offering to buy at 51 if someone is out there selling at 50. This shows something interesting about markets, which is that an individual trader shouldn't quote what *they* think something is worth, but rather what *everyone else* thinks is the price.

2. Because of this, if you ask ten different traders for a price, you shouldn't get ten different prices: they should all converge on a similar price. This will be true even if the ten different traders have totally different views about what the price should actually be.

3. If another guy looks like he knows what he's doing and is making a load of money, and you have no clue what you are doing, then maybe you should just copy that guy.

4. Point 3 is the main driving force in most financial markets.

I know that the first round of the trading competition was not a fair competition. I'd been told the rules three days beforehand, and everyone else heard them only on the day. I know that that is probably a big factor in why I won that game that day, and I know that that was ultimately the first stage in me getting a job that would, eventually, make me a millionaire. That wasn't fair, I know that. But, to be honest, I don't care. The rest of those guys in that room went on to be millionaires because their dads were millionaires. Some of them went on to be traders, because their dads were traders. My dad worked for the Post Office, and I didn't have a desk at my house to do maths homework on. You take your breaks where you can get them, I guess. I went up to that trader at the front of the room and I shook his huge hand.

"Well done," he said. "I'll see you in the final."

"Thanks," I said. "I'll see you there."

It was about three weeks between the LSE round of the trading game and the national final, and I barely went to a single lecture or class in that whole time. Matic had also made it through. I taught all my other friends how to play the game and I holed up in this one room in the library and I just played it constantly for three weeks, with anyone I knew who would join. When I couldn't find anyone to play the game with, I made spreadsheets about it and I memorized them. This was just some stupid numbers game that somebody at Citibank had made up. By the time the final had come round, I must have been the world's preeminent expert on it.

The final was to be held in the Citigroup Tower, which at that time, in 2006, was one of the three tallest buildings in the country, with the HSBC tower and the blinking pyramid dome of the main Canary Wharf tower completing the triangle. Those were the buildings that I'd seen on the horizon, from Ilford, between the lamp posts at the end of the street. It felt like fate. But I still had to win.

By the time the final came round, warm early autumn had become cold early winter. I put on a dark blue checked shirt and a fat blue-and-yellow tie. It was what I used to wear when I fluffed pillows at DFS. The afternoon was already dark when I set off on the underground from the LSE to Canary Wharf. The Jubilee Line trains had a totally different sound to the ones that ran past my bed every morning. They make a spiraling, whirring, ascending sound when they speed up and slow down. They sounded new. They sounded high-tech. To me they always sounded like money.

The game was held on one of the top floors of the tower. In the winter evening, from that height, London is just a huge mass of windows and glowing lamp posts. I had looked up at these skyscrapers every day, as a child, and on another day it might have occurred to me to look out the windows, to try and see my house. But I wasn't there for sightseeing; my brain was full of numbers. Besides, I wouldn't have known which way to look.

Before the game, there was a brief reception of champagne and canapés. I didn't know what a canapé was neither, and I didn't drink any champagne. The other candidates mingled and laughed gently with the traders in attendance. Probably laughing about CDOs, I supposed. But I wasn't listening. I was there for the numbers. Five competitors had been put through from each of five universities: LSE, Oxford, Cambridge, Durham, Warwick. I guess as far as Citibank was concerned, other universities didn't matter. That made twenty-five competitors, including me, and I'd now played with all of the LSE contingent. I fancied my chances.

We settled down to our tables. As the same massive, smiling trader from the first round at LSE delivered some motivational words, I was sizing up the players on my table. My strategy would have to be totally different for this round. Everyone here had played in the first round and done well enough to go through. They should have been good enough to realize that it's nonsensical to quote prices that diverged from the others on the table. That meant there would be no easy money to be made simply by buying low and selling high between different players.

That fact, however—that players would realize the foolishness of quoting far apart from one another—created new opportunities. Through my relentless practice games, I had realized that most players demonstrated a rigid willingness to stick closely to the prices being quoted around them, diverging only slightly. They did this largely by ear, listening out for the prices being quoted, so as to keep their own prices nearby. This presented an opportunity to manipulate the prices being quoted by others simply by quoting prices myself, very loudly. The game operated in a free-for-all style (much like real markets), and if prices were being made around the 62–64 level, loudly quoting 58–60 enough times would often bring the price down to about there. Another opportunity to set the price level would be by immediately quoting a price, again loudly, at the beginning of the game.

This presented a new, potentially profitable, strategy. If I had a high card, I would begin the game by calling out a low price. This is a relatively simple bluff—indicating that I have a low card, to bring the overall price down, so that I can then go on to buy at a low level from a variety of players, since everyone has stuck to my initial low price. The risk of this, of course, would be that other participants would realize I was bluffing, simply buy from me at a low price, and continue trading at a high price. I was counting here on that relatively simple message that had been taught to me some weeks before by my friend Sagar Malde: rich people expect poor people to be stupid. If someone who looks like me, and talks like me, starts the game by loudly declaring what sounds like an excessively low price, the other players are more likely to read it as a simpleton revealing his hand cheaply than any kind of complicated bluff.

After that the plan was to simply ask others for prices incessantly, in order to work out their own strategy, and their hands. Here I was relying on another piece of information that I had gleaned from the LSE players: most of these guys were not counting on winning the tournament, but were hoping to use the final as a networking opportunity. Given this, most players could be trusted upon to employ a relatively simplistic strategy—quote slightly higher than the average if they had a high card, slightly lower if they had a low one. Some might quote a neutral price so as not to reveal information, but that was rare. Very few would ever bluff. Remember, these guys are economics students, they're not poker players.

The key takeaway here is that economists nowadays are ultimately mathematicians, not great thinkers or game players. The other students were playing through calculators, and while they were playing through their calculators, I was guiding their ears, and reading their eyes. Start with a loud bluff, then rapidly assess every other player's intelligence, level of complexity, and likely card. Once that was established, I'd decide whether I wanted to buy (bet the total would be high) or sell (bet the total would be low). If I was a buyer, I guided the price down by loudly quoting low prices, while actively buying from other players at that low level. If I was a seller, I did the opposite.

The strategy worked to perfection, and after the first five games, I was put through to the big final, the final of the final. Only five players now. One internship on the line. That's good odds.

As the five of us moved to the central table, the eliminated competitors grabbed canapés and gathered round to watch.

I sized up the players around me. I had played most of them in the games leading up to this final. They were all good, quick to pick up on price movements and well aware of the maths in the background — but none of them, I thought, had been smart enough to bluff or read bluffing. I figured my chances were good.

The cards came round and mine was a -10. This is a good card. The -10 is the furthest card from the average, which means it has the most power to change the total of the game. But of course, it's only of value if other people don't realize you've got it. Otherwise, they'll immediately start lowering their own prices, and you'll have no way to profit from it. This is another general rule of trading: you don't necessarily make money by being right, but by being right when others are wrong.

I stuck to my usual strategy and immediately declared a high price. If I could establish a high price across the game, then I would hopefully be able to "sell" at high prices continuously, making the most of my -10 card.

Surprisingly, the first player did not "sell" to me, despite my high price. I asked him his price in return. It was even higher. He's giving his game away, surely: he's got a high card.

I asked the other three players. All were quoting high prices. Everyone had reasonably high cards, it seemed. That meant we were going to have a high total, not accounting for my -10, so for me to make any profit, I would have to push the price up. I started quoting higher and higher, and louder and louder, until finally people started selling to me. I was able to push the price a bit higher still, and then I started selling, hard. At this kind of price, and with the -10 in my hand, it was almost impossible to lose. The trick was to quote my own prices high and loud, pushing the market up as if I were an aggressive buyer, but to actually sell when asking prices from the other players. In the chaos and noise of the game, the other players weren't able to keep track of who was buying and selling from their own quoted prices, but the continually repeated numbers being quoted had a strong power to influence the price.

I started to stack up a lot of "sell" bets, confident that it was a near certainty at this price that the end total would be far lower. The time came to turn over for the first of the three central cards. It was a 13.

A 13 was not good for me. Significantly higher than the average card value of 7.65, it drags up the expected total of the cards by about 3 points. With a significant number of "sell" bets on my scorecard, this wasn't good news. Still, I had the -10 in my hand, which nobody knew about, and the prices were high. The maths was all well in my favor. I used the opportunity to ramp the price up even further and continued to sell.

By the time the second card went over, I had used up two full score-cards of sell bets. The second card was a 14.

I should maybe have been suspicious at that point, but I wasn't. Besides, I didn't have time to be. I needed the total to be low or that was my career down the drain, and if it wasn't going to be low, I wasn't going to let that stop me. I ramped the price up and started selling even more aggressively at an even higher price. By the end of the game I had racked up about 300 sells.

The final card went over. It was a 20. The four other players turned their cards over. 10, 11, 12, 15. It was impossible. With the exception of my single -10 card, the other cards were the seven highest possible cards in the game. The odds of that happening by chance are one in eleven thousand, four hundred and forty. 0:0087%. The game had been fixed.

I didn't know how to deal with this situation. For just a moment, my blood ran cold. The crowd loved it. The other players were, of course, delighted. I had made so many sells that their scorecards were all, inevitably, a litany of buys. And the price, in the end, was super high. Who rigged the game? Why? What could this mean?

The table disbanded as the traders and other Citigroup staff members convened in the back of the room to count up the scores. The players all melted into the crowd.

"I'm sorry mate." That was Matic, his hand on my shoulder. "That was unlucky mate. You did your best."

I'm not sure what I said then, to Matic. Maybe I just said nothing at all.

For five minutes the room seemed to be melting. I found I had a flute of champagne in my hand, with those little bubbles that keep coming out of nowhere and flying upward and never seem to run out. What just happened? Who did this? Why would they cheat me?

Shortly after, the trader strode into the center of the room, his huge presence immediately silencing the crowd. A space opened up around him.

"I would like to thank you all for playing," he called out, and his loud, American voice brought me back to the room. "We've calculated the scores, and I can announce the winner."

I don't remember anyone's score exactly. But mine was less than minus one thousand. That's . . . not good. The truth is, I wasn't embarrassed. If you don't shoot, you don't score, you know?

After reading out the scores, the heavy-set trader announced the winner. And the name that he called out was mine. I was the winner. It was me.

I stepped forward, in a daze.

The trader addressed the crowd as he shook my hand.

"Gary's scores in the warm-up games were so far ahead of any other player that we decided to test him. We wanted to see how he reacted when every single thing turned against him, so we rigged the game. It's important to know whether a trader will back himself, or back down. Gary, you backed yourself, and we like to see that. Well done."

The trader reached his huge hand out to me once again, and I took it.

"I'm Caleb Zucman, I'll see you on the desk."

It was cold that night, but I went to the park with my friends, drinking. I got very drunk, so I can't really remember much of what happened. But one memory has stayed with me clearly. It is a memory of me moving very quickly, so that the cold air was rushing across my face. In that memory I am clutching a friend by the shoulders. "I'm going to be a millionaire!" I am shouting. I am screaming in his face, and he's laughing. "I'm going to be a millionaire!"

3

ONE MORNING IN EARLY MARCH, 2007, I WOKE BEFORE THE SUN came up.

We didn't used to have a shower in my mum and dad's house. We had this little rubber hose that you can still buy from Argos for six pounds. I plugged it into the taps and I showered myself, sitting on the cold, early-morning plastic of the bathtub. My dad knocked on the bathroom door before I was finished. He used to start work early too.

I pulled out those old DFS clothes. Dark blue shirt; fat blue-and-yellow tie. Wrapped it all up in some cheap, black, ill-fitting suit from Next, or something, and I gelled up my hair. Then I left. It was still dark at that time.

I grew up in Ilford, but the closest station used to be called Seven Kings. In winter, before the sun comes up, the early morning commuters all stand there in the dark and they shiver as they wait for the train. Their breaths are all white in the air. This was the train that used to run through my bedroom. I tried to look for my window, but I missed it.

Change at Stratford, onto the Jubilee Line. Again that looping, winding, whirring sound, and the train dives underground, heading forward now, into the Wharf. On that day, in March 2007, I was still only twenty, and the sound hit me different. That day, it sounded like the future.

The train plunges underground before it reaches Canary Wharf station. Those stations were all brand new back then, and Canary Wharf's was huge and so spacious, with this crazy high ceiling, like an underground cathedral. You could tell it was all bank workers filing off the trains and along the platforms. Expensive, anonymous haircuts. Expensive, anonymous shirts. They snaked across the station in long, straight lines, heading for the exits. I cut into a line and snaked with them.

Out of the station and toward the building, and I see it now, in the first light of dawn. The Citigroup Center: a forty-two-story skyscraper in gun-metal gray steel and glass that sits on the southern point of a triangle of skyscrapers in the center of Canary Wharf. At that time, the top of the building sported the word "CITIGROUP" in huge, red, glowing letters, with a little red umbrella glowing alongside. For some reason, and I don't know why, thick white steam emanates from the tops of the buildings in the mornings and the evenings in winter. The tube station has these four long escalators that flow upward into a huge circular glowing opening hanging above them, so that when you are leaving the station, it feels like you are boarding a spaceship or something. And then, when you come out, you are in a broad, open plaza with trees and with water but with more, so much more than anything, these giant gray columns of metal, soaring upward, spilling their steam to the navy blue clouds.

Across the streets now, to the building. The wind whips between the skyscrapers, and by the time I reached the vast, warm, brightly lit reception of the Citigroup building, it felt like a sanctuary. Inside there it was all expensive-looking furniture, colorful abstract art and impossibly well-ironed staff. A soft-focus receptionist sent me over to a soft-focus sofa, and I sat down, adjusting my tie.

A kindly looking lady called Stephanie turned up, and handed me a visitor's pass. She walked me through a set of security gates, and around one corner, and into what seemed, to me, to be the world's largest atrium, all escalators and glass. This was a whole new building now, and I could see all the way to the roof, which must have been twenty floors above me. At each level, huge, brightly lit rooms looked out on two sides through thick walls made of windows onto a vast, tall and wide empty space, at the bottom of which I was standing, looking up. Glass and metal walkways and balconies branched out at intervals, connecting offices across the divide. I didn't know about it, at that time, but less than one year earlier, a Citigroup employee had committed suicide by jumping all the way through that central space. He'd fallen twenty floors without even going outside. Some of the traders had gone out onto the balconies, to look down. So it goes, I guess.

Stephanie led me up three flights of escalators to the glass walkways of the second floor. Etched in crystal white onto the vast glass doors were the words "Fixed Income Trading Floor." Words which meant nothing to me. I would spend four years of my life on that floor.

The trading floor itself is a vast room. Entering from the middle, the room seems to spread for fifty meters in every direction: to my left, to my right, and out in front. The thing that jumps out straight away is the monitors. Each trader has eight, nine, ten, even twelve monitors rising up in a huge square or rectangle in front of them. Row upon row upon row of traders, each craning upward to look at these monitor walls above and around them, enveloping them.

The traders sit back-to-back in long rows, mirroring the long strip lighting hanging down from the ceiling above them, each arching up into their screens. The walls to the outside are floor-to-ceiling glass windows, although from where I'm stood, just inside the door, those windows seemed a long way away. Wide, black digital signboards hang at intervals from the ceiling, displaying the time in different cities throughout the world: London, New York, Sydney, Tokyo. Beneath their banks of screens, each trader has a huge, heavy black speakerbox, about a meter wide, covered in buttons and dials and switches. Later in the morning, the room would fill with an ever-rising crescendo of noises from those speakerboxes—pings and bleeps and kachings and shouted numbers—but from where I am, about 7:30 in the morning, the noise was peculiarly calm. The loudest thing was the buzz of the strip lights. Beneath that, a low hum, of voices.

Stephanie led me round to the right of the trading floor, for some distance, and then cut left into one of the aisles that separated the rows. We were moving forward now, into the heart of the trading floor, and to either side of me, I could look along the long rows of back-to-back traders as we walked. White shirt, white shirt, light pink shirt, white shirt. So this is what traders look like, I thought.

We started to move into a section of the trading floor that was noisier. The mismatched melody of electronic signals and warnings and loud human laughing and shouting of numbers that would eventually become the music of my life. I looked around as the noise started rising, and Stephanie cut right onto one of these desks.

We were walking directly between traders now, through the thin space between traders' backs. The noises were getting louder and louder and I could see the multicolored numbers flashing on the huge walls of screens. This desk, far in the back corner of the trading floor, was buttressed on the far end by a vast window, and I could see out of it onto the station and the trees and the water in the plaza and I could see the sun starting to rise.

Stephanie stopped and bent her knees slightly, and leaned into the vast, hulking back of a trader and said something very gently into his ear.

And the trader pushed with his arms against the desk edge and his office chair kicked two feet back and spun around and he stood up, huge, now, between me and the window. And he was so backlit against the brightness of the sun through that window that I could barely make out his huge, beaming smile, but I knew it was Caleb, and I took once again his huge outstretched hand as it reached out, downward, to me.

"Hi Gary. Welcome to the STIRT desk."

4

STEPHANIE WAS GONE NOW. I HADN'T NOTICED HER GOING, BUT SHE was definitely gone. And I was standing, squinting upward, in Caleb's shadow.

With a heavy hand on my shoulder, Caleb walked me away from the window and back toward the central aisle of the trading floor. The STIRT desk had about ten traders in total, seated back-to-back either side of us as we walked, and Caleb gestured to each of them as we walked past.

"This is Bill, he trades sterling."

"This is JB, he trades Aussie, Kiwi, Yen."

"This is Wheeley, he trades Skandis."

In most of these cases I had no real idea what the brief description meant.

Not one of the traders spoke to me as I walked past. A couple of them jerked their heads around, almost instinctively, upon hearing their names, only to quickly turn back. Each of them was deeply involved in the flashing lights and sounds rolling out of their station: one of them wrapped around a thick, heavy brown hand phone; another shouting numbers into his huge speakerbox.

Caleb stopped at the very end of the row. There, half-falling into the central aisle and separated from the rest of the traders by an empty space, sat the man, or perhaps more of a boy, in hindsight, who would be my first ever direct senior in trading.

"Snoopy!"

Caleb shouted loudly and Snoopy turned, with a start. No sooner had he turned than he was up on his feet and wiping his hands on the front of his trousers. He was, I was thankful to notice immediately, the size of an ordinary man, only a couple of inches taller than me. He introduced himself while shaking my hand and smiling and nodding. His real name, it turned out, was not Snoopy, but Sundeep. For some reason, after introducing himself to me, he then turned and shook Caleb's hand as well. Still smiling and nodding the whole time.

With no more than that Caleb was gone, as quickly as Stephanie, and I was left, then, just me and Sundeep. Notwithstanding my lack of direction or instruction, Sundeep too, was very quickly away from me, and back inside his wall of screens. And there I was, standing alone, at the edge of the desk, and it was not immediately clear what I was supposed to be doing, or in fact, where I was supposed to sit.

But that was OK. I had been told about this. I had been warned. This was "the nothing." I'd heard clusters of Pakistani finance society members talking about it while filling in application forms in large huddles in the LSE library. You fill in thirty-five application forms, you write thirty-five cover letters, you memorize the meanings of about one hundred acronyms and you do twenty or thirty interviews. Then, when you finally walk onto your first trading floor, to start your first internship, absolutely roaring with enthusiasm to meet your first team and to make your first million dollars you get given . . . Nothing. No work today. No clear instruction. No obvious job. And in many cases, such as mine, now, also no seat. When you're an intern, the job doesn't get given to you. It's your job to make the job yours. You make your own money on the trading floor, I guess.

There was an empty seat and an entire station of computers and monitors free to Snoopy's left, but for all I knew that could be someone's. So I went and took an empty chair from somewhere else on the trading floor when no one was looking and rolled it over to Snoopy's right, in front of a small filing cabinet. I was half leaning into the central aisle from this position, but I could see all the things that I needed to: Snoopy's screen, just in front of me, and the whole desk of traders to my left. It would be my job to keep an eye on the traders and subtly notice when someone wasn't busy so I could sneak in and talk to them. I could also use the filing cabinet as a kind of makeshift desk. I ripped a sheet of paper out of my notepad and drew a little diagram, writing as much as I could remember of the traders: their names, their roles and where they sat. I showed it to Snoopy and asked him if it was right. He thought that was pretty funny, and made a few corrections. I placed it on the filing cabinet in front of me and made a clean copy on another sheet of paper. I folded that one up and put it in my pocket.

Snoopy was clearly, without a doubt, the desk junior. He couldn't have been more than three or four years older than I was, and every single other trader on the desk looked at least seven or eight years older than him. I tried a couple times to lean into Snoopy's peripheral vision and ask him about what he was doing, but each time he smiled sheepishly and palmed me off. He had the look of a boy copying someone's homework. I liked him immediately. But it was patently clear both to me and to Snoopy that my future would not be in his hands. He knew it. I knew it. He knew I knew it.

I would have to look for bigger fish.

I turned to my left and looked at the members of the STIRT desk.

Even to my young, untrained eyes, they had the air of a ramshackle mob. In the far corner, behind Caleb and next to the window sat a small, middle-aged man. White haired, near-spherical and hobbit-like, he sat too-small in his wobbling office chair, typing furiously with one of those huge brown phones clamped hard between his ear and left shoulder, head cocked to the left. He angled himself away from the desk, toward the window, and occasionally cast suspicious glances backward toward the other traders, as if wary of being caught. Another middle-aged man, tall, wiry, red-faced and completely bald, stood chairless, one pink shirt tail flapping erratically, leaning into his computers, shouting and swearing into the screens in a broad Australian drawl. A swarthy Italian three seats down from me sat in a crumpled, expensive-looking shirt, laughing deeply into his headset. He looked like he'd not been to sleep. Even Caleb, so effortlessly, milkily smooth and charming at the trading game, looked older, less polished, talking amiably on the phone in his oversized American suit.

This was not actually my first ever time on the trading floor. The prize for winning the trading game had been two one-week internships, of which this was the second. The game now was to turn those two weeks into the summer internship, and then turn that into a job. I'd spent my first week, the previous December, on the "Credit Trading" desk, approximately one year and ten months before that precise desk would blow up the world economy. Of course, I had not known about the impending death of the world economy, at that time. Nor did I know of it now, three months later, as I sat falling off the corner of the STIRT desk, wondering what it was that "STIRT" actually stood for, and why the traders here looked so different to those Credit Traders on the other side of this room.

The Credit Traders had been like the LSE students. Polished, starched, uniformed, smooth. The STIRT Traders, well, they were not that. They had accents. Real accents, from real places. I liked that. I also wondered why.

But this was no time for sociological analysis. Time was ticking. I needed a mark.

The choice, at least, could not have been simpler. Whilst most of the traders were absorbed in their screens or their telephones, wiry, bald-head, red-faced pink shirt was a locus of skittish activity. Shouting snippets of jokes into his speakerboxes, hollering things I didn't understand at traders on other desks, over the walls of screens, slapping other traders on the back unexpectedly. Ever standing. Ever moving. He seemed dying to be bothered. I pulled the slip of paper out of my pocket and checked it. "JB. Ozzie. Kiwi. Yen." Whatever that meant.

I got myself behind him and to his right as he was standing, so that I could peek gently into his peripheral vision. In his whirl of noise and motion, he seemed not to notice me at all. I leaned in.

"JB."

JB stopped sharp, like he'd sighted an animal, and stared headlong into the distance, through his screens, for at least five or six seconds. All of a sudden he whipped his head round rapidly to the right, where I was standing, then to the left, then to the right again. I was honestly not sure if it was a skit or if he had genuinely not seen me. No one else looked away from their screens.

"JB," I said again, and JB slowly lowered his gaze to me. I looked upward at JB. JB looked downward at me.

"Hi, JB. My name's Gary." I said, a little stutteringly, as I put out my hand.

JB looked at my hand. For longer, I felt, than really he should have done. He looked, again, back at my face. My hand had been out for a while now, and I looked in turn back at JB. His face had, for whatever reason, remained a vision of shock this whole time.

And then, suddenly, that face was beaming, he whipped my hand round as if taking it off.

"Fuckin oath mate! Where the fuck did you get that tie?"

I looked down at my tie. Blue. Fat. Yellow stripes. JB's hand was still squeezing my hand.

"Erm. I'm not sure mate. I think it's from Next?"

JB waved a beckoning hand which I took to mean to bring my chair over, so I rolled across, perched next to his filing cabinet and leaned in to look at his screens. The flashing lines and numbers could have been the betting markets for the horses for all I knew at that time. In hindsight, at least one of them probably was.

With my arrival, JB seemed to have immediately lost interest in those flashing numbers, and made a half-turn toward me. From this position, talking over his right shoulder to me one second and shouting back over his left shoulder into his computers the next, JB conducted a surprisingly personal interview. JB wanted to know where I came from and what the hell I was doing on the desk. He wanted to know what football team I supported and took a surprising interest in the provenance of my clothes.

At the time, this behavior was confusing to me. My previous stint on the trading floor had consisted largely of uninspiring spreadsheet work and somewhat turgid explanations of Credit Default Swaps. No one had ever asked where my tie was from. It is only looking back now, with the benefit of six years working on trading floors, that I can see how eminently sensible Johnny's (JB's full name was Johnny Blackstone) questions actually were. Twenty-year-old kids do not, in general, just rock up onto the trading floor. Especially not twenty-year-old kids who, as in my case, look and are dressed as if they have been sent by their parents to the local estate agents to ask for work experience. The only twenty-year-old kids you will find on the trading floor are those whose parents run the trading floor. Those people neither sound nor look like me. JB was, I think, amused and intrigued. Looking back, I think I would have been too.

JB was delighted to find out that I was from Ilford, after figuring out that it was, at least in some senses, in Essex. JB's girlfriend and, apparently, many of his brokers (whatever a broker was) were also from Essex. He pressed down one of the million switches on the big black box under his monitors and asked a mystery person if they'd ever been to Ilford. A deep, cockney voice from the pub boomed back.

"Oh yeah, Ilford. Used to go down Ilford Palais all the time when I was younger. All changed down there now though. All changed . . ."

JB was even more delighted to find out I supported Leyton Orient. "Orient!" he shouted out, as if he'd never pronounced the letter O before. He called me Orient for the rest of the week.

JB told me everything about his background. He'd moved to England twenty years previously to study law at Oxford. From his accent I wouldn't have guessed that he'd been outside of Queensland for much more than a day. He'd hated law so had dropped out to play rugby for London Irish. From there, he had gone into broking, and from there, into trading. This was not, of course, the traditional LSE-style pipeline involving writing thirty-five CVs and cover letters while inverting matrices. Something was afoot here, I suspected, but again, there was not really time to get into it. JB also, finally, told me what "STIRT" stood for, which was "Short Term Interest Rates Trading." That was a considerable weight off of my mind.

JB was once again delighted when he learned that I had won the internship in a "trading game." This started him on a long monologue about trading and his journey within it, of which I did not understand much. He showed me graphs and told me many stories. I looked into Johnny's eyes, I looked at the graphs. I looked into the middle distance, and thought. Or at least, I narrowed my eyes to give the sense of thinking. I wondered if he could tell that I didn't understand.

I cannot emphasize enough how much of my early experience of trading consisted of this. Of listening to traders, of nodding along sagely, of pulling the faces of a boy thinking deeply, and of understanding nothing at all. At the time, my lack of comprehension seemed to me so overwhelmingly complete, so painfully obvious, that I could not for the life of me understand how the act was not noticed. After fifteen years in finance and economics, I now know why. Everyone's doing it, all of the time.

Anyway, I must have been good at it, because my nodding was going down a storm. JB and I were getting along like a house on fire. (Fifteen years after this conversation, as step nine of a twelve-step recovery program me, in an old pub overlooking the River Thames, JB would fill in some of the gaps here, as to why he took to me so quickly, and also why he used to speak so fast. At the time, I figured he was just a really nice guy, and that maybe I was just really charming.)

After about two hours of this intense conversation, JB decided it was time to pass me on. He spun his chair round so that he was blocking the central aisle and shouted unnecessarily loudly at the trader behind him, who he was now quite close to.

"Hobbsy!"

Hobbsy vibrated a little, then, a few seconds later, turned his chair around, very slowly, to face us.

"Meet Gazza. Orient fan."

I stood up quickly and offered a hand for Hobbsy to shake.

Hobbsy didn't take my hand, but, instead, looked me once over, slowly, in a way that is quite simply not socially acceptable in this day and age. With him seated, and me standing, hand proffered, he scanned me very slowly, from my head, all the way down to my feet. At that point, he paused, perhaps thinking. And then, up again, to my head.

After another pause, he turned back to his station and opened a tray in his filing cabinet. He took a business card out of the tray, stood up, turned around at a measured pace, and placed that card into my hand.

I looked at the card. On it was printed: "Rupert Hobhouse. Head of Euro Rates Trading."

I looked up, over the top of the card and into the face of Rupert Hobhouse.

It was only then that Rupert Hobhouse offered his own hand to me.

"I'm Rupert Hobhouse," he said. "Head of Euro Rates trading."

"Hi Rupert," I said, as Rupert broke each of my knuckles. "I'm Gary, nice to meet you."

For my part, while Rupert had scanned me, I'd had much time to look at his face. It was at once babyish and concerningly stern, at once handsome and unnecessarily fat. He must have been in his early thirties. Thick black-rimmed glasses framed his eyes beneath a professionally coiffed brown quiff. He had the aura of a man whose parents had dropped him off unexpectedly at boarding school when he was just six years old and had not picked him up until he was twenty-one. I would later find that this was not actually far from the truth. He had the muscular-verging-on-fat physique of a man who has been well-fed for many years, possibly from birth. As if his body was struggling to come up with new ways to use all the nutrition. It was a physique that was at certain points straining at the seams somewhat, as was his, clearly, expensive shirt. It spoke of a capacity for violence.

Rupert turned back without a word and JB wandered off to the bathroom. I took this to mean that I was to sit next to Rupert. I needed only really to turn my chair around and then I was perched looking over his shoulder.

Rupert's body language did not acknowledge my presence, but he immediately launched into a monologue about the nature of his work, which, given the specificities of the circumstances surrounding us at that time, could only realistically have been directed at me. The lack of eye contact spared me significant nodding, so I decided to alternate between taking notes at random and leaning forward and looking at screens.

Rupert Hobhouse was, as had already been established at least two times, the Senior Euro Rates Trader. The Euro was, by far, the biggest and most important currency traded on the desk, and the responsibility was split jointly, but not evenly, between him and his junior Ho Nguyen. Rupert gestured to Ho Nguyen without looking and so I turned and I looked at the guy. I recognized the name Nguyen as Vietnamese and I was wondering if he was maybe an international LSE type, but he quickly turned back to me with a big smile and said, "You all right mate? Call me Hongo," and it turned out he was actually from Norwich.

Trading Euro FX Swaps (it was only at this point that I learned the primary function of the desk—trading FX Swaps—although I had no idea what FX Swaps were) involved a huge number of trades, significant risks and volumes, and constant interaction with all of Europe's biggest banks.

At this point Rupert waved toward one of his screens, on which was a long list of random words and numbers that I now know to be a trade blotter: a full, itemized list of all the trades that he had done on that day. I nodded and chose a few numbers at random, and jotted them onto my pad.

Rupert had still not looked at me once, but, in partial defense of his wholly impersonal style of communication, he and Ho—especially Ho, to be honest—did seem far more busy than JB. Other traders on the desk would shout numbers and words at them frequently, utterances which appeared to require contemplation, digestion and response. Their various screens and speakerboxes commanded them with bleeps at regular intervals and each bleep, it seemed, had to be picked up.

Over the course of about half an hour, Rupert delivered a concise and compact philosophy of trading, generally illustrated with ever longer lists of words and colored numbers, which, whilst only slightly more intelligible than JB's explanation, was radically different in style. What for JB had been passionate and emotional, for Rupert was compulsively precise. I had no idea who was the better trader, but I could guess who made more friends in the pub.

By the time it had finished, Rupert's analysis of Foreign Exchange Swap Trading left me more confused than it found me.

Rupert had asked nothing about me. That was because he already knew everything about me. Or at least, he already knew everything that I had said to JB. This was somewhat disconcerting, as I'd had no idea that he, or indeed anyone, had been listening. What with the constant bleating of speakerboxes from everyone's station, it was something of a wonder that he'd even been able to pick out my voice.

Be that as it may, Rupert must have done so, for he already had most of the details. The one extra piece of information that he wanted added was, of course, what kind of school I had gone to. This was a potential tripwire for me, as I had been expelled from a grammar school for selling drugs, and the fact that I had moved from a grammar school to a comprehensive was clearly visible on my CV, which Caleb, and hence possibly Rupert, had access to. But I had prepared for exactly this question, and I told Rupert that I had left the grammar school to go to a comprehensive because I'd heard that universities had quotas for comprehensive school students. Rupert's face barely moved, but I could tell that he liked that—a thin, English smile played just slightly, somewhat musically, at the corners of his tightly held lips.

With my schooling covered off, Rupert moved on to the question he really wanted to ask me. It was only now that he first looked at me. He opened the top tray of his desk drawer, from where he'd extracted the business card, and drew out a pack of trading game cards. He placed them on the desk in front of me and then, moving only above the neck, like an owl, revolved his head to face me for the first time.

"Tell me how you won the trading game."

The sudden eye contact, combined with this strange way of moving, caught me off guard, and for a moment I was unable to speak. But I steadied myself and explained quickly my thinking: that the ideal strategy depended on the level of player against which one was playing; that weak players could be beaten with simple arbitrage; that the more complex players in the game were still generally uncomfortable with bluffing and could be thrown off by aggressive loudness. Rupert watched me, unmoving, the whole time. When his computer bleeped he ignored it; Hongo picked it up. It struck me that perhaps for some reason Rupert had chosen to forget completely all the finer and undefined spaces that exist between listening and ignoring. One year later, apropos of nothing, Rupert Hobhouse would take me to Las Vegas and explain to me that, with only ten questions, he could ascertain with absolute certainty whether a woman would sleep with him or not. He never told me what those questions were.

Once my explanation of the trading game was over, Rupert simply turned back to his computers and resumed his duties as if he had never moved away from them, and a heavy silence seemed to fall between us. I was still awkwardly straddling the filing cabinet to Rupert's left, which belonged to the unknown trader on the other side of me, and the complete lack of acknowledgment by anyone around me made my already ridiculous physical positioning all the more conspicuous.

It was by now approaching lunchtime, so, in an attempt to assuage the awkwardness I leaned into Rupert's peripheral vision and said, "Erm . . . Do you want me to go . . . get you lunch??"

Rupert did actually react physically to this one. He turned his whole body, much more naturally, with one eyebrow raised. He reached into his pocket, pulled out his wallet and handed me fifty pounds in cash.

"Yes. And get lunch for Caleb and Hongo and JB as well."

I was quite relieved at this response, to be honest. I used to frequently pick up lunch orders for the sales guys at DFS, and it seemed an easy way to both be noticed and get into people's good books. I whipped round and collected everyone's orders, and slipped off of the trading floor.

The skyscrapers of Canary Wharf are all connected by a vast underground shopping center, which I suppose makes them all one enormous building, in a way, and as I walked through these vast, wide, artificially lit hallways, from takeaway restaurant to takeaway restaurant, I felt my sense of balance returning. Something about the conversation with Rupert, if you could call it that, had taken the air out of my lungs.

I hurried back to the trading floor, and wordlessly placed each trader's order on their desks beside them. When I came to Rupert I put down his lunch, along with his change: a £10 note with a few coins piled on top.

Rupert looked at the coins with that instinctive rapidity that people tend to show when they hear money fall to the ground.

"What is that?"

"Erm . . . It's your change."

Rupert didn't move or say anything. He was still staring at the pile of coins. I felt like maybe I'd given the wrong answer so I tried something else.

"Erm . . . It's eleven pounds seventy-four."

I knew that it was £11.74. because I'd taken a quick note of how much everyone's order had cost, so as to make sure that Rupert got the right change.

Rupert opened his top drawer and slid the money all the way across his desk and off the edge so it fell into the drawer. Then he turned to me as if he was going to confide in me, but, instead, looked at me with a ferocious intensity that was impossibly out of proportion with anything like the situation we were in.

"On this desk, we keep the change."

I'd never heard such a thing in my life.

The next few days fell into a pattern. I would wake up in the morning and take a shower with the rubber hose in the cold bath. I would get to the desk extremely early—increasingly early as the days went on, in fact, for reasons that I will shortly explain. Caleb had eventually taken pity on me, and set me to work on some complicated and ultimately pointless spreadsheet, so I spent a few hours every morning working out how to fill an Excel sheet with pastel colors in alternating rows. Once the morning rush was over, I would sit with either Rupert or JB, whoever seemed happier to acknowledge my presence. The truth was, it was always JB who seemed more keen, but I learned to gauge Rupert's subtle moods. Impressing these two would ultimately be my passport to a millionaire lifestyle, so I devoted myself to making them tick.

Working with JB was easy. He just wanted an audience to listen to his stories and jokes, and, in all honesty, they were usually a pleasure to listen to. He wanted to hear about life in East London and pillow fluffing at DFS and weekends with my dad watching Orient draw o–o with Dagenham and Redbridge away in the snow. Rupert was more complicated. I soon learned that there was nothing Rupert liked more than me being wrong. In fact, what Rupert liked was not actually me being wrong, but me being wrong and then fully and thoroughly accepting the blame for it, apologizing unreservedly and devotedly, and then gathering my reserve and staring stoically into the mid distance, absolutely committed to becoming a better man. Rupert liked this so much that I made sure to do it frequently, and I resolved to be wrong far more than I was ever right.

After a morning of this I would offer to get lunch for everyone, it having gone down so well on my first day. Each trader would get something from a different restaurant, and making sure everyone's order was correct and, in fact, just carrying it all back to the office, was no mean feat, but it was a simple way to show a basic capability and reliability and, to this day, I'm convinced it was by far my most important role in that week on the desk. I was initially hesitant to follow Rupert's command to keep all the change, but it had been delivered with such blinding, searing intensity that I felt I simply had no choice but to do it. After a couple of days, Caleb commented that these lunches were getting expensive, with no change coming back, but, when he said it, he looked round at me as if I was his firstborn son or something, and I knew then that somehow, impossibly, what I was doing must have been right. Strange crowd this lot, I thought to myself. I was making like £20 a day.

Through casual conversation I started to pick up strands of information that helped me place people on the desk. I learned that Caleb, at twenty-eight, was the youngest ever Managing Director on the trading floor (I had no idea what a Managing Director, or "MD," was, but it was clearly kind of a big deal), and had been transferred to be head of the London desk quite recently, after a successful career for Citi in Japan. I learned that Bill, the taciturn, silver-haired Scouser in the corner, had been a big money hire from Halifax a few years previously, but, much to Rupert's chagrin and pleasure, had been completely failing to turn in the results. I also learned that, unlike all of the other traders on the desk, Bill had never been to university. Perhaps that was why he kept himself to himself.

In the afternoons, which were generally much quieter, Caleb would wander over to my corner and check out the maths and impressive coloring of my spreadsheet, and comment on my formulas. Caleb had an economics degree from Stanford University in America, and, as such, had by far the closest background to myself. He spoke the language of maths and numbers and formulas, but, somehow, never at the expense of his charm. What Caleb wanted was for me to catch quickly the logical and mathematical connections, and the theoretical workings of the products on the desk. This, for once, was in line with my actual training. Of all the people that I spoke to on the trading floor, Caleb was the only one that I felt could really see through my "I understand this" face. You felt, somehow, that he knew what you knew and what you didn't know. You felt that he really knew *you*.

There was one other trader on the desk who saw completely that I didn't know what I was doing, and that was Snoopy. I learned that Snoopy had not come through the traditional graduate scheme, but instead had been hired as a computer programmer, before being quickly promoted to trader by Caleb. This probably explained why he had the constant air of a sixteen-year-old trying to buy vodka. Snoopy didn't come from a background in finance and economics, and he had not worked on trading floors for long. As a result of this, his mind had not yet become accustomed to the nodding of a hopelessly lost man, and he knew instantly that I hadn't a clue. Fortunately for me, Snoopy had not a clue either.

God knows we hadn't come from the same background, Snoopy and I. Snoopy had grown up a world away, in a golf club somewhere in the idyllic Oxfordshire countryside, next door to David Cameron. He descended from seventeen consecutive generations of well-paid and trusted local doctors and he had never gone to bed hungry (it showed). Somehow, in spite of our differences, we formed an instant and close bond. I knew that Snoopy knew nothing, and Snoopy knew that I knew nothing. I knew that Snoopy shouldn't have been there, and Snoopy knew that I shouldn't have been there. We both knew, on some, deep, instinctive level, that we were surrounded by absolute nutters, and that it was important that they didn't find out. We were stowaways on a pirate ship headed toward buried treasure, and we just needed to hold our nerve until we got there. Maybe, if we stuck around long enough, we could get to that treasure before the rest of these madmen.

With the two of us somewhat separate from the rest of the desk in Snoopy's corner, I confided at the end of the very first day that I had sat at some length with both JB and Rupert, and had barely understood a word of what either of them had said.

"Listen mate," said Snoopy, speaking quietly and leaning in conspiratorially, "don't worry about that mate. No one understands anything. You see that guy over there?"

Snoopy gestured with his thumb over his left shoulder; he was indicating the swarthy, deep-voiced Italian.

"That guy's name is Lorenzo di Luca. He's the stupidest guy I ever met. All he does is go out womanizing. I'm not sure he even speaks English. The other day, he turned up to work three hours late, and when Caleb asked him why, all he did was shrug and say, "Swedish New Year." The guy's a complete idiot. But he still makes millions for the desk. If that guy can do it, anyone can do it. Don't worry mate, we've got this, stay cool."

I looked at Lorenzo di Luca. He was kind of handsome and, yeah, I supposed that he did indeed look a little bit stupid. He was still laughing into a headset in deep bass Italian. OK, I thought. Interesting.

Snoopy was still talking though. "Besides mate, you are never gonna learn anything from JB and Rupert, they don't know what they are doing. You wanna actually learn something, you gotta speak to Bill."

That name again, Bill. I looked over at him. He was still the same, hobbit-like, ball-like, sitting in his chair looking out the window with his big brown phone clamped between shoulder and ear. Everybody mentioned Bill, but I hadn't managed to speak to him. Every time I'd approached him he'd spun his head around like a cat that had been caught licking itself and I'd quickly walked off in some other direction.

OK, Bill. So here was the plan with Bill.

I noticed Bill used to drink a lot of coffees. I asked Snoopy what coffee he drank, and he said cappuccinos. So I got in the next morning at six thirty so that I could have a cappuccino on Bill's desk before he got in. Except Bill was already there at six thirty. He was the only guy there on the whole desk. Sitting there, tiny in the corner, all by himself in the dark. Motherfucker, what time does this guy come in? At least he didn't have his coffee yet, and he wasn't on the phone yet. I went up and asked him if I could get him a coffee. Bill didn't turn around but he slammed his ID card down onto the desk. You could buy drinks with your card at a little coffee shop on the trading floor.

"Yeah go on then, and get one for yourself mate."

I picked up the ID card. It had Bill's little scowling face on it. It said "WILLIAM DOUGLAS ANTHONY GARY THOMAS."

The next day, Wednesday, I came in at five forty-five. Thank fuck the guy wasn't there yet. So I bought a cappuccino and put it on his desk. By five past six Bill still wasn't there, and the coffee must have been cold, so I threw it away and bought another one. I did that again at about six fifteen and luckily Bill walked in just after. I didn't want to look at Bill when he sat down and found the coffee, coz I didn't want him to see me looking at him. But he must have sat down, and he called out,

"Thanks Gal," in his thick Scouse accent.

I must have turned round like I was surprised and said, "Oh yeah, no worries, Bill. No worries."

The next day I came in at six and did the same thing.

The next day, Friday, was my last day on the desk. Bill came in already with his own cappuccino. He put it down on my desk as he walked past.

"Thanks Gal. Come sit with me when you come back."

I was in.

One more little story about Bill, just so you know him a little, and maybe understand a bit more about why I wanted to impress him so much.

Bill was the Sterling trader, which meant he was the guy primarily in charge of watching the UK economy, and on my second day on the desk, which was a Tuesday, some data was coming out in the morning about the UK. I can't remember what it was now, inflation or something.

Just before the data was coming out, the guys on the next desk, who were actually sales guys, not traders, although I didn't know that at the time, were having a hell of a time, listening to music and laughing and dancing. That kind of behavior was not unusual.

Bill, who, like me, was a good seven or eight inches shorter than the average height of the giants on the trading floor, stood up and walked around to the next desk, and asked them to turn the music down.

They did that, and Bill sat, again, watching and waiting, like a hawk, for the data. The data must have been delayed or something, because after a few minutes, the music was back and Bill was back round, a little more adamantly, asking for the music to please be turned down.

Again the music was turned down, and again Bill was intently waiting.

After a few minutes, the music was back again. Bill didn't get up. The other desk was exactly opposite Bill, as in, the salesmen were sitting facing him, but they were separated by the two huge walls of screens, both Bill's and their own. The wires from all the screens fed down into a central hole in the desk itself between them, as did the wires for the speakers from which the music was played.

Bill didn't say anything. He simply opened his desk drawer and pulled out a pair of scissors, and used them to snip the speakers' wires. Calm as you like. You wouldn't have even guessed he had done anything. His gaze barely broke from his screens.

The music, of course, stopped instantly, and it took a while for the sales guys to realize what had happened. Eventually, of course, they did realize, and the head of their desk, a large, blond-haired, big-nosed, unspeakably posh English man named Archibald Quigley came barreling round shouting as if ready to fight.

Caleb, who had of course noticed what had happened, had to quickly jump up out of his seat and physically stop him. Archie was shouting right in his face.

Bill didn't even blink. He was staring at the screens.

I thought he was a fucking legend.

. . .

On my last day on the desk Rupert and Caleb had a surprise for me.

The two of them had been taking some sort of bizarre joy in my lunch trips and had been making them more and more complicated each day. They would ask for individual items from different, distant restaurants, or peculiar specific adjustments to be made to their food. They would ask me to get lunch orders for friends dotted in random parts of the trading floor. Sometimes I wondered if they even knew the people they were ordering for. I think they were maybe trying to test if I could get it right. (I did, of course. It was the only half-complicated thing that I had to do in the whole week of the internship.) More than that, I think they just enjoyed seeing me sweat.

At ten thirty Caleb called me over.

"I'm getting lunch for the whole floor."

He said it like it was nothing. But the trading floor was a big fucking place.

I didn't flap. He wanted me to flap. I knew it. I just looked him back, right in the eyes, and said to him,

"OK, no problem."

He loved that.

It was a big operation. It would have been impossible to do it alone. I went to each individual desk on the trading floor and explained to them what was happening. It must have cost Caleb thousands of pounds. I had to convince each of the managers of the individual desks to lend me their desk juniors for an hour. It was the only way to get it to work. I wasn't always successful in doing that, and I must have carried at least a hundred burgers myself. Looking back on it, I think that some sort of intended humiliation might have been a part of it. But honestly, I didn't give a shit. Just two years before that I had been delivering papers at seven in the morning 364 days a year for £12 a week. I still remember the day when bossman called me in after I delivered the papers and said he was cutting my pay from £13 to £12. Sometimes, I would put a big Sunday paper in the wrong house, and I would end up losing money for the day. These guys were paying me £700 for a week to deliver fucking burgers. And they were my best chance of becoming a millionaire. They could have made me clean the toilets if they wanted to.

By the time I finished delivering all of the burgers it was gone 2 p.m. I sat down on my little corner station, exhausted, half leaning out into the aisle. Rupert and Caleb both had their chairs turned round ninety degrees so that, instead of looking at their computers, they were looking at me. I ignored them.

"Hey Gazza!" shouted out Caleb. He was all the way at the other end of the desk.

I turned round to look at him and saw his beaming smile poking over Rupert's shoulder. They were both leaning back in their chairs.

"You got a passport?"

I did have a passport because two years previously I'd thrown up all over Tenerife with my friends to celebrate my A-levels.

"Go home and get it. You're going skiing."

I was on the tube to Stratford and I was texting my dad.

"Where is my passport?" I asked him.

"It's in the drawer under my bed," he replied.

It was in there, under his underwear.

Did you know, when people go skiing, they actually go right up to the tops of the mountains? And when they are doing it, all around them they can see all the other mountains, covered in snow. I didn't know it was like that, but it is like that. That's what they do.

My mum texted me.

"Does that mean you got the job then?"

"I'm not sure. Probably."

Then she asked me for money.

Part Two

YOU
WANT
SOME?

1

THAT WEEK IN MARCH ON THE STIRT DESK GOT ME THE SUMMER
internship. When I turned up everyone already knew who I was: I was
the kid who'd bought everyone a burger. That little stunt let everybody
know Caleb wanted me, and since Caleb wanted me, everyone wanted
me. The Credit Trading desk made a big push for me, and that made
Caleb want me even more. All this was in spite of, or, perhaps more accurately, with completely no regard for, the fact that I still had absolutely no idea what anyone was doing. I suppose this could be referred
to as a "speculative bubble," and if you sit and think about it for long
enough, you can learn something about how bitcoin works.

The through line was there; I could see it. I could smell every step of
the way. I'd already smashed up my end-of-year exams. Now I was gonna
savage the summer internship. From there, I'd get offered a full-time
job, which I'd start one year later, after I finished uni. I'd hit that, become the best trader in the world, and, at some point, a millionaire.
There were a few details from my plan that were missing, like the fact I
didn't know how to trade, but I was fucked if I was gonna let that stop
me. I killed that whole year on a scream.

That summer I got my head down and focused on winning all the
internship competitions. There were three "trading competitions" and I
won all of them. They all had little tricks to them which you could ex-
ploit, if you figured them out. They were games in the end. There was a
public speaking competition and I won that too. I don't really know
what to tell you about that one. I guess I was just a really competitive
kid.

Matic had also snagged an internship at Citi. He must have net-
worked someone at the trading game final. He was good like that. He

spent the whole internship totally fucked up on coffee and caffeine pills on one of those super-high-tech-futuristic-massive-spreadsheet-million-formula desks known as "Credit Structuring." At that time they were the Gods of the World. Matic barely went home the whole internship. He'd spend the whole day on Microsoft Excel buzzing his tits off, and at night he'd sleep under the desk. He used to set an alarm for like 5 a.m. so that he'd wake up before anybody got in, and no one would know that he'd been in all night. At the end of the internship, Citi offered him a full-time job, but he turned it down to go do a Computer Science Master's at Cambridge. Then, the next summer, he came back to intern again. Some people are just crazy, I guess.

In the evenings, when everyone had gone home, I used to go over and sit with Matic while he was doing his spreadsheets. He was a big, strong guy, but his hands used to shake, just a little, on his mouse and his keyboard, and his tired eyes were darting around.

During one of those conversations, I asked Matic what he thought I should do with my newfound popularity.

Matic's views were clear: "Don't work on the STIRT desk." He referred to the traders as "anachronisms" who were "stuck in the eighties." I didn't really care about shit like that, but Matic's next point was more troubling:

"FX traders don't make any money."

"FX" stands for "Foreign Exchange," and even though STIRT stood for "Short Term Interest Rates Trading," it sits in the Foreign Exchange department for some reason. The general consensus over on the genius-credit-trader side of the trading floor was that FX traders were idiots, and that their roles would soon be taken over by computers. There was no future. They literally used to refer to the FX traders as "monkeys," a nickname which the FX traders gleefully co-opted for themselves. More dangerous and cutting than all of this though, was the damning indictment that they were poor. That was the only bit that worried me.

In spite of that though, and for reasons which I honestly probably couldn't tell you, I think at that stage I'd already made up my mind.

I used to leave Matic a Red Bull, or a coffee, after those conversations. Then I'd fuck off and he'd sleep on the floor.

. . .

Obviously, I got offered a full-time place on the Citi grad scheme at the end of the internship—that goes without saying—and the STIRT boys kept a close eye on me when I had to go back to LSE to finish off my final year. To a man, each one of them believed that they would have been a professional sportsman were it not for some unfortunate teenage injury, or otherwise cruel twist of fate, and my introduction had finally given them access to the numbers needed for a regular football game: no matter how many we were short, I could always pull some kids up from the street back in Ilford who'd be up for a free game and a couple of beers. Football meant that I was seeing most of the STIRT guys every week. The best players were Hongo and, bizarrely, little Scouse Billy, scampering about with his little round belly. You always knew when Rupert was behind you when you were playing. You could hear him growling in your ear.

Caleb and Rupert kept an especially close eye on me, and a series of overtures were made over the course of the year. At the time, I assumed they were coordinated, and it was only sometime later that I realized the two men had hated each other, and they were more like competitive bids.

Rupert got me and some kids from the street to paint his flat in Clapham. Now I'm not no painter or anything, but he offered to pay us £100 each every day. He paid it to me in £50 notes and I couldn't spend them anywhere. I tried to buy some moisturizer from Boots with three consecutive fifties and in the end I gave up and went home. Rupert's flat was fucking enormous. It was three floors with an entire cinema floor at the bottom. The whole flat didn't have any doors except for the bathrooms. Everywhere else it was rotating walls. He wanted us to paint the flat white, even though it was already white. Whatever. It's his money, I thought.

It must have been about April when Caleb called me in and sat me down in a little glass-walled office with a view of all the other little glass-walled offices in the other buildings, over on the other side of the quay.

When you get a job offer from a big investment bank nowadays, you don't actually know what role you're gonna get. You have to do this big "graduate scheme" training/rotation program, where they teach you some nonsense that nobody cares about in some classrooms up on the top floor, and then you spend literally a year and a half rotating around different desks on the trading floor hoping someone will give you a job.

Caleb didn't want me to do that. He wanted me to start straight on the desk. Now I don't know if he knew that I knew that the desk wasn't a top prospect, but he made me two clear offers. Number one: I could start whenever I wanted. Number two: I could start trading from day one. That meant a line on the profit-and-loss spreadsheet, with a clear number next to my name. That's how people get paid, you know. Clear money, next to your name. And it usually takes years to get that.

Maybe that's why I chose the STIRT desk, despite all of the things Matic told me. Maybe somewhere back then in my boyish, twenty-one-year-old overconfidence, I knew that if they gave me a line on the profit-and-loss spreadsheet, within years it would be the biggest in the bank. It would have been a correct premonition. Or maybe it wasn't that. Maybe it was Billy's Scouse accent and JB's rugby stories. Maybe it was Rupert's cinema room and his rotating walls. Or maybe it was just the way Caleb looked at me, in that little glass box that bright April afternoon, with that huge smile, and the way his eyes glittered, like the water, that I could see through the window, in the quay.

My last exam at LSE was "MA303: Chaos in Dynamical Systems." It was on June 26, 2008, which was a Thursday. I told Caleb I'd start on the Monday. I'd need the weekend to buy trousers and shirts.

After Caleb spoke to me, Hobbs took me to LA and Las Vegas. One of the traders there got a nosebleed in a limousine on the way to Carmen Electra's birthday party and I thought that maybe it was because of the altitude or something so I offered him a tissue. He didn't take it. I was wearing a gray waistcoat from H&M that cost £20.

I was supposed to be studying for my exams.

So there was me. Twenty-one years old with all my hair freshly shaved off and a new pair of pointy shoes from Topman. Walking onto the trading floor on June 30, 2008, as the youngest trader in the whole City, just four days after my last uni exam. I don't know why I shaved all my hair off. It just felt like the right thing to do.

I always remember that after my first one-week internship, a year and a half earlier, I had gathered together all the business cards that I had collected and sent everyone a personalized thank-you email. In those emails, among other things, I had included a request for any advice or suggested reading material that might help me in my nascent career.

One scary-eyed-looking middle-aged Englishman named Clarky had sent me a short, curt reply. All it had said was:

> It was nice to meet you, Gary. Don't rush onto the trading floor. Takeyour time, see the world, enjoy your youth. Once you get in, you'll never get out.
>
> All the best,
> Clarky

Well, I hadn't listened to Clarky. Looking at it now, it seems like much smarter advice than it did at the time. Why didn't I take it?

If I try to put myself back into the shoes of me as a twenty-one-year-old, all I can tell you is this: I was hungry. Probably I'd been hungry for a long time. Sleeping on broken mattresses will do that to you. Do you know what I mean? Do you?

If you were gonna rob a bank, and you saw the vault door there, left open, what would you do? Would you wait around?

Besides, how you gonna see the world with no money?

Fuck it man, it was my time to shine.

I knew from day one things were gonna be different. This was no longer just "impress the boys—buy some burgers—get a job." There's a profit-and-loss line next to my name now. That's *my* money. Money for *me*.

So what do we do? There's a double-pronged plan of attack.

1. Learn to trade.

2. Get a book.

Simple plan, right? What's a book?

Well, the way the STIRT desk works is that everyone's a trader for FX swaps. If you don't know what an FX swap is, don't worry. At this stage I didn't really know either. All you need to know is, you can trade an FX swap in every currency, and the STIRT desk ran ten currencies—Euros (EUR), British pounds (GBP), Swiss francs (CHF), the three Scandinavian currencies (SEK, NOK, DKK), Japanese yen (JPY) and the Australian, New Zealand and Canadian dollars (AUD, NZD, CAD), all of which were traded against the mighty US dollar (USD).

Each trader gets responsibility for one or more currencies. So, as you know, Rupert was the senior trader for euros, a "book" that he shared with Ho Nguyen. Bill ran the British pound book. Caleb ran the book for the Swiss franc, and JB ran the Ozzie (AUD), Kiwi (NZD) and yen (JPY).

So what's the big deal with a book?

The big deal with a book is, when you run a book in a currency, all the customers and all the trades in that currency come directly to you. Why's that good?

Well, remember what we learned from the trading game. Anyone can ask anyone for a price at any time, and that person has to make a price with a "two-point-spread." For example, 67–69, meaning "I will buy at 67 or I will sell at 69." Now imagine there's a bunch of outside customers in that game who are willing to trade on a bigger spread: for example, the four-point spread 66–70, meaning "I will buy at 66 or I will sell at 70." That's a little bit how real markets work. If that were to happen, then you could, say, buy from those outside customers at 66, and then immediately turn around and sell what you bought for 67, securing an immediate and guaranteed profit of 1. If you were willing to hold on to the risk for a little bit longer, you might even find someone willing to pay 68 or 69, potentially doubling or trebling your profit. That's what "getting a book" means. It means access to customers who are willing to trade at worse than market prices, and that means nearly guaranteed profit for you—which, I probably don't need to tell you, is a very good thing. (This, by the way, if you think about it, is exactly what Thomas Cook are doing to you on your foreign exchange money, every time you go on holiday.)

You might be asking yourself at this point, why are customers willing to trade at worse than market prices? That would be a very good question, and it is one that I, at twenty-one years old, didn't think to ask. But don't worry about that. Give it time.

For now, how to get a book.

Well, the flip side of all that free money is that once you have a book you need to be available to make prices at any time. You never know when someone is going to need an FX swap in Swiss francs or Australian dollars or whatever the fuck book that you trade is. And Citibank offers a 24-hour pricing service (there are also desks in New York, Sydney and Tokyo) so if you are taking a piss or are in Las Vegas, someone needs to be making that price. That's why everyone on the desk had an allotted partner whose job was to make the price if they, for whatever reason, were off the desk or otherwise incapacitated (some traders were incapacitated more often than others, as we'll see).

This role is known as "cover trader," and it's an important job. If you are off the desk, and the cover trader quotes a price in your currency, that trade still goes in your book, not his, and the profit (or loss) goes to you. As such, as a junior trader, cover trading was a very important role. You could make (or lose) money for the senior traders on the desk. You could prove your ability as a price-making trader. You could basically stake your claim for a book of your own. If you could prove you were an adequate or even a very profitable cover trader, the senior traders would be fighting to have you covering them when they were away. This would immediately make it clear to everyone that you were rightfully next in line for a book, and perhaps even serve as a reminder to the bossmen that the tired-looking, graying trader in the corner maybe didn't need to be running three whole books to himself.

But when you're green, no one wants you as cover. You're a risk. You're a liability. You first have to win someone's trust. And this is where the two goals coalesce. Win someone's trust, prove to them that you're a good cover trader, and then, hopefully, they'll teach you to trade.

OK, so once more we need a mark. Let's analyze our options here.

First choice, that's an easy one: Billy. Bill has already established himself in my eyes as a bit of a legend and has been officially accredited by Snoopy (whose opinion I respect) as being the smartest trader on the desk. Not only that, but he's British, he's short, and he's not a posh dickhead. So really, we've got a lot in common. That could work. Only problem is, as soon as I turn up on the desk, I see that Snoopy's moved over into that corner and is definitely claiming that space. Snoopy's got like a year and a half experience and seniority over me. That's gonna be a hard one to get.

The next two obvious options are Rupert and JB. I've made an impression on both of these guys and they both seem like they'd be keen to work with me. I could probably get in with either, but there are problems as well. The most obvious being that they both seem kind of insane. JB first. JB is a lovely guy, there is no doubt about it, and by now I've heard all of his stories and had more than a few beers with the guy. I was on this desk for five weeks on the summer internship, remember. The problem is he speaks at a million miles an hour and I don't understand a word that he says about trading or anything else. He might not be the best spiritual guide. Not only that but some young-ish Frankenstein-looking trader seems to have been brought over from New York and he's sitting right next to JB. So that spot could be taken as well.

Now that leaves Rupert. The positives are kind of obvious here. Number one the dude took me to Las Vegas. Number two, I've painted his bedroom. That seems like a good basis for a friendship, am I right? Rupert splits the euro book with Hongo, but Hong is already in his thirties and there seems to be a space for a junior. He's the senior euro rates trader, which is the biggest trading role on the desk, so he must be a good trader, and he seems to have a sensible, disciplined trading style that could be a good basis from which to learn. On the debit side he is maybe a psychopath. I've spent enough time with him by this point to know that that definitely is a risk. But nobody's perfect, you know?

There was also Caleb, of course. There was always Caleb. But come on, Caleb is the bossman. We can't do that—I ain't no teacher's pet.

So I settled on Rupert. Or should I say, Rupert settled on me.

See with Snoopy moved over into Billy's corner down by the window, I got put into Snoopy's old seat, far from the window, half spilling out into the aisle. From there I was a bit separated from most of the traders by the empty station to my left. I don't know why they kept this station permanently empty. Maybe it was as a physical reminder to me, and previously to Snoopy, that the desk junior should know their place. To the left of that empty space was Rupert, who spent the entire first half of my first day completely ignoring me.

I didn't get to lunch that day until about 2 p.m., and when I came back Rupert had moved himself into the empty swivel chair next to mine, and was swinging it about from side to side. That worried me, but

I tried to pretend as if nothing was up. I sat down and looked straight forward into my screens, but both of his huge round knees were pointing straight into me, so it was hard to pretend he wasn't there.

"Where have you been?"

I turned to him as if this was all nonchalant and normal. He was squeezing the fuck out of a neon-orange stress ball.

"Oh, I just went to get lunch?"

"What did you eat?" Rupert responded kind of too quickly before I'd managed to get my question mark out.

"Erm, it was like . . . sausage and . . . beans and . . . tomato?"

"Where did you get that?"

"Erm . . . I got it from the canteen, downstairs."

Rupert did that thing again where he was just silent and looking at me for way too long, and it would have been awkward for everyone in the situation, except it was only just me and him there.

"I've worked on this desk for twelve years. And I've never even once gone to that canteen. We eat. On. The desk."

Then he just kept on looking at me for ages, and I didn't really know what to say.

You know, only just two months before this, me and Rupert had been standing by a swimming pool on a warm and dark evening, at Jay-Z's afterparty, in LA. And Rupert had been asking a pretty girl in a yellow bikini what her Chinese zodiac sign was. Rupert was a tiger, by the way. So was I.

I can't remember what the girl was.

OK, I thought. So that's how it's gonna be, yeah?

No problem.

This was not an isolated incident. In my first few days, during which I spent most of my time trying to install software programs on my computer and talking to a guy named Jimmy John in Bangalore on the phone, Rupert picked up a habit of grabbing me suddenly, firmly, and directly from behind by both shoulders and shouting things out like

"WHAT IS UK CONSUMER CONFIDENCE???"

Or

"WHAT'S THE US SERVICES PMI??"

I knew the correct answer of course was "I don't know." But horribly unfortunately, that turned out to no longer be an adequate reply.

"That's not good enough anymore Gary! You're a trader now! You have to know!"

This was distressing for a couple of reasons. Firstly, the "I don't know" strategy had been so phenomenally successful throughout my internship that parting with it felt like losing a leg; and, secondly, I didn't even really know what PMI stood for. Three-letter acronyms have always been a weakness of mine. At one point, physically grabbed and raised from my seat during another long-distance phone call, I, in my panic, hazarded another strategy and hastily shouted something like

"Forty-seven point one!"

As a guess.

The response to this could fairly have been described as no less than righteous fury, and, given that the number shouted was both incorrect and made up (never a good combination at the best of times) I suppose, even in hindsight, that was probably fair.

For the sake of my nervous system, I did two things.

The first thing was, I snuck over to Snoopy and asked him what the fuck a PMI was and how I was supposed to know its exact number on any given day.

Snoopy showed me an "Economic Release Calendar," which is a full list of all the economic data released, all over the world, on every single day, and the exact time of the release. The amount of data points on any given day is enormous, often more than fifty or sixty, although they are generally released all at the same time for any given country, which means that there would normally only be three or four significant times in each day when data would come out. From then on, every day, the first thing I would do every morning was check the times of all the data releases and set a load of alarms on my little Nokia mobile phone for five minutes before. After that, I never got a number wrong, and after a couple of weeks Rupert stopped grabbing me. That was a relief. I never stopped setting those alarms though, every single weekday, for three whole years after that. By then I didn't give a fuck about data releases, and no one would have dared grab me anyway.

You know, that was a long time ago, but still, sometimes, even now when I'm at my laptop and I'm not concentrating, I find I've opened that calendar up. Today, on the day that I am writing this, UK Inputs Producer Price Inflation came out at 7 a.m. It was 22.6 percent. That's pretty high.

The second thing I did was, I decided, that if there were any other option, any option at all, I wouldn't be learning to trade from Rupert Hobhouse.

2

SO THAT'S HOW I ENDED UP WITH SPENGLER.

Theodore Barnaby Spengler III was, for want of a better word, an idiot.

That's probably not fair, to be honest. He was more of an idiot savant.

Spengler had not been my first choice as a mentor. He had not been my second and he'd not been third.

Once I'd decided that I was going to escape Rupert, I'd tried to see if there was any chance with Bill. I managed to convince him to let me manually input some of his trades into the computer systems, but I messed one up in my first week of doing it which led to him screaming "You cost me forty FUCKING grand you fucking TWAT!" halfway across the floor.

Forty fucking grand was twice my dad's salary. So it was somewhat with my tail between my legs that I fell back to my final safe haven and, just like I had done on my very first day on the desk, rolled my swivel chair over next to JB.

But there was a new presence next to JB now, the oversized, Frankenstein-headed frame of Theodore Spengler.

Theodore Spengler looked exactly like Herman Munster, from the Munsters, and I'd noticed his gurning, bobbing head bouncing next to JB's the first moment I'd stepped back on the desk as a full-time hire. The previous winter Caleb had fired three traders. I assumed that Spengler must have been some kind of up-and-coming star brought in to replace those guys.

I quickly realized this wasn't the case.

What had actually happened was that Spengler had been hired by the New York STIRT desk from the US graduate scheme about a year previously, but they had quickly recognized this as a grave error of judgment and had somehow convinced Caleb to take him off of their hands. What Caleb received in return for that cursed gift, I will never know, but I do hope it was something good.

What was so bad about the boy?

Spengler was a huge, lumbering presence with the body shape of a muffin, who walked like a farmer falling over. He would cascade onto the desk every morning at exactly 7:29 a.m., which was precisely one minute before being officially late. Upon falling into his seat, he would invariably flip up one of the little switches on his speakerbox and call out to one of his brokers. The broker's name was always a normal name with a *y* on the end, so he would shout out something like

"Hey Granty!" or "Hey Millsy!" or "Hey Johnathany!"

In some sort of completely incomprehensible accent, because he was from Johannesburg or Cape Town, or somewhere like that.

And the broker, who for some reason would half the time himself be from Essex or East London, would inevitably reply with something along the lines of:

"Hey Spengler! How you doing you old rogue/you big charmer/you maniac, last night was wild, wasn't it! Were you all right getting home?"

In one of my very first mornings sitting with Spengler, it turned out that he had not, in fact, been all right getting home, but had actually pissed himself in a taxi. I know this because he told this to his broker quite openly, quite gleefully in fact. The broker himself seemed to find it hilarious, which I found surprising, because to me it seemed pretty disgusting. JB cast a look over his shoulder at Spengler which told me I was not the only one feeling that way.

I can't remember which broker it was that Spengler told this story to. I think it was Granty. But it doesn't really matter, because Spengler then flicked up every single one of his switches, one at a time, and told the same story, in identical words, to seven different brokers. Every single broker laughed hilariously, even the three Danish brokers, all of whom were called Carsten. The whole process took about thirty minutes. This is how I learned that brokers are paid to laugh.

Public stories of poor personal hygiene were not Spengler's only peccadillo. He compulsively, constantly, endlessly regaled me with terrible jokes. Inappropriate jokes, unacceptable jokes, and JB would scold him every time. That did absolutely nothing to slow down the boy, who seemed only to revel in scorn. Every single time JB upbraided him, the boy's pained gurn would stretch at the seams, and something would rise in those dull eyes: a sparkle, a glitter, a smile.

The jokes were sometimes anti-Semitic. A deeply unwise move for a South African giant sitting no more than three meters from a Jewish boss with the power to determine his pay. He once made one of these jokes while Caleb was walking behind him, and Caleb firmly grabbed the back of his swivel chair and instantly spun him 180 degrees. Caleb said nothing but stared down at the boy, and the boy looked up at the face of the man who was only three years older than he was and he looked deep into his eyes, and his mouth seemed to be trying to form words but he said nothing and then in the end his lips stopped moving altogether. He looked like he was going to start sucking his thumb. They stood like that for about fifteen seconds before Caleb sighed deeply and turned Spengler's chair back around and walked off muttering.

"Think about what the fuck you are doing you fucking retard."

Spengler would scratch his arse endlessly and swallow down burgers at troubling speed. More than that though, what I most remember, are Spengler's phone calls with his mum. Once a day, at 3 p.m. precisely, the boy's mother's phone call would come through. They would speak for exactly an hour, inexplicably, in Flemish. I'm still grateful that I don't speak Flemish, even now, to this very day.

The maddest thing of all was, I quite liked the boy.

Why?

Probably because he was a fucking good trader.

I'd been sitting with Spengler and JB for about a week and a half when Rupert turned around and dropped a meaty hand on my shoulder and said:

"You're coming for lunch today with me and the brokers."

I'd met brokers before. There'd been brokers in Vegas. There'd been brokers on the ski trip. But I'd never been on a broker lunch before. And it had never just been me, and Rupert, and the brokers.

We took a black cab into the center of the city, even though a train would have been quicker. Rupert filled his seat amply, looking forward, as the car edged through traffic, and I perched on one of those little fold-out chairs that look backward.

I must have seemed nervous, because Rupert literally asked me, out of nowhere:

"Are you nervous?"

I told him that I was fine, and then he asked me if I'd ever eaten Japanese food before. I replied, honestly, that I hadn't. Then he asked me,

"Is it because you've never used chopsticks?"

And for the first time that I had ever seen it in him, an expression crossed his face of what seemed to me to be a genuine kind of brotherly, or fatherly, concern.

He placed his brown, expensive-looking bag down on the floor of the taxi, and he pulled out two pens.

"Look," he said to me. "You place your little finger and your ring finger like this." And he squashed his two fat fingers together and he showed me.

"This creates a little crease between the two fingers, here, you see? And you can place the first stick into that cradle, like this, and then you can hold it there with the base of your thumb."

And he did that with one of the pens.

"That leaves the tip of your thumb and your other two fingers free to hold the other stick," he said, flexing his fingers, "and then you can use the two sticks to pick things up."

And he used the tips of the two pens to pinch the flesh of my left hand.

"Here," he gave the pens to me. "You try."

And I tried to do it and I dropped both the pens to the floor, and Rupert smiled.

Rupert didn't know it, but the actual reason for my anxiety was that I had no idea how much the restaurant was going to cost. It had had some kind of obscure Japanese name that I didn't know how to spell, so I hadn't been able to Google the prices, although I suspect that that might not have helped. Before leaving, I'd gone to the cashpoint, and withdrawn £200 from my bank account, because that was my daily limit for withdrawal, and added it to the £40 that had already been in my wallet. I was worried it wouldn't be enough.

I picked the two pens up off the ground and returned them to Rupert.

Rupert put them back into his bag and he leaned back into the seat of the taxi, exhaling deeply and spreading his arms out wide across the backs of the seats.

"Don't worry about the brokers," he said to me, "they're only brokers. If they weren't brokers, they'd be bus drivers."

I still hold chopsticks that way to this day.

So what is a broker?

People sometimes use the terms "broker" and "trader" interchangeably. In fact, they are quite different worlds. This was obvious to me even at this point, because it seemed almost all of the brokers were from Essex or East London, despite the fact that on the trading floor, which was conspicuously *in* East London, there were no such accents to be found.

In fact, as Rupert had expressed so succinctly, the differences were more than linguistic. By 2008, it was almost impossible to get onto a trading floor without a degree from an "elite" university. Even on the STIRT desk, every single trader had one, including me, with the single exception of Bill. Most brokers hadn't been to university at all.

It is the cockney voices of the brokers that bounce out of the speaker-boxes on the desk. Their dulcet tones endlessly sing numbers in a back-to-back rhythm that in some ways harks back to fruit and veg street markets. Strawberries, pound a pound, three-month euros, 4.3 4.6. It's been nearly ten years now since I've worked on a trading floor in London, and I wonder if those musical voices are still so cockney. I hope they are, but I fear that they're not.

The brokers don't work for the banks. They work for these cartels called "brokerages" and their job is, technically, to make connections between traders. The traders make the deals, and the brokers just match them together. That's important: the brokers don't carry any risk if the trades go bad, only the traders do. The brokers are kind of like estate agents. They get paid on commission, which means that they always want you to do more and more trades, regardless of whether the trades are good or bad.

Theoretically, the brokers allow you to buy something without tipping off your opposition to the fact that you wanna buy. This can be useful if you're a big player, like Citibank, and you wanna buy without moving the market. The theory is, if you wanna buy something at, say, 36, you tell your broker, and he starts shouting "36 bid 36 bid 36 bid" down every speakerbox in the City, and hopefully he finds someone who wants to sell there. The deal can happen without anyone ever knowing that you, specifically, wanted to buy, and that's good, because if everybody knows you're a buyer then they might push the price up before you can buy.

That's the theory though. What's the reality?

Well the reality . . . is they do broker lunches.

Back in the cab with Rupert, we eventually pulled up at some fancy restaurant in Central London. I'd love to tell you the name of the place, but I have truly no idea what it was.

What I can tell you is that it was a Japanese restaurant, and that an immaculate hostess in an immaculate outfit greeted us immaculately in a small but impeccable reception area that was far too dark for that time of day. Somewhat dazzled by all the perfection, I was led up some stairs, or it could have been down some stairs, and into a vast dining room area that was simultaneously both flooded with light from huge windows and, internally, curiously dark, due to the fact that all of the furniture was black.

It was not yet midday and the tables—which were huge, jet-black, perfectly round, alien-looking things—were almost all totally empty. The hostess walked us through the great and spacious dining area for quite some time and then round a corner formed by a wall of glass bottles. This led us into a secluded area where the largest and blackest of all the tables stood bathed in sunlight right next to a floor-to-ceiling window which cast a harsh angled light onto the faces of three brokers, who sat, huddled together on the table's far side.

Our entrance dissolved the huddle in an instant, and the three brokers stood up at the same time and all of them rushed to shake both our hands.

I took my measure of the three. There was a young one: brutish, confused-looking. A middle-aged one, seductive and serpentine. And an older one, whose hair was thick and a pure white, and who must have been at least sixty years old, and who looked as if his head had never stopped growing a day in his life.

That one, the one with the big head, introduced himself to me in an impossibly deep voice:

"Hi, my name's Bighead."

The *h*, of course, isn't pronounced.

A dance ensued in which the five of us tried to seat ourselves around the enormous circular table in a way which did not seem awkward. It was difficult, and I found myself separated from Rupert by some distance, round the other side of the table, next to Bighead, which I liked because his deep cockney accent and his thick shock of impossibly white hair and the pure size of his head all reminded me of my dead grandad and put me at ease, and it also meant that I was not next to Rupert. The conversation all flowed, like a river, in one direction, from the brokers toward Rupert, and I liked that as well, for it meant that I didn't have to say anything, and I had a lot of time to observe.

Although Bighead was the eldest, he did not lead the conversation. That was done by the middle-aged trader, whose name was Timothy Twineham and whose own hair was also thick but impossibly black. The conversation was perfectly smooth. It was like honey. And there was never a break or a pause. Sometimes gaps were left intentionally, for dramatic effect, and Bighead would fill them with his contrabass voice. The young broker, who was seated between Timothy and Rupert, said nothing. He simply swung his face back and forth between the two as if it were a tennis match, endlessly nodding, enthusiastically, and occasionally rocking that face backward for a cackling laugh.

When the young broker did that, I laughed too, but more gently. Rupert never laughed.

White wine was served, and a very large platter of sashimi. I did not, at that time, know what sashimi was. It is basically sushi without rice. Rupert explained to me (with some difficulty, for there was really quite some distance between us) that sashimi is better for one's health than sushi, and that eating it can keep the weight off. I looked at the size of the platter, and I looked at the size of Rupert. I nodded quite deeply. I reached some distance into the middle of the table and stabbed a small, pinkish-white piece of fish with an immaculate chopstick and tried to balance it over to my plate.

The white wine was being drunk quickly, and I was drinking it too, even though I don't really like wine, because I didn't want to make a faux pas. There was an anonymous kind of deep bassy music playing in the background that I have since found to be almost ubiquitous in expensive London restaurants, and after a time, the music and the wine and the conversation started to coalesce into one, and I started to find that I could barely hear the actual words that anyone was saying at all. It didn't matter because I didn't have to say anything. All I had to do was lean earnestly forward, into the table, and look deeply at whoever was talking, and look off into the distance sometimes and nod. I tried to use the chopstick technique that Rupert had taught me, and I dropped three pieces of fish onto the table and one piece of fish onto the floor.

It was quite some time before the second course arrived, and I had been awaiting it quite eagerly because I was already starting to get quite drunk by then, and I had encountered some technical problems with the first course, which were largely that it was slippery and quite far away.

Unfortunately, the second course was no more straightforward, for what came to the table was an extremely large plate of nothing but raw chicken and raw beef. Now, you probably know that raw chicken is inedible, or, at least, not safely edible, and I did also suspect that as well. But until just an hour or so previously I had held a similarly strong conviction about raw fish and that had clearly turned out to be wrong. I waited a few minutes to see what others were doing, but they were deeply embroiled in a conversation about the Morgan Stanley Senior Euro Dealer, and eventually I had to relent. I reached out and picked up a piece of raw chicken between two sticks and was, for the first time, able to get it, unsullied, to my plate. I ate it. It was quite disgusting.

The disgustingness was sufficient for me to question this Japanese convention and I leaned over to Bighead, with whom I was rapidly developing an unspoken, grand-paternal bond, and nudged him gently under the table.

He turned and leaned over to me, conspiratorially.

"This chicken," I said to him, under my breath, "don't you think it's . . . A little . . . Disgusting??"

Bighead, who had himself drunk quite some wine, looked at me quizzically. Then he looked at the large platter of beef and chicken then he turned and looked at me again.

"Did you eat some of that chicken?" He was looking quite bemused.

"Yeah, of course I ate it, it's fucking chicken. What the fuck else am I supposed to do to it?"

And my new grandad laughed deeply and loudly and he stood up and he removed a part of the surface of the table and would you believe there was a whole fucking grill under there and nobody had told me, and he didn't stop laughing for ages and nobody really quite understood why because he didn't tell anyone that I'd just ate some raw chicken and, to be honest, I was grateful for that.

At the end of that lunch, two hours after its beginning, nobody paid.

Well, somebody must have paid, but I didn't see anyone pay. All I knew for sure was that it wasn't me. And nobody asked me to pay.

And then all of us, who were by then quite well drunk, went back to our offices and did work.

And I didn't really know what that meant.

Once Rupert had taken me out, that popped the cork for Spengler.

See, the thing about Spengler was, Spengler was lonely. People don't talk to their mums on the phone in Flemish for one hour every day at work unless they're lonely. If you've got someone at your workplace doing that, you should check in and make sure they're OK. Spengler was a long way from his mum and a long way from his hometown and he didn't know how to make friends.

But if you're a trader at a big London investment bank, in some ways you don't need to make friends. For there are some people who are paid to be friends with you and those people are the brokers. And now, also, for Spengler, there was me. And Spengler was happy about that.

So it was only two days after my first lunch with Rupert that Spengler took me for a lunch of his own. Snoopy had to cover the Scandinavian currencies (that was Spengler's job, the Scandinavian currencies), and me and Spengler went off in another cab, this time to eat steaks.

In the cab, Spengler didn't teach me how to eat steaks (although to be honest I probably could have benefited from that). Instead, he gave me a detailed lowdown of the three brokers and one trader who I would be meeting, and the significance they played in the Swedish Krona Foreign Exchange Swap markets. That's all Spengler ever talked about when it was just me and him together: Swedish Foreign Exchange Swap Markets and the people who were in them. I wouldn't have asked for anything else. We would be meeting:

1. Granty: swarthy, middle-aged, charming, head of Swedish FX swaps broking.

2. Jonesy: bald, significantly older, self-deprecating, shouldn't really be doing this anymore but he's on his third divorce.

3. Bushead: Young, Scouse, Swedish FX broker. Once again named for the size and the color of his head.

4. Simon Chang: Young, up-and-coming Swedish FX trader for HSBC. Very smart and has enormous calves. From Hong Kong. Everyone calls him Jet Li, but it's OK because he doesn't mind.

It was of no significance to anyone that not a single person at this lunch was Swedish. Less than eighteen months after this I would myself be made senior Swedish FX swap dealer having not spent a single day in Sweden in my life.

The steak restaurant was deep in the City of London, at the end of a number of meandering alleyways, and the dining room itself was, upon entering, set cavernously deep into the ground. Not a trace of sunlight entered the large room and, whilst I'm sure it must have had electric lighting, that lighting was sufficiently dim and atmospheric that in my memory the place was lit by candles, which lent an air of surrealism and conspiracy to a meal eaten in the middle of the day.

As we approached the table I saw the four men sitting together and started to match their heads to the descriptions I'd been given. In particular, I recognized the red, bulbous head of Bushead, who, unbeknownst to Spengler, had been with me and Rupert in Vegas.

No sooner had I noticed the brokers, than the brokers noticed us too, and, at the moment they saw Spengler walking to their table, they stood up and began cheering and jeering, and wailing and clapping and going wild. I had not been expecting them to do that—Spengler didn't normally get that kind of reception in the office—and I turned round to Spengler in confusion, and I saw that the boy was gurning an enormous smile that looked fit to crack that Frankensteinish face of his, and I saw that beneath that, he was starting to blush.

A few things happened at that meal with Spengler.

The first was that Bushead, who had spent three days with me in Las Vegas, never once mentioned, to anyone, that he knew me.

I knew Bushead, and I liked him. You could even say I knew him quite well. I had once seen him, very drunk at three in the morning outside a nightclub in Los Angeles, gesture to Lindsay Lohan's girlfriend, via a winding movement of his right hand, that he wanted her to roll down her car window, and then, upon receiving her somewhat generous acquiescence, thank her by shouting, "Your car's fucking shit mate!" Right into her face, before proceeding to piss in a bush.

He had honestly had no idea who she was; he had simply just disliked her car.

I had felt that that had been a bonding experience between us, compounded by the fact that we were from similar backgrounds, but the moment I sat down Bushead gave me a look and I immediately knew what it meant. That was then, and this is now. And I instinctively knew he was right.

Spengler's riotous reception led into a solid ten minutes of aggressive ribbing and cussing and Spengler squirmed and smiled and giggled throughout it and turned his face down like a young blushing bride. He loved it. You could tell.

Once that was over, they got to the real talk. Swedish Foreign Exchange Swaps and red wine. Spengler was a fiend for the both of them. I've never seen any man consume more of either.

Spengler and Simon Chang were machines. They were heavy. Once you got them started talking about FX Swaps, the conversation never slowed down. At this stage, I still didn't really know what an FX swap was, and I wasn't in the conversation. But I sat across the table and stared at them, and I watched the passion, the love, in their eyes. They wanted to know if the three days at the end of September were particularly cheap due to a mispricing, or whether it was that Ingmar at Handelsbank Stockholm perhaps knew something that they didn't know. They wanted to know if the Riksbank were having another dinner in October and, if so, which traders were going. What about Anders at DNB Copenhagen? How was his alcoholism going? How were things between him and his wife?

They were fiends, they wanted to know everything. And while I understood almost nothing of what they were saying, I wanted to know everything too, just like them, and I watched and I watched and I listened and listened and as the time passed and the plates were brought over and taken away and as bottle after bottle of red wine continued to flow, I started to think to myself that perhaps that seat that I'd fallen into, behind JB's left shoulder, and behind Spengler's right, was perhaps not such a bad seat after all.

I'd said nothing, almost this whole time. I'd not needed to. The madness of Spengler and Simon had filled up the space. I had, at first, intended to drink the wine at the same pace that Spengler did, but having seen the speed at which he inhaled his first three glasses, I recognized instantly that I couldn't do that and, lacking a pacemaker, and engrossed in vicarious conversation, I ended up not drinking at all.

I had been watching them for over an hour, and the food had been and gone long already, when, for the first time, Spengler turned his huge face toward me and gurned an attempt at a smile, and his teeth were all horrid and purple and he said to me in his deep Afrikaans drawl that was rolling and stumbling,

"Gary . . . That's a very expensive . . . red wine you're . . . Not drinking."

And I did the only thing I could have done in that situation. I turned to my wine glass and I looked at it and I picked it up, and I tilted it at him and I drank some, and then I put it down and then I turned my face to his face that was glowing and purple and I smiled and I said to him: "That's lovely, Spengler. That's really lovely."

From there, the drinking outings just multiplied, and a kind of inverse proportionality rule became established, where I went out with each trader with a frequency in exact opposite proportion to that which I would have chosen had I been given the choice.

Spengler and Rupert took me out (separately, obviously) at least once a week, and each of their behaviors became increasingly atrocious in ways that were peculiarly specific to them.

The broker lunches became broker dinners, and Spengler was much worse in the evenings than he was in the daytimes and his teeth were much redder and there was one young broker from Essex who couldn't have been a day over nineteen, and when Spengler was drunk he would kick him in the backside and shout, "Take me drinking, Broker Bitch Boy!"

And when that would happen the boy wouldn't look back at Spengler, he'd turn and he'd look at me, and he wasn't much younger than I was, and his face would have an air of solemn complicity about it, and he wouldn't smile and I wouldn't smile back at him, and all I'd do is I would try to meet his stern gaze that burned into my eyes and I'd try my best to match his solemnity, and then we'd both nod.

Rupert used to want to take me out in the evenings in Clapham, where he lived, Ilford's polar opposite in London in more than just geographical ways.

It used to take me hours to get back from there and sometimes we would stay out so late that I would miss the last train, and Rupert would have to pay for me to get a taxi all the way home, so I didn't like going, but I didn't really have a choice about it, because Rupert wanted me to meet all his friends.

And his friends all had beautiful shirts that were monogrammed and freshly ironed and they had expensive haircuts, and my shirts were from Topman and I'd bought them on the premise that they were "non-iron," and they all started calling me "Gary the Geezer" and I started talking a little bit more Essex than was really my voice.

And one of his friends had been with us in Vegas, and he was a trader at Goldman Sachs and his name was Pippy-Holloway or something, and he'd been the guy who'd got a nosebleed in the limo that time, and he was always there when we went out. One day at a fancy-dress house party at Rupert's fancy place, where I had come dressed as Robin and Rupert had let me bring Harry from the street, who had come dressed as Batman, and it was the first time we'd ever seen anyone take cocaine in the flesh, that guy Pippy-Holloway had introduced me to his girlfriend.

And she was beautiful, of course, in a porcelain kind of a way, and she was all dressed in white like she'd come as a fairy or something, and I was so shocked to find out that Pippy had a girlfriend after all the things that I'd seen him doing in Vegas and I looked at her and I kind of felt bad for her, but she seemed happy, you know, she was smiling, so what could I do? I smiled back at her and I put out my hand and we shook hands and I said: "Hi, I'm Gary, yeah it's lovely to meet you too."

I didn't talk to her for very long, but I asked her how long she'd been dating Pippy-Holloway for, because I'd been wondering, and it turned out they'd been dating for years.

But it wasn't just Rupert and Spengler who were taking me out, everyone got involved at some point. JB was always in the pub drinking with the brokers, and I could join him whenever I liked, and Hong would come and Snoopy would come too and sometimes even Caleb would come along. And Snoopy would take me out with his brokers too, whenever he got the chance, and I would always be happy to go with him because I felt safe with him and he himself would always seem happy as long as he was being fed expensive food. And every Wednesday we'd go out and play football and Harry from the street would come along to every game, and maybe some other kids from the street too, and some brokers, and then after that we'd go out for beers.

What fascinated me most about hanging out with the brokers, was that you would often see the same brokers in different places, with different traders. Bushead, for example, was Spengler's broker, because he broked Skandis, but he had been in Vegas with me and Rupert and all the other euro traders. Jonesy, despite having been at my lunch with Spengler, was actually a Canadian dollar broker, which made him Snoopy's broker, and he was often out for lunch with Snoopy. Bighead, my adopted city grandad, had been for lunch that time with me and Rupert, but he was not actually Rupert's broker, he was actually a Sterling broker, of Bill's.

What was interesting about this was not simply that the brokers were attending lunches and dinners of different traders, it was that the brokers *themselves* were totally different, each time. The Bushead that was with me in Vegas, wantonly insulting the transport choices of celebrities, was unrecognizable from the Bushead in the steak restaurant, with Spengler. The Bighead who seduced Rupert with sushi was nothing like the Bighead drinking in old pubs by the river with Bill. When the brokers were with Rupert they were controlled, they were stoic, they spoke of the euro trader at Deutsche Bank in ways that were cutting and cynical and harsh. When they were with Spengler they were wild and abrasive and insulting, and they spoke only about the boy himself and the market. When they were with JB, they spoke about rugby. When they were with Snoopy it was all golf and food. The brokers were chameleons, even their voices changed. And they seemed to know exactly what each trader wanted. Spengler wanted red wine and white tablecloths followed by nightclubs. Rupert wanted expensive sushi and bars. Caleb, when he went out, wanted prestigious sporting events. Billy wanted a pub lunch and a view of the Thames. The brokers never seemed to ask what the traders wanted, or where they wanted to go. They seemed to osmose it. They just knew.

I was offered cocaine once by a broker. Exactly once. I turned it down. I was never offered it again. I wondered if it had gone on my permanent record. I wondered what else would end up on there.

3

THE EVENINGS WITH RUPERT WERE GETTING MORE AND MORE FRE-
quent, and later and later, and it was inevitable things would blow up. I
was young, but I was only human, and I was still getting into the office
at six thirty every day.

The thing that I liked about going out with Spengler was that he was
always drunk out of his mind by about 9 p.m. I could just go home and
get a good night's sleep without saying anything and he wouldn't even
realize I'd gone. You couldn't pull that shit with Rupert. He'd drink and
he'd drink and he'd never get drunk. He knew where you were at any
given time. He saw everything. I went home when he wanted me to go
home.

One evening, at a fancy bar in Clapham somewhere, with a stomach
full of sashimi and mojitos, we were getting close to the time of the last
train. Timothy Twineham was there, Pippy-Holloway was somewhere.
At last-train time I would always try to make a move because I knew that
if I left at about that time it would save Rupert the taxi fare and that
meant he was more likely to allow me to leave.

But he didn't allow me to leave.

"Stay out. I'll get you a taxi."

But I didn't get a taxi.

Over time, "get a taxi" became "stay at my place," and that meant we
were drinking until 4 a.m. Remember, I start work at six thirty.

My alarm went off at 5:10 a.m. and I was sleeping on an enormous
sofa in an enormous cinema room and I felt immediately that I was
gonna be sick. Throwing up in Rupert's cinema room seemed like the
kind of thing that a man could be killed for, so I held it in and somehow
I got into the office without being sick on the tube.

I didn't last much longer than that.

By seven forty-five I was locked in a toilet cubicle throwing last night's sashimi into the bowl like those banking retrogrades in the movies. I staggered my way back to the desk about half an hour later and it must have been obvious what I had been doing because Caleb sent me immediately home. He didn't seem angry or anything, he just walked over as soon as I got back from the bathroom and put his hand on my shoulder and told me, "Go home."

I thought that was the right decision, to be honest, so I left.

That wasn't the big problem though. The big problem was what happened next.

I was obviously keen to redeem myself the next day, so I got in at about 6 a.m. to be the first on the desk.

Billy, as always, was the next guy to get in and he didn't say anything as he walked past me, he just laughed as he walked past with his cappuccino and he gave me a pinch on the back of my neck. Remember, my seat was on the very edge of the desk, so every trader had to walk past me as they walked in, and everyone was giving me some light-hearted shit. When Caleb walked past he was in high spirits, and he said, more at me than to me, "What happened to you yesterday, Gazza? You feelin' better today? Was it Hobby who did that to you?"

And I laughed and I thought nothing of it. Five minutes later Rupert walked in.

"Morning Rupert," Caleb said, without turning his face from his screens. "Gary's back today. He told me you did that to him."

I, like Caleb, did not need to turn and face Rupert to know what his reaction would be. I began to concentrate very hard on looking forward.

For about five minutes, nothing happened. No one on the desk said anything at all to anyone and I didn't see anything because I was using every muscle available to me to look directly and exactly at my screens. At that time, there was still an empty station to the left of me, and, to the left of that, Rupert's station. I was certain that if I turned my head even an inch sideways, I would see Rupert staring at me.

It was after about the sixth or seventh minute that I started to hear it, a kind of low, guttural moan. It was difficult not to react to that, but with great effort, I succeeded, and the volume of the moaning started rising and rising until it became more clearly and more distinctly a growl.

Many years later, I encountered a wild boar in a temple on a mountain in Kyoto, and it made a very similar sound. The growling, again, was difficult not to react to, but I felt that I had settled on a path now, and had I turned and faced Rupert at this point, it could only make the situation worse. Besides, I couldn't be the only person hearing the growling, and no one else had said anything. So I sat there, perspiring lightly, looking very intensely and purposefully forward, and endeavoring not to react.

Then the banging started. A thump and a cracking bang, and then a pause, and two more loud thumps and two more cracking bangs. It was humanly impossible not to react to this, and it also occurred to me, on an instinctive level, that I might be in danger now, physically, so I turned to my left to look at Rupert, and when I saw him, this is what I saw.

Rupert's large hands were spread flat on his desk and his elbows were out at right angles, and his arms were holding his upper body upward so that it was leaned forward and twisted round and his head was projected quite some way forward, not toward his screens, but up and around and over the vacant space that was between us, so that his face was less than two feet from where mine was. He was baring and gnashing his teeth whilst growling loudly, like a dog. Under each trader's desk were two small doors which could be opened inward to reveal the computer towers of the computers that we were using and, at infrequent intervals Rupert must have been kicking his legs out wildly at those doors, for his body was jerking and loud cracks were emerging from beneath him which must have come from the doors smashing and bouncing off of the metal brackets behind.

I took all this in, of course, in a moment, and in that moment, I didn't know what to do. The sight was, quite simply, fantastical. It was amazing. And I couldn't tear my eyes away.

I got myself into trouble, a few times, when I was a kid. A few times, it had been with genuinely dangerous people, and I'd known people who'd been seriously hurt. I knew what it was like to be threatened. But no one had ever gnashed at me like a dog.

I knew that I should turn around and look back at my screens, but I couldn't stop looking at him. And so he looked at me, and he swung his head round at me, and he gnashed at me for what must have been twenty seconds, and I have no visual memory of anything other than

Rupert's taut, spasming, animalistic body, lashing out from its pink-shirted cage at me. But nothing happened. No one intervened.

And then suddenly, after this wild twenty seconds of wonder, I snapped back to my senses, and I remembered that I was there, in this place, for a reason, and that looking at this flailing, lurching wolf of a man was insane, and I swung my head back toward my screens, and I could still hear the growling, but the gnashing stopped, and the growling subsided slowly, and I didn't look around for an hour, after that, but the noise calmed and, eventually, it stopped.

And neither I, nor Rupert, ever mentioned a word of those twenty seconds to one another, ever again.

And the maddest thing was that, after that happened, for the rest of the day, and forever afterward, he didn't seem mad about it at all.

But I tell you what though, I started going to Clapham less.

Things changed soon after that.

I wanted to introduce brokers, and broker lunches and broker dinners, into this story, because a lot of the important things that happen on trading desks don't actually happen on trading desks at all. They happen in the bars and the restaurants and the pubs of the City, and at Wimbledon and at Wembley stadium and in the Venetian in Las Vegas and on yachts in Båstad in Sweden. In all this, brokers are a big part of the social fabric that holds the trading floor together. What's more, before long one particular broker will start to play a big role in my life.

But when I look back at that time, it's funny the things that I do and don't remember.

I remember the names of almost none of the bars, restaurants or pubs that I went to. Years later, some time after I had retired from trading, as a special occasion for a friend's birthday party, I went to Hakkasan, which is a fancy Chinese restaurant in Central London. It wasn't until I walked in that I was flooded with a strong sense of déjà vu and I realized that I had been there, not once, but probably a number of times before, and it was literally only at that moment that it occurred to me that I had probably already been in most of the most expensive restaurants in London. At the time, I had never really viewed these places as restaurants, as places to be enjoyed. I had always viewed them only as work, and as

Spengler and Rupert sipped at their expensive wines that tasted like shit to me, my priorities were only ever to learn, to impress, to fit in.

There are only a few restaurant names I remember. L'Anima was the first place that I ever ate veal. It was delicious. Locanda Locatelli was the restaurant in which a broker stole my shoe and promised to give it back to me only if I promised to do more business with him, which is why I went home with one shoe.

There are a couple other evenings I remember. The first time Billy took me out, when I realized that he was not always taciturn and sober, but was in fact a prodigious drinker. That night we had been accompanied by one of those great rarities, a young female broker. She had that East London air of a fighter about her, and when Bill, in an unfortunate fit of drunkenness, accidentally tipped his eighth pint, in its entirety, into her expensive handbag, I swear on my life I saw her physically suck a single tear back into her eye. I respected that a lot.

I never saw her again.

I also remember the first time Caleb took me out to go to my first ever England game, something that, when I was a child, was an impossible dream.

I remember, at halftime, Caleb, and I, and the brokers, drinking, in the comfortable bar area which sits behind the seats in Wembley's plush corporate zone, and I remember checking my phone and suddenly realizing the second half had started, and grabbing Caleb by the wrist and saying, "The second half's started! We've got to go!"

And I remember Caleb and the other big men with pints in their hands laughing deeply and bouncing their beers and saying they'd go when the drinks were all done. And I remember we left early, too.

And I don't remember who England played that day, or what players were playing or who won or who scored the goals. But I remember that Orient had been playing that day, too, and that I didn't have any time anymore to go to Orient with my dad since I'd started the job, and that, back when I did go with my dad, we never used to miss a minute: the start of the first half, the start of the second half, the end of the second half. Even if we were losing by a few goals and it was cold we'd still stay. And I remembered how my dad would never forget a single scoreline or goalscorer, Northampton at home, Grimsby away.

And I remember that at the end of those long evenings I would take the train home or sometimes the taxi and I would often not get home until 1 a.m. or sometimes much later, and that everyone would be sleeping in my house, my parents, my sister, and that I'd been in that house for so long that I knew exactly which parts of which stairs in the dark, steep, narrow staircase didn't creak when you stepped on them. The outer parts of the fifth and the sixth steps, and the ninth and the eleventh steps, and I remember that even in the pitch-black I could creep up the stairs stepping only on those parts of those steps, so as not to wake up my parents, or my sister, and then I remember getting into my bed and setting my alarm, and that I'd set it for 5:10 a.m.

4

WHILE ALL OF THIS WAS HAPPENING EVERYWHERE, THINGS WERE changing on the desk.

I was still there on the floor every day before seven in the morning, sitting behind Spengler's shoulder, trying to learn what an FX swap was. For all of Spengler's faults, he was a good teacher as well as a good trader, and he taught me.

An FX swap is, quite simply, a loan. In more detail, it's a collateralized loan. Think of it like this: you go to the pawn shop, you give them your gold watch, and they lend you £200. This is also a collateralized loan. You have received a loan of £200, and you've lent the pawn shop your gold watch as "collateral." "Collateral," in this case, means simply a security you give to the lender, which they can keep if you don't repay the loan. That makes the loan much less risky. This loan is, in a sense, also, a "swap." The lender has given you money for a period of time, and you have given the lender, for the same period of time, your gold watch. Then you both give it back, so it's a swap, isn't it? It's a "cash-for-gold-watch" swap. An FX swap is exactly like that, except, as collateral, instead of giving a gold watch, you give foreign currency. You borrow £200 and, as collateral, you give an equivalent amount of euros, which, at today's exchange rate, would be €232. That's a collateralized loan, and it's also a "currency-for-currency" swap: an "FX swap."

This raises a question though. When you go to a pawn shop, you are the one who pays interest, not the pawnbroker, because *you* are the one borrowing money. But in an FX swap, you are *both* borrowing money — one of you borrows pounds, the other borrows euros — so who pays interest? The answer is simple: you both do! One of you pays the interest rate for pounds, which, at that time, hovered around 4.5%, and the other pays the interest rate for euros, 3.5%, give or take. Those cancel out, don't they, and, in the end, the borrower of pounds, which has the higher interest rate, pays the difference, about 1%, to the borrower of euros.

So who uses these things? Well, basically, everyone. For any investment fund, hedge fund or corporation with incomes in one currency and investments in another, FX swaps are the go-to product. That could be The Gap opening a sweatshop in Bangladesh, or your grandad's pension fund buying Japanese stocks. All of that stuff is foreign exchange swaps. By daily volume traded, they are one of the biggest financial products in the world.

Got that? Great. That is pretty much the best explanation of an FX swap you will ever get, I promise, and it is pretty much exactly how Spengler explained it to me, although his explanation was much more boring, and longer.

It turned out that it was a good time for me to learn what an FX swap was, because FX swap trading, which had for so long been a little backwater of the trading floor, was becoming, somehow, profitable.

The reason that I knew this is because a part of my job as desk junior was collecting the desk PnL. PnL, if you don't know, stands for "Profit and Loss," and it's the only thing that matters in the world. At the end of each day, I went round to each trader and collected their PnL estimate for the day.

Back in 2007, when I'd been interning, it had generally been considered that a very good STIRT trader made ten million dollars in a year. That works out at $40,000 a day, and very often a trader would make that. Of course, no trader would make that *every* day, and every trader would sometimes make a loss, but a good trader would be batting for that run rate, and would have that ten million figure in their mind as a goal, or, as the STIRT traders would call it, ten bucks.

I should probably add at this point that this is the money that the traders make for the bank. It is not the money that they make themselves. The traders themselves are working on a pretty regular salary (my salary at the time was £36,000, which I considered to be enormous), and at the end of the year they get a "bonus" based on their PnL. How the bonus gets calculated from the PnL was a process that was highly mysterious and about which, at that point, I had not the slightest idea.

About that time, coming into the late summer of 2008, those daily PnLs started to grow. Traders who would previously have been happy telling me they made $50,000, started to make $100,000, or even $200,000, maybe one or two times in a week. One day in late August, Bill made over a million dollars in a single day. This was unprecedented.

Now the PnL numbers that I collected daily were just estimates that got put in an email and sent to New York. But the computer systems calculated a precise daily, monthly and yearly PnL for every single trader, that got sent to everyone in an email at the end of each day. By the end of August, five traders—Rupert, Billy, JB, Spengler, Hongo—had *already* made ten million dollars for the year. Three of those—Billy, Spengler and Hongo—were already above twenty.

It wasn't just the STIRT traders who could see one another's PnL. It was all available on an internal website that everyone on the whole floor could see. This meant that every trader on the entire floor knew that, at that moment, moving into the final third of 2008, the bank's top three traders were, in order—an old gray Liverpudlian who looked like a hobbit, an Afrikaans idiot, and the junior euro dealer on the STIRT desk.

STIRT PnLs had already been unusually high when I'd turned up in June, but most of this money had been made since then, in July and August, and I didn't really understand why. The only people who seemed to have any sort of structural understanding about it were Billy and Caleb, who insisted that it was because "the LIBOR had shot up." That might as well have been "because Venus is in retrograde" for all that I knew. The other traders didn't seem to know or care why it was happening; they were focused on the only thing that mattered, which was that finally, after perhaps many years of underappreciation, they were making the PnL that they felt they deserved. You could see it in the way they carried themselves, and in the way they got looked at as they walked round the floor. JB was chirpier than ever, and, as a result, barely on the desk. Caleb, already a star of the trading floor, was increasingly viewed as a legend. Even Billy started talking a bit. The only guy who didn't seem to be enjoying himself was Rupert, who, as you may have noticed, hadn't quite made the top three.

I was surprised by this development, although obviously pleasantly so, but no one else seemed surprised at all. They all acted as if after ten years they were finally getting a birthday. Besides, what's the point in being surprised? You have to make hay when the sun shines, I guess. They were making as much hay as they could.

I would've loved a bit of hay of my own, to be honest, but, while I now knew what an FX swap was, I still didn't really understand how all of this money was getting made, and whilst I wanted to ask Spengler to tell me, he, like everyone else, was pretty focused on making the cash. Besides, I still had to learn how to cover trade.

So that's how the days were passing and passing. I'd come in usually at about six twenty in the morning which meant I would get a bit of time with Billy, and, as we moved into August, he would be saying more and more that the global economy was going to blow up. That should have worried me, but he was kind of laughing and smiling as he said it, and he said that he was going to make a ton of money from it, so I figured it was just a turn of phrase.

Then when everyone else came in I would do some admin tasks on my computer for an hour or two and for the rest of the day I'd sit with Spengler and try to learn to cover trade until one of us went off on a broker lunch.

Cover trading was not difficult, to be honest. You get called for a price, you check where it should roughly be with a couple of the brokers, all of whom I knew by now, you stick the dates of the FX swap in a little software program that was specially made for the desk and it makes some price suggestions, you shift that price up or down a little bit to reflect whether you want to borrow or to lend, and then it's done. After that, you decide whether you want to hold on to the trade (because you like it), to hedge out immediately for a small and quick profit, or to try and haggle around for a little bit just to make some more cash. Before long, I was cover trading for Caleb and Spengler and Snoopy whenever they were off of the desk.

As we moved into September a couple of things happened. Firstly, the regular grad scheme started, which meant a bunch of green-as-you-like kids around my age were brought in to do a load of classroom work upstairs on the top floor, in preparation for their financial exams. I had to do my financial exams as well, of course, which meant I, too, was up on the top floor. Secondly, the end of the world started to get a bit serious.

There was a little button on all of the speakerboxes, which was next to and identical to the buttons for the brokers. If you pressed it you could speak "on the hoot," which meant that your voice came out of every single speakerbox on the floor. This was always good for a laugh when a trader came back from a broker lunch four beers longer than he should have been and tried to rancorously harangue the broker that he'd just been out drinking with, but accidentally pressed the wrong button and ended up on the hoot.

Caleb started to do a little morning meeting on the hoot every day, and in that meeting he would talk about the LIBOR number, which I still didn't fully understand, and what that meant for the global banking system and the world economy.

It started to become apparent that the collapse of that global banking system was quickly moving from the realm of "impossibility" into the realm of "almost certainly not going to happen," and then onwards to "very, very unlikely," which was not actually as reassuring to me as it might sound.

Nobody on the STIRT desk really seemed that bothered about it. In fact, they seemed pretty happy. Because the higher that "LIBOR" number went, and the more the global banking system capitulated, the more money everyone seemed to make.

What had happened was that the guys on the credit desks—the credit trading desk upon which I'd interned the previous summer, and the credit structuring desk under which Matic had slept—had sold the world a lot of apparently worthless bullshit for billions of dollars, and that would have been quite fine if it weren't for the fact that they'd sold quite a lot of it to our bank as well. That bit had been a real big mistake. Not only had they done that, but the guys at Credit Suisse and at Deutsche Bank and at JPMorgan had all done the same thing, and now it was becoming increasingly clear to everyone that every single bank was going to go bust.

The take on the STIRT desk regarding this was nuanced. Firstly, we regarded the role that our employer was playing in the demise of both the global banking system and the global economy to be a moral failing on all of our parts. That's a joke, obviously. Nobody thought that, of course. Why the fuck would we think that? The credit traders were all pricks and they sat on the other side of the floor anyways and look at them all fat like pigs in their pink shirts. They've been making more money than we've made for years now so fuck those guys, it's our turn to get paid.

The traders started making a million dollars a day, two or three times a week. The imminent bankruptcy of our own employer was of no concern to anyone. We all knew that we'd get bailed out.

"What are they gonna do?" they'd all joke to each other. "Send the guys with brown overalls in to run this whole thing?"

And then we'd all laugh and we'd make loads of money.

Well, except for me. I wasn't making any money, and I was really trying quite hard to figure out what it was exactly that everyone was doing to make so much of it, but it really wasn't easy to tell. I still laughed, though, when everyone laughed.

And that's when it happened.

Nobody thought that Lehman would go under.

I had two friends who were working at Lehman. Remember that guy Sagar Malde? From LSE? The Kenyan guy. Fucking nice guy. He was working at Lehman. He'd just started the graduate scheme, as a trader. And a mate of mine, from my old grammar school in Ilford. His name was Jalpesh Patel. He'd just started at Lehman as well. He'd got in through a scheme to improve representation for ethnic minorities.

They didn't think Lehman would go under.

Bear Stearns, another, slightly smaller American investment bank, had died like a canary in the coalmine just a few months earlier, and they'd gotten bailed out, so everyone thought Lehman would get bailed out as well.

At least that's what Caleb used to say every morning on the hoot.

But they didn't get bailed out. And Sagar Malde lost his job and Jalpesh Patel lost his job too. And they both had only started those jobs just a couple of weeks previously and they had been given little "Lehman Brothers" duffel bags they used to carry around.

And a little part of me felt bad that they lost their jobs, but another part of me said well, that's the way it goes, isn't it? You guys should have picked better banks.

But another part of me said what the fuck are you talking about? You won your job in a fucking card game and you didn't do no research and not only that but your bank is under as well, mate, and if the cards had fallen in another direction that would be you on TV packing your shit into a Citigroup bag.

But I'm not really sure if a part of me actually said that or if I'm just making that up to make myself feel better. Because the main thing I thought was, man, I'm still dancing. There's money to be made here, and the music ain't stopped.

Of course, there was one specific problem with that plan, one kind of elephant in the room, which was that my employer was also by this point conspicuously bankrupt, and anyone with half a brain knew. Even I knew.

So when Caleb announced on the hoot that the near-term foreclosure of our own bank was no longer "very, very unlikely" but was actually now "we estimate less than a 25 percent chance," it was weirdly more reassuring to me than "very, very unlikely" had been.

But at 9 a.m. on Monday, September 15, when I went to the top floor to learn about bond mathematics with all the other twenty-one-year-olds on the grad scheme, and I told them about that "less than 25 percent chance," it was clear that they definitely hadn't known. You should have seen the looks on their faces.

Caleb was right though, or maybe he wasn't right. It's very difficult, philosophically, to judge accurately the correctness of a probabilistic forecast like that.

We did get bailed out though. And I kept my job. I didn't have to pack my shit up in that Citibank duffel bag. And what is there to say about that really, except to thank God?

Which is something that none of us did at the time.

I went in at 6:10 a.m. the Monday after the bailout, the beginning of October 2008. I was still twenty-one. Billy was already in. When I walked onto the desk it was only him and me there, and it was dark outside, because it was still very early. Bill was sitting down, small, in the corner, and I could see the dark sky through the window behind him and he was already looking in my direction, and he was grinning from ear to ear at me, like a little Scouse monkey, and he was nodding at me like a madman. All of this was entirely out of character, for Bill, but Bill had made thirty million dollars in the previous week, and now that the bank's not going to go under, he's probably going to get paid. That's why he was happy. To this day, I am still relatively convinced that, in that week, Bill had actually made perhaps well over one hundred million dollars, and had spent the entire week hiding the cash. I'll shortly explain how Bill made so much money, but the main thing that you need to know now is that Billy was happy. And I liked Billy, a lot. So that meant I was happy as well.

Caleb came in next, before six thirty, which was uncharacteristically early for him. All of the other traders came in very shortly afterward, which was much earlier than usual for everyone. Hardly anyone else was there on the whole trading floor, and we were all there, sitting down at our glowing walls of screens, in the darkness. It felt like a midnight mass.

No one said anything, and then at one moment, Billy spun his chair around into the aisle, so that he was right next to Caleb, and he shouted to Caleb in a broad Scouse, "So Caleb, what do you think of the bail-outs then?"

And we all turned and we looked at them but Caleb didn't turn to look back at Billy but he looked forward and he reached up with his left hand and supported his chin, and he thought for a little while and he looked kind of sad, and then he said, "I don't know Billy . . . It feels like getting bailed out by your dad."

And it was the first time and the last time and the only time that I ever heard anyone on the trading floor talk about the bailouts in anything that was anything like ethical terms.

And then everyone turned back to their screens, and they all started trading, and they all made more money by doing it than anyone had ever made in their lives.

So. Why were the Lehman crisis and the bailouts so profitable for the STIRT desk?

Well, at that time, pretty much every major bank in the whole world, but especially in America, went bankrupt. As a result, banks stopped lending to each other, for two simple reasons:

1. You probably shouldn't lend someone money if they are about to go bankrupt.

2. You probably shouldn't lend someone money if *you* are about to go bankrupt.

These are good rules for life. Write them down.

Now, if nobody's making loans, then loans become expensive, and, as I've explained to you, an FX swap is, basically, a loan. Not only is it a loan, but it's a collateralized loan, which means you don't make a huge loss if your borrower goes bankrupt, and, when the whole world is on the verge of bankruptcy, these are the only loans you are able to make.

We were the only game in town.

The way that we saw this happening was that all the spreads blew up. Remember the spreads in the trading game? 67–69? I-buy-at-67-and-I-sell-at-69? Well imagine if suddenly that's 47–89, and you've got people trading with you regularly on both sides. As soon as you get one buyer and seller, that's a guaranteed profit of 42, when you used to be playing with 2's. Welcome to the buffet, eat as much as you can.

And they did eat. And no one ate as much as Spengler.

Spengler had always been a fiend. He loved to make money and he loved to rip customers. He was a trader right down to his bones. Once, back in July, he'd ripped a customer so hard that the salesperson had come back and complained to Caleb, and Caleb had asked Spengler what he had been doing and Spengler, who was seated, had looked up at him as if aggrieved, with his arms spread out wide, and said to him, "It's not my fault Caleb, it's my job!"

And Caleb had looked down at Spengler like a father looks down at his son and put his arm round his shoulder and leaned into him and said, "It's not your job to rip the customers Spengler. Your job is to rip them, and leave them smiling."

And I always remembered that. But I think Spengler forgot it at times. After Lehman he forgot it a lot.

One day that week, after the bailout, Spengler ripped a customer so hard that he made two million dollars. Two million dollars in one single trade.

After he did that, he got so excited that he leaped out of his swivel chair and into the aisle, and he dropped into a deep lunge that must have made his cream chinos see their whole life flash before their eyes. His heavy head started to bounce, with his huge mouth agape, and his arms were fist-pumping and the sight was so obscene and so absurdly horrific that everyone turned their chairs round to watch.

Caleb jumped from his chair immediately and grabbed the boy in the same way that a football steward grabs and wraps a streaker, and then he was holding him by the shoulders and leaning into him and their noses were almost touching and he was saying to him quietly, "What the fuck are you doing? What the fuck are you doing?"

And he was just saying it again and again and Spengler was arching his head backward and his mouth was trembling and trying to form words but nothing was coming out and all he could say was, "B–b–but—I—b–b–b–but I—"

"Shut the fuck up," replied Caleb, and he was talking in a whisper and he pointed over across the trading floor and he said to Spengler, "Look over that way. Look over that way. Do you see those guys? They're losing their fucking jobs this week. Do you understand that? They're losing their fucking jobs this week and you're standing here fist-pumping like a maniac. What the fuck are you doing, Spengler? Do you want to get paid here? Yeah? Do you want to get paid?"

Remember that question. "Do you want to get paid?"

Through all of this there was a problem, a big problem. You might have already spotted it.

The traders on the STIRT desk are making money here because the spreads have gone massive. And who gets the money from big spreads? I'll remind you, it's the owners of the books. Spengler was making all the Skandi spread money because he was the trader for Skandis, and JB was making all of the yen spreads because he was the trader for yen. Rupert was making all the money for euros, and Bill made the money for pounds.

And what was I the trader for? Nothing. So what money was I making? Jack shit.

That's the problem.

So, we need a new plan.

OK, so how do I make money here, when everyone's making money, if I can't access the money from the books?

Well, there's one guy who was making more money than anyone, and that guy was Bill.

What was Billy doing?

Well, what Bill was doing it turns out, was this.

Bill had been skeptical about the global economy for some time. He didn't believe you could run an economy simply by lending money to dickheads and he could see global debts going up. He had long suspected the math-genius-credit-traders to be the spoiled rich idiots that, in hindsight, they probably were, and he'd been expecting their shit to blow up.

The problem was, he had been a little bit early, and he'd been betting on this blow-up for years. This had probably cost him a few million dollars in PnL in each of the previous three years, which explained both why he had not, thus far, been particularly profitable for Citibank, and why Rupert thought that he was an idiot.

Billy was not an idiot.

What Billy had actually been doing was that he had been betting that different kinds of interest rates would diverge. OK, imagine this: imagine you need to borrow money for three months. What do you do? Well, you go to your bank or your mum or the mafia or whoever it is you go to to get your loans and you ask for a loan for three months, right? Simple. But if you're a big bank or an investment fund or a corporation, there's another thing that you can do. If you're a big institution like that, then you could call a big, institutional lender, like Citibank, and you could ask for a loan for *only one day*. OK, you're thinking, that doesn't fix the problem, because I need money for three months, not one day. Well, that's no big problem, actually. When the loan comes due, tomorrow, you go back to another big lender, maybe Deutsche Bank this time, and you borrow the money again for a day. Now you're good for two days. Do that every day for three months, and you're laughing. Basically, if you want to borrow money for three months, you have a couple options— you can take one loan for three months, or you can take ninety separate loans each for one single day.

So which do you choose? Which would you prefer? You are probably thinking, I'd rather take the three months because then I can have it all sorted and know the whole interest rate in advance. But in the international money markets, you can easily arrange ninety single-day loans in advance as well, so in both cases, you can fix your interest rates in advance.

The correct answer is that if you are the *borrower*, you prefer the ninety-day loan, and if you are the *lender*, you prefer the single-day loans. The reason for this is that if you lend someone money for ninety days, and they go bankrupt on day twenty-five, you are fucked, but if you only lent them money for one day, you are not. And if you are a borrower, and you borrow money for one day, and on day twenty-five people realize you're going bankrupt, you are fucked, whereas if you borrowed money for ninety days, then you might have a chance.

Of course, before 2008, none of this mattered, because banks didn't go bankrupt back then. But in 2008, that all changed. The ninety-day lending market totally evaporated, whereas the one-day lending market remained virtually unchanged. Little gray Billy was the only guy in the whole City, it seemed, who realized that was going to happen. He'd been betting on it happening for years. When it happened, he made tens of million dollars in a single week, and much more than that after that, too. Turns out, when he had been saying the global economy was going to blow up, it had not been a turn of phrase, after all. He was right, after years of being laughed at. And let me tell you, he fucking enjoyed it.

Wouldn't you?

Problem is, though, that didn't fix my problem. Because that bet had already gone. I should have made it two weeks ago. Once a guy's made forty million dollars on a trade, you can bet that now is probably too late.

So what did I do? I went back to Spengler.

Other than Bill, Spengler was the one other trader on the desk who was making far more money than he should have been.

Technically, Spengler was not the desk's second most profitable trader—that was Hongo, who would go on to make over a hundred million dollars that year, just like Bill. But Hongo was on the euro book, and Spengler was trading the Skandis. There was a clear hierarchy on the desk of which books were most profitable, and the Skandis were down near the bottom.

So how was Spengler making so much money? If I could convince him to show me, then maybe I could make some as well.

In the immediate aftermath of Lehman, there hadn't really been much time to think. Nobody wanted to do any cover trading, because they were all making so much money on their own books, and Caleb was off the desk all the time in meetings with the bigwigs trying to make sure everyone would get paid. Because of that, I was covering most of the time.

But once we got into November, the markets started to calm down, just a little, and Caleb came back to the desk. That meant I was able to get back, once again, behind Spengler, who, by that point, had already made an absolute ton. It was clear that he was going to end up as one of the bank's top traders that year, despite being one of the youngest, and it was getting to his massive head. For me, though, that wasn't a problem. When Spengler was feeling big for his boots, there were only two things he wanted to talk about: trading, and himself. Our interests were perfectly aligned.

I asked Spengler how he'd made so much money and he showed me an enormous spreadsheet that he used to use. It was a masterpiece. It broke the whole Swedish aka "Stokkie" FX swap market down into individual days. How much does it cost to borrow Stokkie on December 14? What about May 23? Every single day was isolated and analyzed and a comparison was made between the current price in the market, and what the price, in Spengler's mind, should have been. He sent me that spreadsheet, and I used it for years.

As we were looking through the spreadsheet, Spengler explained all the features of his "position," which is what traders call the list of all the different trades they've made at any given time. In the case of the Stokkie FX swap market, that meant how much Swedish krona he had borrowed, or lent, on any given day. He always had some random esoteric reason for every individual trade.

But there was one thing I noticed as we looked through Spengler's position. He'd borrowed Swedish krona on *every* single day. Remember, an FX swap is a loan, right? But it's also a swap, which means it's a two-way loan. You don't just borrow a thing, you also lend a thing. In the specific case of Spengler's Swedish krona book, the thing he was lending in return for all the Swedish krona was US dollars. The situation struck me as a little unusual. You might have thought that he would borrow Swedish krona on some days, when it was cheap, and lend it on other days, when it was expensive. But he wasn't doing that, he was borrowing Swedish krona and lending US dollars against it on every single day for the upcoming two years. The only difference was how much he was borrowing.

Why was he doing that?

Later that afternoon, when I got a bit of time, I went and had a look through the other traders' FX swap books. Billy was also lending US dollars, on every single day. So was Snoopy, albeit in smaller size. Caleb and JB were doing it too. They were all lending dollars on every single day for the next two years.

Before the end of the day, I went back to Spengler, and I asked him.

"Why's everybody lending dollars? Why's nobody borrowing dollars?"

Spengler looked at me like I was an idiot.

"Why the fuck would we borrow US dollars? Borrowing US dollars is fucking retarded."

I tried to strike a pose with my face that made me look like I wasn't "retarded." But it must not have cut the mustard because Spengler let out a deep sigh and opened his spreadsheet.

"Look, what's the interest rate for dollars right now? It's 1 percent, right? And it's going down to 0 percent. But look what interest rate we can get in the FX swap." He started to fiddle some numbers around in the corner of the sheet. "We're getting over 3 percent. It's free money."

I didn't need to hear that twice. He was still talking, and I wasn't listening, because I was trying to work out how to ask him if I could get some of the trade. I didn't need to think long though, because I was still trying to figure out what to say to him when I suddenly realized he was looking directly at me and saying:

"So? Do you want some?"

Well, what do you think?

So let's open up here and make sure you're still with me.

An FX swap is a loan. It's a two-way loan where both people borrow one currency from one another. They both pay interest, which means, in the end, only one person pays the interest differential. If pounds are 3% and dollars are 2%, then the pound borrower pays the difference, which would be 1%.

But who sets the interest rates on the individual currencies?

So there's a real fancy old building somewhere in your capital city, or in Frankfurt if you're European, and that building's called the "Central Bank." It will probably be called the Bank of England or the Bank of Japan — basically the bank of wherever you're from. In the US it's called the Federal Reserve or Fed. In Europe, it's the European Central Bank (ECB). In that fancy building a bunch of posh mummy's boys who never left university try every year, and desperately fail, to prevent your economy from slowly collapsing. Then, they go and have a fancy dinner in a wood-paneled hall. These guys are important to your life, even if you don't know it, and they are important in this story too.

At this point, though, the only thing you need to know about these guys is that they set the interest rates for every country in the world, including yours. (Another related fact, that you don't *need* to know, but might find interesting, is that Bill had his own designated taxi driver, who would drive him home after broker dinners to his Hertfordshire manor whenever he missed the last train. One time I had a drink with that driver — his name was Sid — and he told me that whenever Bill was extra drunk, as a point of principle, he would make Sid stop off outside the Bank of England, so that he could sneak into an alley round the side of it and take a piss on the back of the Bank. Sid said that Bill would insist on that, even if it was not at all on the route home. I respected that a lot.)

So at this time in history, late 2008, central banks all over the world were rapidly slashing the interest rates to zero, in the desperate and ultimately futile hope that it would somehow stimulate their economies. This was happening to almost every currency on the desk: pound, euro, Swiss franc, Swedish krona and Danish krone, and the American and Canadian dollars. Once you add in the Japanese yen, which had already had zero interest rates for nearly twenty years, almost all of the major currencies would soon be at zero.

So what does that mean for FX swaps? Well, if the payment on an FX swap is equal to the interest rate differential, and almost all interest rates are going to zero, then the interest rate differentials must all also be zero, as well, right? And then all the FX swaps should be free!

But as Spengler had pointed out to me, the FX swaps weren't all free. The very, very short-term FX swaps, the one-day ones, *were* free: the price was effectively zero. But for anything longer than a couple of weeks or a month there was a really huge premium for borrowing US dollars. This created an equally huge opportunity for FX swap traders to lend dollars for three months at a time, and then just borrow them back every day. It was, as Spengler explained to me, free money.

Except, nothing's ever really free money. Is it? Could it really be that easy to make cash? If it was that easy, why wasn't everyone doing it? Well, the truth is that everyone *was* doing it. But was it really free? What were the risks?

These are all the questions that I could have asked myself that day, as I sat there, behind Spengler, and he was swinging his massive spreadsheet around. But I didn't ask any of them. I nodded, and I said, "Yeah man, for sure, I want some."

And Spengler just pressed the button and he spoke to Granty and he put the trade on for me, and just like that I'd lent two hundred and forty million dollars, for three months, in a dollar/Stokkie FX swap with Danske Bank Copenhagen, and I went home that day thoroughly happy, and it was the first medium-sized trade of my life.

It wasn't until I got home, and I was eating dinner with my parents, and watching a little tiny fuzzy black-and-white television that you used to change channel on with a dial, that I thought to myself: "Wait a minute, what the fuck am I doing? I don't know anything about dollar/Stokkie foreign exchange swaps. I've never been to Sweden in my life. And what the fuck do I know that Danske Bank Copenhagen doesn't know? And isn't two hundred and forty million dollars like, kind of a lot?"

The truth is that two hundred and forty million dollars, the size of trade suggested by Spengler, was not really a big trade to the STIRT desk, who frequently traded in billions and referred to them as "yards." But it was a hell of a lot of money to me, and talking about a trade really feels very different to actually having a trade. I didn't sleep much that night.

The next day I went in super early. I had to talk to Bill.

I was actually waiting for Billy when he got in that morning, and that surprised him. All the questions that I should have asked the previous day had at last crystallized in my mind. Putting your own money, and your reputation, and your career on the line, on what is basically just an opinion, will make you think long and hard about whether those opinions are actually right. Think about that when you're watching the news.

Billy was looking at me askance when he came in and he saw me, already sitting next to his chair, and I told him what I'd done before he'd even sat down.

"I lent $240 million of three-month Stokkie."

Bill was laughing immediately. He thought that was funny as fuck.

"Fuckin hell, did ya? Finally grew some fucking balls and lent some fucking dollars, yeah? Why the fuck'd you do that then hey Gal?"

He was pissing himself.

I didn't sugar coat it.

"Spengler told me it was free money."

I told him the truth, and he looked at me as if I'd been an idiot. To defend myself, I added:

"Everyone's doing it. I checked everyone's position. Everyone's doing it. You're doing it too!"

Then Billy smiled and he nodded and his attitude changed. And he probably would have ruffled my hair if I hadn't have shaved it all off, but I had, so he just pinched my nose. He turned away and he looked at his screens.

"Not as dumb as you look are you, you fucking cockney twat. We're all doing it are we? Well, it looks like you're doing it too." And he laughed and he booted up his nine monitors and he pulled his *Financial Times* out of his bag.

"Why's everyone doing it then? What are the risks?"

Bill dropped his *Financial Times* to the floor, then, and he turned and looked into me with an air of seriousness.

"Well, well, well, well," Billy said, and he was fucking loving all of this. "Somebody really has gone and grown a pair overnight, haven't they? What do you think are the risks?"

"I don't know. Spengler said it's free money. Maybe that means there aren't any risks."

"Good fucking answer, why the fuck did you do it if you don't know what the fucking risks are?"

"I did it because you're doing it, Bill."

And Bill smiled at that. "Good fucking answer again. Well, I'll tell you why I'm doing it. I'm doing it because the world needs US fucking dollars and we're fucking Citibank, and we're the biggest American bank in the whole fucking world and we've got the dollars and they don't fuckin have them, so we'll charge them whatever we want, and we're all gonna get paid. OK? Do you understand that?"

I nodded.

"And now I'm gonna tell you something even more important, right? Don't you ever fucking tell me, in your whole fucking life, that there's a trade that doesn't have a fucking risk in it. OK? That's what those cunts over in Credit thought and look what the fuck happened to them. And I'm gonna tell you one last thing, the most important thing of all of it, and then you're gonna fuck off and sit back in your corner. This trade will blow up, and we'll all lose our fuckin arses, in one situation. The trade will blow up if the global banking system collapses. And if that happens, this whole place goes under. You'll lose your job, and I'll lose my job, and the whole global economy comes down with it. We're betting that's not going to happen. And we're gonna be right, right? And we're gonna get paid. And then we're all gonna go and have a good few drinks afterward, and now you're gonna do it as well. And you should probably go back to your seat now and have a good long think about what all of that means. And you make sure it's the last fucking time you ever do a trade that you don't know the risks of. It's a good fucking trade though Gal. Well fucking done."

And he was already back in his screens, and I was back in my seat, and it wasn't the last fucking time that I ever did a trade that I didn't know the risks of, and if it had have been, I could have saved myself some big trouble, over the years. But despite all of that, and exactly as was told to me by both Bill and Spengler, it was indeed a good fucking trade, and by Christmas I'd made seven hundred grand.

Looking back at those first few months on the desk, going out drinking, eating raw chicken, learning about trading, running around covering all the different traders when they were out on the piss, making my first seven hundred grand PnL, I can't believe how fun it all seemed, at the time. The days became nights became days became nights and it all seemed to blur into one. And JB was always there with a joke and a smile and Caleb always seemed to notice the good work that I did. And even if Rupert was dangerous and Spengler repulsive, none of it all seemed to matter, because everyone was making the cash.

Well, I wasn't making much cash, at that point, of course, but even that was coming, I could feel it. The PnL was appearing, and my thirty-six grand salary was more money than I'd ever had in my life anyway. And I was going to restaurants, which was a thing that I'd never done, and I was walking around making trades on the trading floor wearing pointy shoes and a little Bluetooth headset. What more could you want?

But more than that, more than any of that, it felt, for the first time in a long time, like I was a part of a family. And Billy and Caleb were like two separate and opposite fathers, one small and scrappy and sweary and the other huge and impossibly smooth, and Rupert and JB were the one mean and the one friendly uncle at Christmas, and Snoopy and Spengler were like my big brothers.

And in the few evenings when I went home to have dinner with my actual parents, they'd harass me for rent and they'd ask me for money to fix the car. And I did have to give them the car money, but I told my mum that I was paying the rent to my dad, and I told my dad that I was giving it to my mum, and neither of them realized that for ages, and everything felt like it was just coming together in the world.

5

AND THEN SPENGLER WAS GONE.

I didn't realize at first. Spengler was always the last guy to arrive in the mornings, so when Caleb walked past about fifteen minutes before Spengler usually appeared, and said, "You're covering for Spengler today," as he walked by, I didn't think anything of it. But though it wasn't unusual for Spengler to be late, which often happened if he'd been out heavy drinking, it was unusual for him not to come in at all, especially without texting me or anything. But I figured anyone could get sick.

What was strange was that no one said a word. Everyone took the piss out of Spengler all the time, and him not turning up without any notice was something that would have usually at least merited a joke. But it didn't. No one said anything at all.

By then I was used to covering for all of the traders, and so I had my speakerbox set up with a couple brokers on it for each of the different currencies. The way it worked was that every broker had an open line to the bank which you could add to your speakerbox, and whenever that broker shouted down to us, it would come out of the box of each of the traders who'd put that specific line on their board. You could turn the volume up or down, or even off (the innermost fear of every broker) for any line you wanted, so if for example I got called in to trade Skandis, like in this situation, all I had to do was turn the volume up for the two Skandi brokers that I had on my board.

Spengler, who always traded Skandis, had far more Skandi brokers on his own board, five or six. I'd told the two on my board that I was covering, but the other three or four didn't know, and they kept chirping, unanswered, out of Spengler's box into his unoccupied seat. After about an hour of this, one of the Danish Carstens started to wonder why he wasn't being answered, and began to shout, "Spengler! Spengler! Are you there? Are you there?" for about fifteen minutes, before JB, who was sat next to the speakerbox, slammed both of his hands angrily down onto his own desk, got up out of his seat, wordlessly, leaned over to Spengler's speakerbox and turned the volume on every one of his broker lines down to "off," then sat back down. It was then that I realized something was up.

Barely anyone said anything that whole day, beyond the unavoidable shouting of numbers. Even JB—perhaps especially JB, usually the loudest and most sociable—was completely silent.

It wasn't until mid-afternoon, when the morning rush of trades had passed, that Billy walked toward the aisle, grabbed me by my right ear and pulled me physically out of my seat.

There was a little mini Starbucks on the trading floor, where an enormous Brazilian barista used to sing falsetto and listen to samba while he made you your coffee. Whenever me and Billy went for coffee, we would always go there. But we didn't go there. We went to a little Italian café out on the wide, open Canary Wharf plaza, away from the bank. Bill said very little as we walked over to the café, then he bought two cappuccinos and he sat me down. It was early December by then, so the afternoon sun was already low in the sky and was filtering onto our wooden table through large white-painted wood windows that were designed to pretend to look old.

"Do you know what's happened?" Billy asked me.

"No. I don't know what's happened. What's fucking happened?"

"Rupert's fucked Spengler."

That hadn't actually been what I'd been expecting. Spengler had always seemed to me to be the kind of guy to fuck himself pretty badly. I tried not to betray any emotion and just said, "OK. What happened?"

"You remember when Spengler was covering Rupert?"

I did remember that. About three weeks previously Rupert had been away from the desk for two weeks on holiday, because even though Rupert would not normally have taken holiday at such an important time, it was legally mandatory for every trader to take one two-week chunk of leave every year, and Rupert had not taken his yet. Because the euro book was too big for Hongo to do on his own, and deemed too important to be covered by me, Spengler, who had been trading his own

Skandi books so excellently, had been given the cover job while Rupert was away.

I nodded, and Bill continued.

"And you know Spengler made a fuckton of money for Rupert?"

This much I knew too. Spengler had made significantly more in his time trading the euro book than Rupert had been making himself, even though he had been trading his own Skandi books at the same time. (Remember, though, the euro money still goes to Rupert.) We'd all noticed this, and we would all have been taking the piss out of Rupert about it only we knew he'd blow up if we said anything, and, besides, we could all see him steaming over it anyway. It was funnier to not say a word.

"Well Rupert came back and he checked all the trades."

That was a bit crazy, but it was more than believable. The euro book was massive, and hundreds of trades would go through it every day, but it was well within Rupert's nature to check every one of them. Sometimes salespeople would try to book trades at slightly the wrong price, to try and pinch a bit of money, and then claim that it was an accident when they got called up on it. You could bet Rupert never missed a single one. Checking all the trades that went through your book *in the two weeks while you'd been on holiday*, though, was a different level of anal retention, especially when you consider how busy the trading desk had been during that time. He must have stayed in the office late to do it. And what was he doing it for? Just to find out precisely the exact ways that Spengler was better than him?

"OK," I said, "and what did he find?"

"Turns out Spengler made even more money trading for Rupert than we thought he did. So much so that he figured he'd take some for himself. He transferred three million dollars out of Rupert's PnL account and into his own."

My immediate reaction to this was not that it was wrong, or that it was immoral. Fuck me, if I could have taken three million dollars out of Rupert's bag and got away with it, who knows, I probably would have done. What struck me immediately was that this was incredibly stupid. Of all the people to steal from and expect not to get caught for it. Turns out Spengler did fuck himself, after all.

But at the same time, I could just see him doing it. I could see him sitting there, trading for Rupert, who everyone knew hated him, and making so much more money for him than Rupert would have made himself, and just thinking, "Why should I let Rupert take this money? I'm the guy sitting here. I'm the guy making it. I'm a better trader than he is. Why shouldn't I take my piece? Just a bit. Just a piece."

Yeah. I could see it. It was too easy to see.

But still. It was stupid as fuck.

Now Bill's face took a more serious turn, and he fixed me directly in the eye.

"Listen. I don't give a fuck about Spengler. He stole. He's an idiot. He got fucked. But let me tell you one thing. He's not the only guy stealing on that trading floor. He's not the first and he won't be the last. I've seen it too many times. But listen kid, there's one thing that you're gonna learn from this. I'm an old man, and you are still young. You're gonna be in this game for many years more than I will, and maybe you'll steal at some point too. But whatever the fuck you do, what*ever* the *fuck* you do, you remember these three letters—C-Y-A. You know what CYA stands for?"

I didn't know, and I communicated that fact.

"CYA stands for Cover. Your. Arse. Cover Your Arse. Whatever you do, Gal, you Cover Your Arse. I don't care who you steal from in this game, as long as it's not me or my mates. But if you ever steal from anyone, or do anything dodgy, even one percent dodgy, you do not leave a trace of you on it, not a *trace* of you on it. Do you hear me? Not even the tiniest hint of your smell. I mean it. Coz you're popular now, and you're doing well, and everyone likes you. But one day, at some point in the future, somebody's not going to like you, and trust me now, they'll scrape through *all* of your shit. So you make sure every inch of it is smelling like roses. OK? Do you hear me? Coz otherwise, how the fuck do you sleep at night? Don't let these fuckers have one single thing over your head. Whatever you do Gal. Cover. Your. Arse."

And I never forgot that, and thank fuck that I didn't.

The next day, Spengler was still gone. And I was trading Skandis for that oversized invisible boy from my seat on the corner of the desk. Rupert was still two seats to the left of me, beyond the empty seat, and in quiet moments, when he wasn't looking, I'd try and catch a glance at him. I wanted to see if there'd been any kind of change in him, any visible hint of what he'd done.

There wasn't. He looked calm. He looked totally collected. If anything, he looked calmer than before. He looked happy. He looked, dare I say it, peaceful, even zen. At one point he pulled a book out, right there on the desk, and he put his feet up on the dustbin and started to read it. The book was called *How to Conceive a Boy*. I asked him if it was possible to conceive a boy, specifically, and he said it was a matter of sexual technique.

And while he was sitting there, reading that book, with his thick legs propped up on the dustbin and pointed toward me, I was able to look at him, and I wondered how it must have felt. What must it have felt like to have destroyed someone as utterly helpless and stupid as Spengler? A man who was little more than an overgrown boy.

And I looked at Rupert again, leaning back comfortably in his big swivel chair, and I wondered if his children would actually turn out to be boys. This all happened years ago and he's probably got children now. I wonder if they're boys. I hope they're OK.

The day after Spengler's disappearance, Rupert asked me to go with him for lunch.

It occurred to me that Rupert might have been doing this so that he could explain what had happened, why he'd chosen to fuck Spengler. He knew, of course, that I was close with Spengler, in a way, and I even briefly considered that he might be planning to apologize. But Rupert didn't apologize, and he didn't explain anything. Instead, this is what he did:

Rupert wanted to go to an expensive Spanish restaurant that was located on the west bank of the Isle of Dogs, the huge round peninsula encircled by the River Thames in East London upon which has grown Canary Wharf. This meant that we would not take a train or a taxi, but would rather walk beneath the skyscrapers. It was sunny that day, but being December, little light reached the ground as we walked.

Rupert said nothing to me as we started walking. That wasn't unusual. When Rupert and I were anywhere together, just the two of us, we talked when Rupert wanted to talk. Often that wasn't very much of the time.

Then Rupert spoke to me, neither turning his head or breaking his stride,

"Gary. You know, when you first came to work here, we walked once through Canary Wharf, like this, and I remember you looking up, and all around, as we were walking, at the tops of the towers."

He stopped talking after that, without asking a question, and his words hung before me in the air.

I filled the silence with something anonymous and banal and some time had passed before he picked it up again, as if I'd said nothing. "You don't do that anymore. You don't look up at the skyscrapers."

Again, he had not asked a question, and this time I just waited and eventually he said, "You know, this place, it's like *Watership Down*. The only people you see here are the survivors. What you don't see is the people who lost."

And I thought to myself, "What the fuck is *Watership Down*?" And I looked it up when I went home and it's a book about rabbits.

There was a pause after that where we didn't talk, but just walked on, side by side, through the cold, and the highest skyscrapers were eventually behind us, and a little bit of sun reached us, then, on the ground.

"You know, Gary, I've got a problem."

This was an uncharacteristic statement from Rupert, and it took me by surprise. He wasn't looking at me, but forward and upward, in the direction he was walking, toward the sky.

"Whenever I meet someone," he continued, "I need to know immediately, as soon as I meet them, whether they're better than me or worse than me."

And I didn't say anything. I was just watching him as we were walking. I really wanted to know what he'd say.

"And then, if they're better than me, I hate them, I *hate* them, for being better than me."

And then a pause.

"But if they're worse than me, then, I *despise* them, and it's even worse, because they're worse than me. I despise them for that."

And I didn't say anything in response to that. What on earth could I possibly have said? And we walked together, to the west end of the Isle of Dogs, to that expensive Spanish restaurant by the river, and there, together, we ate a whole baby pig.

There was a mad tone on the desk after that. While nobody had ever really liked Spengler, except for me and I guess maybe JB, everyone knew what Rupert did was wrong. You shouldn't just fuck a guy like that. There should have been a discussion.

It turned out that Rupert hadn't even spoken to Caleb, he'd gone over Caleb's head, to Caleb's boss, in New York—a giant slug of a man who was unable to breathe without making loud noises and left silvery trails wherever he went. The Slug had been visiting London a week previously, and Rupert had gone straight to him. That meant that no one had had a say in the matter, not even Caleb. Not JB, not Bill, and of course not Spengler himself.

The unease was palpable, and it lingered in the air, and its scent mixed in with that of the other big question whose stench dominates every trading floor at that time of year. The question which would one day come to dominate my own life, the big question.

Do you want to get paid?

One of the maddest of the many mad things about trading floors, back then, was the way that the traders got paid.

That year both Billy and Hongo made over a hundred million dollars, each, for the bank. And a couple others were not far behind. But that doesn't really count for anything unless you get paid. These guys were on salaries that were far more than mine, I was sure. I guessed they were making probably, seventy or eighty K, although I really didn't know. But even if it was double that, it's a lot less than a hundred million dollars.

So how much do you get paid on a hundred million dollars? I absolutely had no idea. The numbers were so much higher than anyone on the STIRT desk had ever been used to that I think, quite possibly, nobody did.

It was not even certain that you would get paid at all. Do you remember Simon Chang, from Spengler's dinner? Three years later he would go on to become the most profitable trader in the whole of HSBC.

When bonus time came, the bank didn't pay him anything, they just fired him instead.

This created, inevitably, an atmosphere of tension. Everyone was sitting on these huge PnL numbers, ten times more than they'd ever made for the bank in their lives. But no one knew what they'd take home. Everyone was asking the question. Are we gonna get paid?

Whether you got paid or not, and how much you got paid, seemed to be based on a whole host of mysterious factors. I knew this because the traders spoke about them all of the time. Sure, the desk had done well, that was obvious, but the bank as a whole, even more obviously, had not had a great year. This was a factor, apparently, and it didn't look good.

A lot of human factors were also involved. What was the relationship like between senior management and the desk? It would be the Slug who would decide how much money went to Caleb, and then Caleb would divvy it up. So what did the Slug think? Did he like us? Did he know that we called him "the Slug"? Hopefully not. This is why Caleb had been off the desk so much of the time. He had to butter up the Slug and the other big dogs. That's how we'd all be able to get paid. Nobody was better at buttering up than Caleb. There was no better man for the job.

The Rupert/Spengler thing didn't make us look good though.

Everyone was talking about this, constantly. But no one ever spoke about specific numbers. There's this weird thing on the trading floor. No one *ever* tells you how much they get paid. Ever. I literally thought it was a sackable offense. That's not a joke. All of the graduates thought it was a sackable offense to tell someone your bonus. It wasn't until years later I found out that that wasn't true. This meant that I had no idea of the numbers, and it never even occurred to me that I would get paid anything at all on my measly 700K, which was more than 150 times smaller than Bill's PnL.

Of course, I still wanted them to get paid though. If they got paid, I'd get paid the next year.

And then, just like that, as we were all waiting around nervously for bonus day, suddenly, Spengler was back.

Caleb didn't have any special love for Spengler. No one did. But he damn sure wasn't going to let Rupert go over his head like that. He must have gone and dropped some special magic salt on the Slug for that one, and Spengler rolled in one day without any forewarning, shambling onto the desk with a big sheepish grin.

Caleb hadn't told any of us in advance that Spengler was returning, or at least he hadn't said anything to me, and I'm pretty sure it was just because he wanted to see Rupert's reaction. JB was delighted when the boy turned up. He jumped up and grabbed him by the shoulders and was slapping him on the side of the face. Billy was laughing and Snoopy was trying not to. Just like everyone, I was trying to sneak glances at Rupert. He wasn't moving. He was sitting perfectly still, looking straight forward, one hand on his keyboard, one hand on his mouse. His face showed not one trace of emotion, but his shirt collar was straining to burst. Within a few months, it would be Rupert himself who'd be gone. I wonder if he already knew.

Then Caleb went and got everyone paid.

6

BONUS DAY HAPPENS IN JANUARY, LATE JANUARY NORMALLY, AND back in those days it was the only thing that mattered. Laws were later passed limiting bonuses as a multiple of salary, which led to an enormous increase in salaries and, I'm told, a decrease in the drama and significance of bonus day. But back then, in early 2009, it was still a religious event.

On bonus day, each desk head gets allocated their own little meeting room, and they call each of the traders in one at a time. The traders on the STIRT desk would go and have their meeting with Caleb, and come back to the desk. Of course, when they reappear on the desk, everyone's reading their body for signs.

To call in the first trader, Caleb called up the desk on the phone line. At that time, it was my job to take all the phone calls, which was a bit problematic because no one could understand my pronunciation of the word "Citi." On that bonus day, it meant that I was given the privilege of sending the first trader over to see Caleb. It was Bill.

I couldn't look at Bill when he came back to the desk. I don't know why but I just couldn't look. When Bill came back, he told Hongo to go. When Hongo came back he sent in Rupert. When Rupert came back, he sent Spengler, and, like that, each of the traders went in in descending order of PnL.

I couldn't look at any of them. I don't know why I felt so personally invested. It wasn't my day, I knew that, but still I felt sick.

And then when the last trader, Snoopy, was done, he came back, and he told me to go. I hadn't been expecting to be called.

Caleb's room was in the bowels of the trading floor. It was not Caleb's normal office and it took me some time to find it. When I did find it, I was first struck by how dark and depressing the artificially lit, window-less room was, and how poorly matched it was to Caleb's huge smile and sparkling eyes.

And sparkling was the word. Caleb was jubilant. It was immediately clear he'd delivered the goods.

He sat me down and he pushed a piece of paper across the table. It was £13,000. I'd not been expecting anything, and I was surprised.

Thirteen thousand pounds is a lot of money. I know that. But I don't remember any feeling of happiness. I don't remember feeling anything, if I'm honest. All I remember is the darkness of the room, and Caleb smiling.

Weirdly, at that moment, in that small broom cupboard of a room, I recalled the day that I'd been expelled from school, for selling and smoking cannabis. I had just turned sixteen and my dad, who was very religious, had been called into school to pick me up. On the drive home, he'd not said anything. I was pretty stoned and I was watching the houses fly by, and then he turned and he asked me one question.

"How did it feel?"

And my answer was just,

"It felt fine."

That night, in the middle of the night, I woke up, and my mum, who was also very religious, was sitting, crying, on the end of my bed, which was the bottom bunk of a bunk bed.

When I saw her there, I thought to myself, "Why are you crying? I'm the one who is going to fix this. Not you."

That's how I felt when Caleb gave me £13,000.

Two things happened after that bonus. The first is that I got my first book. Immediately after getting my bonus, on the same day, JB took me for a coffee at the little Starbucks. He told me that he'd seen how I'd been working, how I'd been progressing, and he wanted to give me the Kiwi dollar book.

The Kiwi dollar book, more properly called the New Zealand Dollar FX Swaps book, was a shit book. He knew that, I knew that. It was the shittest book on the desk. But still, in a way, it was a big deal, and I rec-ognized it as a sign of respect.

The next thing that happened was not such a big thing, but it's always stayed with me. JB and Caleb insisted that I had to buy something, as a treat, for my parents.

According to them, now that I'd got my first bonus, that was something that I just had to do.

Up to that point, in my whole life, I'd never bought "as a treat," anything, for anyone. I'd never even done it for myself. I was at a complete loss as to what I should buy.

So Caleb asked me, "What does your dad like?"

And I told him, "He likes football, I guess."

And that is how I came to buy my dad a Sky Sports subscription. And on Saturdays, when previously we would go to watch Orient together, me, him, and Harry from the street, I would instead go to Fitness First in Ilford, and lift weights, and when I'd leave my dad would be sitting on the sofa, watching the Premier League, which is something that neither of us had ever done in our lives, and I'd ask him what the score was and then I'd go out.

I canceled that subscription a year later, the day I left home.

I didn't care about the £13,000 though. And I didn't care about the Sky Sports. I cared a little bit about the Kiwi book, but not really. The only thing that I really cared about, or that I really, *really* cared about, was that seven hundred thousand dollars that I'd made, and how easy it had been for me to make it. Because if I could make seven hundred thousand dollars then I could make seven million. And that's what I was going to do.

It was round about then that Harry's mum died. I don't actually remember who told me. Someone called me up. Was it the work phone, or my mobile phone? I suppose it must have been my mum.

Harry grew up on my street. He's four years younger than me. In my mind he is always a ten-year-old, but by then he was nearly eighteen, and a big strapping kid with strong shoulders and rosy cheeks, and whenever he could get away with it, a ball at his feet or a beer in his hand.

When we were kids, he lived with his mum, who was a solicitor with beautiful, curly brown hair, exactly eight doors down from my house, and ever since he started school, when he was four or five years old, my mum started childminding him, which meant that he'd come home with us after school until his mum got back late in the evenings.

I've never had a little brother, and Harry became that for me. I always loved computer games when I was a kid, but my parents could never afford a console or anything, and when Harry's mum bought him a Play-Station, neither of them could figure out how to get it to work, so I went round to his house and set it up. After that we were inseparable. Every evening at his house playing PlayStation, or football in the street.

Harry's house was identical to my house, in size and in floorplan, but in no other way. It always felt so quiet with just the two of them, whereas mine was always crowded to bursting, and his mum was always so intel-lectual and calming while mine was always wild and insane, and some-times she'd ask me if I wanted to stay with them for dinner, because she was cooking a bolognese, and she'd drink red wine from a big glass while we ate it and she'd talk about books.

I'd known she'd had cancer for a long time, but for some reason, I'd never thought she was going to die. Maybe Harry had been thinking the same, I don't know. But my mum, who had also had beautiful, curly brown hair, told me that he'd cried, when it happened, and I was angry at her when she told that to me, because I felt like it wasn't hers to say.

I stood up and told Caleb that I needed to go home. I didn't give him a reason, but he just looked at me and nodded and that meant "OK then, go home."

And Harry wasn't close to his dad, so I sat next to him at the funeral, and he wore a big fat orange tie with his top two buttons undone, and he didn't cry, and after that I didn't know where he'd go, but he went out to Essex, to live with his dad.

And I spoke to JB, and I spoke to Rupert, and I spoke to Billy. I spoke to each of them one at a time and I told them that I didn't know what Harry was going to do. They all knew him because he used to play foot-ball with us every week, and they all liked him because he was that kind of guy, a good footballer, who always passed when he could have shot, and always ready with a joke and a smile.

The next time Harry came to play football, each of those guys went up and they spoke to him, one at a time, and I remember watching Rupert talk to him, with a heavy hand on his shoulder, and an honest, deep look of openness, of intimacy, and I hoped that it was what Harry needed and I'd not been able to give to him, and it was only then that I noticed how big Harry had gotten, and that he wasn't ten anymore, and I wondered if we'd move on, together, in our lives, from there.

I don't know who it was who did it, whether it was Rupert, or JB, or Billy, but one of them got him a job, as a broker.

And that's how Harry joined me in the game.

As Harry entered, Rupert left. Maybe it really is like *Watership Down*.

Rupert's days had been numbered ever since he tried and failed to fuck Spengler. Caleb was out to get him.

Caleb couldn't fuck Rupert over properly though. Rupert was too good for that. Rupert knew how to Cover His Arse. And so Caleb promoted him sideways. A classic move in the City. There's a new job available, far away. You don't want to go? You don't understand, you have to go.

The specific job available for Rupert was about as far away from Caleb as possible, in Australia: head of the Sydney STIRT desk.

I don't know if Rupert wanted to go, but he went though. He put on a brave face at least. He told me that it would be good for his career, and that it was close to Vegas.

I checked a map though, I don't think that it is.

Rupert leaving meant promotions for everyone. JB got promoted to senior euro trader, and Snoopy got promoted to junior euro trader. Hongo got given JB's old job—Ozzie and yen trader. Promotions and new books for everyone then. Nothing for me. Except with Snoopy going onto the euro book, I got the one thing that I'd really, really wanted. I got to go over and sit next to Bill.

And then came the big one. Probably the first real big shock of my trading career.

I hadn't expected it at all. Caleb was still just twenty-nine, you know. And when he stood up at seven thirty one morning, coming into the busiest time of the whole day, and he marched the entire team off the desk and toward one of the little corner offices, I honestly thought someone must have died.

I had been moved into the back corner next to Bill now, and Caleb was heading the long line of traders off the floor, so when I'd gulped down my coffee and thrown off my headset to chase after them, it was JB, not Caleb, who turned around to me and called out, "Not you Gary, someone's got to stay on the desk."

And so I just stood and I watched them, and I thought to myself, "What the fuck?"

But I didn't think that for long because Snoopy's speakerbox started bleeping, and then Hongo's, then Spengler's, then Bill's, and I was running and spinning between each of them and making prices in euros and in yen and in krona and in pounds and flicking up the little switches to everybody's different brokers, all of whom I knew by now, and making all the prices and in that moment I felt just like Roy Keane, or Steven Gerrard, marshalling the whole thing from the middle and I thought to myself, "I've got this, I can do this, I'm good enough, I've figured this out."

And then I thought, "Damn, I can do this all by myself, maybe I don't need the rest. Maybe just me, Snoopy and Bill . . ."

And I was so taken by this wild dance that I didn't even notice that all the traders had marched their way back to the desk, and Billy punched me so hard in the shoulder that my Bluetooth headset fell off of my head and he shouted, "Caleb's gone and fucking quit!!!"

Caleb was leaving, Caleb was retiring at just twenty-nine, Caleb had got married and just become a father, and was going to build a big fuck-off house in California and spend the rest of his life there as a family man. Nice for him, I suppose.

What did it mean for me?

My first thought, of course, was concern.

Caleb was the guy who hired me. Caleb was my big sponsor. It had been Caleb who had promised me that I would be able to trade from day one. I was still only just twenty-two. It was highly unconventional for a guy of my age and experience to be allowed to run their own trades, to have their own PnL. What if the new boss didn't keep to that deal?

Then there was the question of who the next boss would be. Would it be someone from the desk? Would someone be brought in from outside? Billy, having been the most profitable trader in the whole bank in the previous year, would surely be offered the job as a matter of course, but we all knew that he wouldn't take it. Billy hated the bigwigs and made no attempt to hide it, the only thing he wanted was to trade. Taking the promotion would mean more time politicking and less time trading. No, there was no way that Billy would take it. Snoopy was convinced that if Billy didn't take it then they'd offer it to one of the Slug's traders from New York, a horrible guy who looked like a frog.

But of course Caleb leaving was not the only new piece of information. Caleb was leaving to *build his own house*, in Northern California, and never to work again, at the age of twenty-nine. How the fuck much money had this guy made? I knew that the desk had made a lot of money the previous year, it had probably made about half a billion dollars in total, but I didn't know such things could be possible. And even the concept: leaving, *retiring*, at twenty-nine. What did that mean?

I had two leaving dinners with Caleb. One was a huge dinner, with the whole desk, out in the early May sunshine, in the same Spanish restaurant by the water where me and Rupert had eaten the pig.

The weather was turning, and it was beautiful. The sun had its warmth again and the evenings were getting later and the mood was one of joyous celebration. Everyone was happy for Caleb. Caleb was living the dream.

Every trader on the trading floor talks about quitting. They say, "I'll go next year, after my next bonus. These fuckers don't deserve me, I'll go next year . . ."

But no one ever actually goes, not till they get pushed.

Traders talk dreamily of a house in the mountains, or by the sea, of the family that they'll have in the countryside. The younger ones, who might still be single, talk of travel, of how they'll cycle to India, of how they will sail to Chile.

But no one actually goes.

But here he was, Caleb was going. Twenty-nine years old, still young and still handsome. He hadn't lost any of his hair yet; not even the first hint of gray. What a hero. He was doing what everyone wanted to do, and he hadn't pissed anyone off. Well, no one I liked, anyway.

We all sat around this long rectangular table, and on it were endless plates with little bits of cheese and chorizo and olives and other things that I didn't understand, and if I'm totally honest I didn't really like that kind of food, I would have rather have had a proper dinner, but I was glad to be with everyone, laughing and eating and joking as the high sun sank into the river, and I was just happy there was no baby pig.

At one point, Billy asked Caleb, "What about your deferred stock?"

Which was a question I didn't know the meaning of, but Caleb smiled that smile that I recognized from the Trading Game, the smile of a man who can't lose, so he caught my attention, and I watched as he answered,

"Don't worry, I took care of it."

"Charity?"

"Charity."

"But the Slug though?"

"One year with no bonus."

"And he took that?"

"He did."

And the other traders were not really listening, but I was shifting my gaze between Caleb, who was nodding deeply and smiling, and Billy, who looked much more serious but was nodding as well, and though I didn't understand what they were talking about, I remembered it. It would turn out to be important that I did.

Then, later, as the sun had almost set, and everyone was well drunk, JB asked Caleb, "Do you have any regrets?"

And Caleb looked out to the sunset, and he thought for a while, and then he said, "Only one, that we couldn't fuck Rupert. But don't worry. Give it time. We will."

And we all laughed and we all raised our glasses, and we drank beer until late in the night.

I had one more leaving dinner with Caleb, just me and him this time. Actually, it was more of a leaving lunch.

Caleb came up to me after he made his announcement to the desk. He apologized that I couldn't have been there in the meeting when he told everyone, but I understood, and he apologized for leaving so soon after hiring me, and for making promises that he now couldn't keep. He told me he'd make sure that I would be looked after, and that, to make it up to me, he would take me out for lunch to any place that I wanted, and that I could ask him any one question and he'd answer truthfully.

I asked him to take me to Chili's. They do good buffalo wings there. With the blue cheese dip. So we went.

Since we used to start early on the STIRT desk, we ate lunch quite early as well, and when we got into Chili's, which was a huge and well-lit fast-food restaurant high up somewhere in the Canary Wharf shopping center, it was not yet midday and totally empty. I got my buffalo wings.

It was sad, sitting there, just the two of us, in that big, open restaurant. We sat opposite one another on a small, square, plastic table, separated by twenty-four buffalo wings and two small pots of blue cheese dip. Only seven years of age were between us, but there, sitting across from me, and double my size, to a stranger he might have looked like my dad.

I looked at him. Huge head framed by that black helmet of thick dark hair. He looked tired. But he looked happy. He looked like a man who had finished his work. At that time, I had known him for two and a half years. I knew that I'd miss him. It had, a little bit, that feeling of the last day of primary school. You know you'll miss your friends, and your teacher, but you don't know what to say.

I didn't tell him any of that, of course.

"So," I looked him dead in the eye, "I get one question?"

"That's right."

He was smiling broadly and squinting slightly from the bright light of the sun, which was coming through a skylight and scattering sharp beams all over our table.

"And you're gonna answer it honestly?"

"Of course I will, Gazza."

Big smile, widening.

"Any question I want?"

"Any question you want."

I put down the wing I'd been holding.

"What do I need to do to get paid a hundred thousand pounds?"

Caleb laughed loudly and reeled backward; he placed down his own wing, now just bone.

"A hundred thousand pounds? Bonus??"

"A hundred thousand pounds. Bonus."

There was a pause while he looked at me incredulously.

"It's not possible. You can't make that in your first full year."

Caleb laughed again, but I wasn't laughing. I held his gaze. I was only twenty-two years old at that time. I tried my best to look like a man.

Caleb stopped laughing.

"Tell me what I need to do, and I'll do it."

He was starting to see I was serious now, but his answer still remained the same.

"You can't get a hundred-thousand-pound bonus in your first year as a trader. It's not possible. You just can't do it."

"Tell me what I need to do, and I'll do it."

Caleb didn't say anything for a while. He brought his hand to his chin, and he watched me.

"You'd have to make ten million dollars for the bank."

That afternoon I went to the printer next to the desk and I opened it up and took out two blank, white A4 pieces of paper.

At the top of the first piece of paper I wrote, "12 MILLION DOL-LARS," in big capitals. The extra two million dollars were margin for error. Under that I wrote out five trades, each calculated to make exactly twelve million dollars profit for the year. The trades were:

1. Lend one billion dollars one year Swissy FX Swap

2. Lend one billion dollars one year Yen FX Swap

3. Lend 1.3 billion dollars one year Sterling FX Swap

4. Lend 1.5 billion dollars one year Canada FX Swap

5. Lend 1.4 billion dollars one year Stokkie FX Swap.

I folded the piece of paper up and I put it in my desk drawer.

I wrote the exact same thing on the second piece of paper, folded that one up, put it in the back pocket of my trousers, took it home, and kept it in my underwear drawer which was under my bed.

They were big trades and I was too junior to execute them. Plus, they weren't my currencies. They were other people's books.

How could I get one of them on?

CALEB'S ACTUAL LAST DAY WAS IN LATE MAY. HE'D ALREADY MOVED all his stuff off of the desk in the previous week, and so on the day itself there was not much to do but shake all of our hands. He left in the afternoon, a couple of hours before the end of the workday. It was probably about 3 p.m.

As he walked off the desk, and started walking down the aisle, JB shouted down the hoot, "Caleb Zucman is leaving the building!"

And we all stood up and started clapping, and then everyone else on the whole floor stood up and clapped too.

And I watched the huge back of the great, hulking man walking off, all alone, down the aisle. The first trader I'd ever known. And he didn't turn or raise a hand or acknowledge the applause in any way. He simply walked off and didn't look back.

We all wanted to know who the new boss would be. Bill turned it down, like we knew that he would. We were all worried that it would be the Frog, from New York. But it wasn't the Frog, it was Chuck.

Chuck Mathieson was a giant.

I know I have liberally described traders as large throughout this book, and that is probably because almost all of them were incomparably larger than me. Chuck was the biggest, by a lot.

Chuck was Canadian. I'd never been to Canada back then. He was probably from Toronto or Vancouver or another of the big cities, but the moment I saw him I imagined him as a lumberjack in some frozen, snowy wasteland, carrying huge trees to his home, on his back. He must have been about six foot seven. Despite a bulbous stomach that he carried quite gracefully, he did not come across as a fat man, merely as a giant. An honest goliath. Belying his size was a friendly face that prevented him from being intimidating, although I only ever really saw it from below. In his early fifties, square jawed, with a crisply cut salt-and-pepper side parting, he looked a little bit like an enormous version of my father. His combination of gigantism and amiability captured me, and I was intrigued to know more of the man.

Chuck was a legend of the trading floor. He traded the Russian rouble. As you know, the STIRT desk traded only "rich-world," "Western" currencies. Places where the trains ran on time. The currencies of countries like Russia and India and Brazil got traded on the "Emerging market" desks, which physically sat not far from our desk, but might as well have been a different world. Chuck had been trading the rouble since before I was born. People said he knew Vladimir Putin.

While none of us on the STIRT desk knew Chuck personally, his reputation and size preceded him. Whenever he stood up and walked around the trading floor his vertiginous head bounced over the tops of the screen-walls so everyone on the trading floor could see where he was at any given time. In the weeks after Caleb left, the rumor started to spread that he was going to be the new boss. This is how I found out that the rumor was true.

After Caleb's departure, there was no desk head until such time as a new one was appointed, and there was also no Swiss franc trader. As a result, Bill had to fill in as temporary manager and I had to fill in as temporary Swiss franc trader. This wasn't like covering for someone: the trades themselves did not go into Caleb's book, which no longer existed; rather, they went into mine. The Swiss franc book was a decently profitable book, back in those days, and I was making a fair bit of cash.

Bill hated managing and Bill hated admin, and since I was Bill's junior, a lot of admin rolled down to me. That meant that I often had to stay behind after everyone had gone home, which I didn't mind, because, as I've said, I was making the cash.

In one of those late afternoons, about two or three weeks into this period, I was the only person left on the desk, doing boring admin, sending emails and booking some trades. Chuck, who had not yet been formally announced as the new head of the STIRT desk, wandered over to the desk, and to me.

I looked up at Chuck. With me seated and him standing, the distance between our faces was enormous. In order to look at me, Chuck had to bend his neck fully forward, as if looking down at his own shoes. He was positively beaming. I smiled.

Chuck offered me a hand, which I shook. He already knew my name. "Hi Gary, I'm Chuck."

Then he wandered off to get a chair to sit in. Because all the other STIRT traders had gone home, there were empty chairs everywhere, so this should not have been a procedure, but for some reason he disappeared and it took him about two minutes. Maybe he needed a reinforced chair.

Chuck eventually returned and slowly rolled the chair in next to me, and lowered himself into it in installments. The incredible size and weight of the man lent a great gravity to all of his movements. I felt very much like a boy.

Once Chuck had gotten himself into the chair, he didn't say anything, he simply smiled mischievously at me, for some time.

I didn't quite know what to do with this, so I smiled back myself, somewhat awkwardly, and continued booking my trades.

That went on for about two minutes, which was utterly ridiculous, and then Chuck leaned in and said simply, "Hey."

He was still smiling like a madman, or maybe more like a schoolboy, so I turned round to him and said, "Hey?"

At this point, Chuck brought his right hand around, which I hadn't realized he'd been hiding behind his back the whole time. In the hand was a copy of the magazine *Sports Illustrated*, which, as you probably know, is some kind of swimsuit magazine.

I looked at the front cover of the magazine and then I looked back at Chuck's face. He was wiggling his eyebrows at me.

Chuck opened the magazine. Not in such a way as to read it himself, but in such a way that made it clear that we were both to look at the pictures, together. The picture was a double-page spread of a woman in a bikini.

I looked at the picture and I looked back at Chuck. He was still wiggling his eyebrows. He wiggled them for a little bit longer, and then he said,

"Yeah. You like that, huh?"

And of course, I replied, "Yeah. Yeah it's nice."

And so Chuck turned the page.

On the next page was another double-page spread of a woman in a bikini. I looked at Chuck with his wiggling eyebrows and he said, "Mmmm, yeah. That's real nice."

So I said, "Yeah, that's nice."

And I nodded a bit.

This then went on for a long time, far longer than could possibly be reasonably explained. I didn't quite know what was going on, but I realized, perhaps on the third or fourth bikini, that it must indeed be true that Chuck was the new head of the desk. There was no other possible explanation. The feeling established itself with greater certainty as we worked our way through the magazine.

Eventually we finished, with all the bikinis, and Chuck rolled up the magazine and stuffed it into his ample trouser pocket. Then he stopped smiling and looked meaningfully off into the distance as if, now that introductions were over, he could finally get down to business.

"So, what do you do then, on the desk?"

I looked Chuck in the face, and Chuck looked at me, and suddenly, Chuck looked very young.

It was simply inconceivable that Chuck, who within a week would be taking over the STIRT desk, did not know what my actual job was. Wasn't it? Or was it?

I looked him in the face, deeply, and I tried to take a measure of the man. What was he doing here? Was this a bluff?

Since Caleb had been the Swiss franc trader, I had assumed that the new boss would take over that role, and I would be left as humble Kiwi trader and cover for Bill. Surely Chuck knew that was my job. Or did he?

I kept looking at him. Was it a game? Was he clueless? I tried to read it in his face. I probably looked at him for longer than I should have done, because after a while, he started to smile again. That big, wide, mischievous, childish grin returned to his face, and then, as he smiled at me, I started to smile too, and I said to him, "I'm the Swiss franc trader, Chuck. I'm the Swiss franc trader."

And Chuck kept on smiling and he started to nod real deeply, and he lifted himself, slowly, out of his reinforced chair and he kept ﾃ at me at intervals while he was doing it, and nodding. And then he got himself back round the side of the chair and he started to roll it away with him, and as he was leaving, he turned back to me one last time and he said, "It was really nice to meet you Gary. I'm looking forward to working with you."

And then Chuck left and I was alone on the desk once again, and I sat and thought about what had just happened.

And then I flicked up the switch to a guy called Morley, who was my favorite Swiss broker, and I started shouting his name, "Morley! Morley! You still there?"

And I flicked the switch down and a bit later Morley's cockney voice sang back at me, "You alrite, Gal? What you doing still here?"

"Don't worry about that mate, listen, do you reckon you can get me some one-year? I wanna lend US dollars."

"Well, everyone's gone home mate, but I can maybe get you some from New York. How much you wanna do?"

"I wanna do about a yard mate."

A yard is a billion dollars.

And I did it. I became the Swiss franc trader. And I did trade number one from the sheet that I wrote.

And by the end of the year, it had made me just over twelve million dollars.

Which is exactly what I wrote on the sheet.

8

NOBODY HAD EVER MADE TEN MILLION DOLLARS IN THEIR FIRST year before. They told me that once it was done.

I suppose, then, that raises the question: why was it that I was the first?

I'd like to tell you that it was for my intelligence, or maybe because I was brave.

That nobody had ever had the nerve before, to put on such big trades at such a young age.

The truth is, though, those weren't the main reasons, although I suppose they may have played their parts. There were two main reasons I made so much money that year: it was easy, and it was allowed.

It was easy because everyone was doing it. Everyone was still doing that same trade. Lending dollars out for the long term, at 2%, and borrowing them back, every day, for free.

And it was allowed, I suppose, for the same reason. Because everybody around me was doing it, all of them on a much bigger scale. Bill made a hundred million dollars again in 2009, for the second year in a row, and became, once more, the most profitable trader in the bank. No one else made a hundred million dollars, but a couple made seventy-five. Who was there to be concerned with me? Sitting in my corner, scraping by to make twelve million bucks. No one cared. Hell, even Snoopy made thirty that year. Sometimes Chuck lumbered over to me like a pine tree and cast his huge shadow over my screens. In those moments he wouldn't say anything. He'd simply smile the smile of the mad or the enlightened and rock my chair gently backward and forward while looking away. I think it is genuinely possible that he still did not know what my job was.

Of course, beyond the question of how I was able to do it, there's a bigger question: how were all of us able to do it? Why were we all allowed to do the same huge trades, and make so much money? Wasn't there a risk, if we all did the same trade, of it all going horribly wrong?

It wasn't until midway through 2009 that I even thought to put that question to Billy, and he told me that right at the beginning of the crisis, Caleb had gone to the big bosses—not just the Slug, but the Slug's boss, and the Slug's boss's boss—and he'd gotten special dispensation for us all to do the same trade. The way Billy told it was that, if the trade made money, we all would make money—Billy, me, Chuck, the Slug, the Slug's boss, all the way up. Hell, even the CEO got paid on our PnL. If it went wrong, the whole banking system would blow up, and we'd all lose our jobs, so who cared. That's why it was allowed. A fish rots from the head down, I guess.

I looked over at Chuck and I wondered if what Chuck was doing, and what all of us were doing, was wrong somehow. Chuck was smiling and nodding, at nobody, like he always did. He had just poured an enormous pile of loose change out onto his desk, from his drawer. He was counting the individual coins and placing them into piles.

You might think that making my first twelve million dollars would have been a big thing for me, a thing I'd remember. You might think that I'd have a clear image in my mind of a grand seminal moment. Something to treasure to this day.

In reality though, it happens slowly, a bit at a time, by degrees.

It took me over six months to make that twelve million dollars. That's only two million dollars each month. What's that then? A hundred thousand dollars a day? A little bit less?

And that's how it really was, dripping in, every day, a hundred thousand dollars here, a hundred thousand dollars there. Maybe only fifty thousand dollars one day.

And what was I doing while it was happening? What do I remember of that time?

You know, numbers are powerful. Numbers can hypnotize you. And I remember every day that spreadsheet was going around with everybody's name on it, and everyone's number. And my number was slowly ticking upward. One million dollars. Two million dollars.

Late one evening, on a weekend, I saw my best friend's car, a little pokey silver Peugeot 106, stopped up at a traffic light in Shoreditch, so I ran over and started knocking on the window, and when the window rolled down there was a girl's face there, looking straight at me, with big bow lips and short, black hair, and it was the most beautiful thing that I'd ever seen, and she became my first serious girlfriend.

Three million dollars. Four million dollars.

Gordon Brown was talking one day in parliament, about taxing the banks, and when that happened I felt a pang in my heart, but I looked around at Billy, and he was shaking JB by the shoulders and they were both laughing, and Big Chuck was laughing as well, and even though I didn't really understand what was happening, I took a big breath in and I breathed it all out. We would be OK.

Five million dollars. Five and a half million dollars.

She lived in northwest London so I needed a car to get to her, and my friend needed £750 because he was studying Fashion Design at Central Saint Martins and he needed to buy a mannequin with collapsible shoulders, so I gave him £710 for his Peugeot and he borrowed the rest from his mum.

Six million dollars, seven million dollars.

And Harry was living out in Essex, with his dad, now, but whenever I got time I'd drive out to get him and we'd go to the gym, and I'd ask him how his job was going and he'd say that it was going really well, and I'd ask him how things were going with his dad and he'd say they were OK.

Eight million dollars, nine million dollars.

And every weekend I'd drive round to her tiny studio apartment in northwest London, and I'd stay there all weekend, and the walls were covered in hand-drawn pictures of deer skeletons, and the floor was covered with bits of material and clothes, and when the winter came, she refused to turn the heating on, because she said it was too expensive and that she could save money that way.

Ten million dollars. Eleven million dollars.

My dad was still watching Sky Sports in the evenings and the weekends, but that was OK, because I wasn't at home much anyway. My friends couldn't get jobs because of the financial crisis, so whenever I was free, I'd just hang out with them and play PlayStation and bust jokes.

Twelve million dollars.

Job done.

It wasn't until ten million dollars that I even really stopped to look up. It was the end of November by then.

Winter is a strange time to be a trader. It's cold and pitch-black on the way in and it's cold and pitch-black when you leave.

I didn't really have a proper coat back in those days. Just this skinny little black kind of pea coat kind of thing that I bought from Topman for I think £30. I've still got it. To avoid getting cold in the mornings I used to sprint all the way to the station and time it to get there for exactly when the train arrived. I couldn't time it for the second train though, which would be sitting, frozen, waiting for me on the platform at Stratford, and I remember standing, perched on the little window seat cushion at the end of the carriage, shivering, waiting for the train to start and to plunge underground.

We'd work for the first two hours in darkness, and then, slowly, the sun would come up over a horizon that we couldn't see for the thick clouds, and would take us from a blackness into a dark gray. We'd work for five hours, in the grayness, then the blackness, again, and then all of us would get up and go home.

By this time I was well established as Bill's junior, and Caleb and Rupert were both gone. The only person who I bought lunch for was Bill, and I would do that every day. The takeaway lunch restaurants are all buried in the underground shopping center, which you can access directly from the Citigroup building, but I'd take the long route through the park at the back of the building, every day, just to get outside and see if I could find the sun. Bill himself rarely left the office. I wondered when he saw the sun. I imagined he lived in some big, luxurious country manor. I guessed they had sun in those places on the weekends.

In December the trading floor starts to wind down and the world becomes one never-ending broker lunch. I was through ten million dollars by then, but not quite at twelve yet, which had immediately become my new target, so I didn't take my eye off the ball, but it was difficult because every broker and trader in the City said that I owed them at least one Christmas drink.

Billy and JB were taking me out frequently, which was a significant improvement on Rupert and Spengler, and I started to realize how much the two drank. I got a text from Hongo one time saying he was in a bar down in the Canary Wharf main square drinking with JB, but he needed to go home, so could I come and take JB off his hands. When I got there, JB was staggering and swearing, and Hongo dropped him onto my shoulder and went to the bathroom.

I slumped JB onto a stool and balanced him a bit from his shoulders, the way you might balance a vase on a plinth. He tottered slightly, then slumped forward off of the chair and back onto me again, and I could see he was going to cry.

He started saying something about his sister being sick, back in Australia, and how he wanted to go back and see her, and I looked over both my shoulders to see if anyone was looking at us, and I saw Hongo was coming back, so I started slapping JB on the cheek and whispered, "Come on mate. Hong's coming back. None of that boss, yeah? None of that."

And JB looked left and saw Hongo and he started laughing, and he pinched my nose so hard that I had a bruise on it for the next four days.

We all went out in central London for a team Christmas dinner at Nobu, which is some super fancy restaurant that is supposed to be Japanese, but to be honest is just Mayfair, and Bill drank so much that I had to take him to the bathroom, and while I was hobbling him over there like a physio carrying an injured footballer he suddenly started and jumped and grabbed me by the shoulders and started shouting, "MAIKYKANE!" in my ear.

"MAIKKKAIM! MYKOKAIN!" he was shouting, and slurring his *k*'s considerably.

I had no idea what he was saying. I thought it was something about cocaine, but I was pretty sure Billy didn't do that, so I was leaning in and asking him what the fuck was going on but all he could do was shout, "MAIIKKYYKAIMMM," about seven more times.

Then, suddenly, Michael Caine emerged from the darkness and walked right past Bill's shoulder and in my shock I let go of Bill and he started to reel backward and he pointed right in my face and shouted, "It's MICHAEL CAINE you fucking cockney TWAT!"

And then he fell backward onto the floor.

.   .   .

Back at home, my parents had put the Christmas tree up, and three stockings on the wall. One for my brother, one for my sister, one for me.

The Christmas tree was not huge, but it filled the whole living room, such that you could not watch TV from either of the sofas, and instead you had to wedge yourself between the TV and the tree. That was fine for me, I never watched TV anyway.

Whenever I got back late that Christmas, after drinking, all the lights would be off in the house, but the Christmas tree's fairy lights would be on and lighting up the living room. In purples, in oranges, then pinks. It reminded me of being a kid. Maybe I still was a kid.

I didn't buy anyone any presents that year. But they still all bought presents for me.

9

I WASN'T SCARED ABOUT BONUS DAY. I MEAN, I KNEW, DIDN'T I? I knew what it was going to be. Caleb had told me. Ten million dollars was a hundred thousand pounds. So twelve million dollars had to be something like one twenty.

There hadn't really been any big reason why I picked a hundred thousand pounds that day, in that conversation with Caleb. I guess it had simply been the biggest amount of money that I could imagine, back at that time. It was a crazy big amount to me. You've got to remember, just four years before that, I had been delivering newspapers, every day, for £12 a week. After that, I had been fluffing pillows for £40 a day and even *that* had felt like a lot of money to me. I was still living with my mum, you know? A hundred thousand pounds was inconceivable. I couldn't even imagine what you could do with that.

So I wasn't scared on the day itself. Not a bit. What I do remember is that I had expected to be called into the room last, because the previous year had been done in reverse order of PnL, and my PnL was the lowest on the desk. But what actually happened was that Bill got called in first, as I had expected, and when Bill came back to the desk he told me to go in.

The bonus meetings weren't in the broom cupboard that year. Big Chuck had somehow snagged a beautiful office right on the corner of the building, with windows facing out over the quay in two directions. That was such a Big Chuck thing to do. It was sunny that day, I remember. And Big Chuck was sitting there in the sun, with his hands flat on his knees, super calm and placidly smiling, like a huge golden statue of Buddha. Honestly, I can see the whole thing vividly, I remember this like it was yesterday.

Big Chuck didn't say nothing. He just smiled. I sat down opposite him, and I placed my hands on my knees to mirror the man. There was a single white A4 piece of paper placed perfectly centrally on the table between us, angled so as to face neither one of us, pointing, instead, toward the door.

I looked at Chuck, and he looked down at me, calmly, and it was quickly clear he was not going to speak. So, instead I looked down at the paper.

There were some words at the top of the paper. My name, including my middle name, Gary Walter Stevenson. Beneath that was a small table with a number of numbers. None of them were the number I was expecting, which was, as you know, £120,000.

I realized that there were a few more sheets of paper under the top sheet, but I was near certain that the number itself would be here on the front page. I pointed at the first number at the top of the table, which was the largest: £395,000.

"Is it that number?"

There was no strategy behind me saying that. In fact, I don't remember the actual saying of the words. I remember it happening. I remember seeing my arm reaching out and pointing, and hearing the words that I was speaking.

I looked up at Chuck. Chuck started to smile broadly with his whole face and his eyes, and very gently, he started to laugh.

"Yes, it's that number."

"Wow," I said. "That's a lot of money."

I remember that. I remember that so clearly. Then after that, everything's blank.

The next memory I have I am back in my seat. I am at my desk, right hand on my mouse, left hand on my keyboard, and ridiculously, absurdly, pathetically, I am feeling that I am going to cry, and I'm trying not to cry.

I feel, on my right cheek, that Billy is looking at me. And I turn instinctively to see if he is actually looking at me, and he is, so immediately, too quickly, I look back. And I'm holding it but I'm clearly not holding it very well.

And Bill stands up and he comes round to the left side of me so that he is between me and the other traders on the desk, so that the other traders can't see me, and he puts both of his palms flat down on the desk and he leans in very close to me and he says, "Go outside. Go sit down in the park for a bit. Take a moment. You'll feel better. It's OK."

And the next memory I have I am sitting down, like a child, on the grass in the park, and it's really not a park at all but a medium-sized square of grass surrounded on three sides by enormous skyscrapers, but at that time of the day the sun is on the fourth side, so between the long shadows I am sitting in the sun.

And in my daze, I'd forgotten to bring anything, my scarf, or my jacket, even the black fingerless gloves that I often wore on the desk because I got cold when I was working, and I suddenly realize how cold I am, but at least there is sun.

And the first thing I thought of, when my senses came back to me, was my dad.

My dad worked for the Post Office for thirty-five years, and when I was very young, he used to start work very early, before I woke up. As you know, the train from Seven Kings into the City used to run right past my bedroom window, and my mum used to come into my room and gently wake me up, very early, in the pitch-black of the nighttime, to look out of the window, and try to catch sight of my dad in the train as it flew past.

Sometimes the trains were very fast, and it was all a blur, and I wasn't able to catch him. But other times, the trains were slower, and I was able to see him, all lit up in the warm glow of the train carriage lights, always looking back out of his own window, for me, and smiling and waving.

And then, because it would still be very early and dark and cold then, especially in the winter, I'd go back to sleep and my dad would be at work. And I wouldn't see him again until late in the evening, or, at least, what seemed to be very late in the evening to me, then just a young child, and he was always tired then, and he was always friendly even though he was tired.

And I thought of all the years that he'd done that, woken up early, gotten the early morning train, in the dark, in the cold, come back late, in the dark, in the cold. For us. For me, I guess. For what? Twenty thousand pounds a year?

And here was me, small in the shadow of the skyscrapers that had grown around me as a boy, sitting, cross-legged, with no jacket and no scarf, in a small triangle of light, on a small square of grass, just turned twenty-three years old, and just having received three hundred and ninety five thousand pounds.

What could that mean?

I sat there for a while, in the cold, and I calmed myself. And I thought of the other dads. I thought of this guy Ibran Khan who I went to primary school with, and his dad was disabled and he didn't have his own bedroom and he slept on a sofa in the front room, so he didn't have to climb the stairs, but they were all very kind to me. And they gave me food that was too spicy for me to eat and they gave me tea that was too spicy for me to drink. Why hadn't I kept in touch with him? Where were they now? And I thought of another boy called Muzzamil, who came over from Pakistan when we must have been just seven or eight, and he couldn't speak English, and he would spend all playtime and lunchtime just running around endlessly doing cartwheels and shouting the only word he could say that we would understand, which was his own name. "Muzzamil! Muzzamil! Muzzamil!"

What could all of that mean?

And the next thought was, what do I do now?

And the thought after that was, what did the rest of them make? If I made £395,000 on twelve million dollars, then what did Hong make, on his seventy? What had Rupert made the previous year, with eighty million dollars? What did Bill make on one hundred million dollars, two years in a row?

And what about the credit traders, with the pink monogrammed shirts, who had blown up the world? What had they made before they blew up the world?

And then I thought: It was so easy to make twelve million dollars. I can make twenty. I can make fifty. Maybe I can make a hundred. I was smarter than Rupert. I was smarter than JB. I knew it. Maybe I wasn't as smart as Bill, but if I really put myself into it, I could get there. I was definitely smarter than the credit guys in the pink shirts. I could make more.

And what would it mean if I could make fifty? Maybe I'd get paid two million pounds. What could I do with two million pounds? What couldn't you do? You could do anything. You could retire. You could be free. You could be your own man. You could build a house in Northern California, maybe. You could sail to Chile. Maybe. Where's Chile again? Maybe I can do it. No, not maybe, I know I can do it! Why should the pink shirt guys and the Ruperts be millionaires and not the Ibrans and the Muzzamils and not me? Why not me? I'm not worse than them. I'm better than them. We're all better than them. And I'm better than all of them. I'm the best. I can be the best.

And I think there, in that cold January sun something about me changed, and my career changed, and it wasn't a career anymore. From then on, it was bank robbery.

Part Three

GO HOME
AND ASK
YOUR MUM

1

I DIDN'T WANT TO GO HOME THAT DAY, I'M NOT REALLY SURE WHY. So I messaged my girlfriend and I asked her if I could stay round at hers, and I took the Jubilee Line over to northwest London.

It was cold that night, one of those frosty London nights where there's no clouds above you, and you can actually see a couple stars for once, and you can feel how cold the universe is.

I didn't do anything once I got there, it was like I couldn't move. I just lay on her bed in her tiny apartment. She used to have a part-time job hand-drawing t-shirt designs to make money to pay for her bills while she was studying fashion, and she'd stuck all the old drawings up onto the walls. It was all horse skeletons and deer skeletons and other, anonymous skeletons, and I lay there and I counted the skeletons as a tiny rotating portable heater cast warm, dancing, orange shadows all over and across them and she padded around in her cold, bare feet on the wood floor, preparing a dinner for us both.

We'd spoken before about bonus day, and she'd known I'd been looking forward to it. She'd told me that I didn't have to tell her how much it turned out to be, and as we sat, eating at her tiny little table, with sewing machines and scraps of fabrics and dresses all pushed to the side, she didn't know how much I appreciated that. I don't think she understood why I was being so quiet though. I don't think I understood either.

In the middle of the night I woke up and she was crying. It was loud and I maneuvered her around so that she was below me and that I was above her and I looked down at her and asked what was wrong.

"Why didn't you tell me? Why didn't you tell me?"

She was speaking between sobs and she was staring up at me and I was stroking her hair and I was trying to calm her. I hadn't really decided who I was going to tell yet. I didn't know if I'd tell anyone. But I figured, at least, that I owed it to her, or maybe I just wanted her to stop crying, or maybe I just wanted to speak the words out in the real world, to see if they existed, to see if they worked.

So I told her.

And she stopped crying, instantly, in a moment. And her face was totally calm and unmoving, as if receiving a vision, and she was just looking, silently, up at me, through me, beyond me, and in that moment she looked very much like a young child. And her eyes seemed to grow until they became enormous, and I could see the whole circles of her unmoving irises, and the vast seas of white that seemed to open around them, and I'd never seen eyes move like that before.

Straight away, I wished I'd never told her.

A few months later we broke up.

After that, I thought I should probably tell no one, but just that weekend my mate Jalpesh called me up to play Pro Evolution round his mum's house with some old schoolfriends. Jalpesh was the guy who lost his job at Lehman in the 2008 crisis, but since then he'd managed to get another job trading at Deutsche Bank. A couple other of our friends had also managed to get jobs in investment banks, although in roles that weren't as glamorous as trading, and as we passed around PlayStation controllers the conversation turned toward bonuses.

Jalpesh had been given £6,000, and he was pretty happy with that. He threw the question over to Hemal. Hemal had received only three. When Mashfique got asked he said he'd got nothing. You could tell he was pretty pissed off, but he was always pissed off.

The whole time I didn't say nothing. I was sitting there playing the game. Eventually the question made its way round to me.

"What did you get Gaz? Did you get a bonus?"

I'd decided, of course, to tell no one. But I wasn't really sure what to do. Those guys in that room were some of my best friends. I'd known them for over ten years, since we were kids. What could I do, you know? Was I going to lie to them?

I decided, in the moment, just to say it, just to try it.

"I got three hundred and ninety-five thousand pounds."

And you could feel it, the oxygen leaving the room. You could hear it, like a gust of wind. And after that, ten seconds of silence, and then the plasticky sound of a PlayStation controller, bouncing twice as it drops to the floor.

Things were never the same after that.

2

THERE WAS ONE GUY I STILL HAD TO TELL THOUGH. HARRY SAMBHI.
Harry had to know. I wasn't gonna tell him the exact number, I'd seen
the power of what that could do. But I had to tell him that I'd gotten
something, and that it was good. Harry had known me since I was eight
years old and he was four. I'd told him about the first time I'd kissed a
girl, the first time I'd gotten drunk, the first time I'd smoked weed. The
kid looked up to me, you know? Besides, we were in this together now.
I had to give him something to run with.

So I got in my car on a Saturday morning and I drove out to Essex, to
Harry's dad's house. I didn't tell him in advance that I was coming, but
I got to his place sufficiently early that I knew he would have to be in.

I rang on the doorbell, Harry's dad answered. I never really knew
Harry's dad all that well. He was looking a bit worse for wear. He propped
himself up on the frame of the door and when I asked him if I could see
Harry he was scratching his ruffled hair and his stubbled chin as if he
wasn't quite sure of the name.

Eventually the words fell into place for him, and he said Harry was
sleeping in the living room. I was confused about why Harry would be
sleeping in the living room instead of his bedroom, but while I was
thinking that, his dad had shuffled away up the stairs. I'd never been
into Harry's dad's house before. I walked into the now vacated dark hallway, and went through to go look for Harry.

The living room was spartanly furnished. Fake wood floor, white
walls, television, old brown sofa. Although it was a bright winter morning, the dark red curtains were pulled tightly closed, and one single
shard of light crept between them to penetrate the gloom of the room.

Harry was lying face down on the sofa. I mean literally face down. His entire face was plunged deeply into an old, dark brown pillow. I momentarily wondered how he could breathe. His body was too long for the sofa, so both of his feet were propped up by the sofa's far arm, which gave him a vague semblance of being in prayer. He was fully dressed: trousers; white work shirt; one pair of comically enormous black shoes. One of his feet had popped out at the heel, as if a cursory attempt had been made at removal but the idea had not been followed through. His right arm hung crookedly down to the ground, where his hand lay, bent ninety degrees at the wrist.

Despite Harry's slovenly comportment, his appearance was only the second most eye-catching thing in the room. The thing which immediately caught one's attention upon entering the space was not Harry's heartfelt, fully dressed prayer to the sofa, but what lay behind it, and above it, screaming itself loudly and erratically from the white wall.

In huge, bright red, heavily painted letters, in a wild and oscillating hand, stretching from one edge of the wall to the open door, were the words

HARRY KING IS CHAMPION SAMBHI

I stood for a moment, wordless, and I took in the sight. The lone shaft of morning light cut across Harry's waistline and onto the wall, pointing upward, to the word "KING." It was a work of art.

Harry stirred. A moan of muffled anguish escaped from the pillow.

I jostled Harry with my fist on the side of his hip and I tried to lift his head by the hair.

"Harry! What the fuck you doing Harry? Why the fuck you sleeping with your shoes on?"

Harry lifted his heavy body up sideways and turned his face toward me and smiled. The lines of the sofa pillow were imprinted on his cheeks.

Through cooperative effort, we got Harry into a sitting position. He was smiling and making noises that were not words. It was pretty clear that he was still drunk. Eventually we got him speaking English, and I asked him the questions I wanted to ask.

"Harry man, what the fuck are you doing? Why you sleeping on the sofa?"

"Ohhh it's . . . Oh don't worry about that mate. Jussst . . . out with the lads. Lads from work!"

He pointed to the left and then to the right when he said this. His words were a jumble of slurs.

"Why you still wearing your shoes?"

He grinned at me and kicked his right shoe off. It nearly hit the telly. He kicked his left foot a couple times, but the shoe didn't come off. He giggled a bit and gave up.

"Harry. Do you know that you've written HARRY KING IS CHAMPION SAMBHI in massive fucking red painted letters on your fucking wall? Where the fuck did you get the red paint from!? It don't make no fucking grammatical sense!"

Harry looked surprised for just a moment, and he twisted round to look at his work. His surprise seemed to pass quickly and he paused for a while to admire it, then he read the words, slowly, back to me.

"HARRY. KING. IS. CHAMPION. SAMBHI."

He turned back around and was nodding contemplatively, and he rubbed his temple with his hand.

"You're right mate. It don't make no grammatical sense. I think KING and CHAMPION should be swapped around. But don't worry about that mate. I did that fucking months ago. It's been there for ages. Don't you like it? I think it's good!"

And so, I moved out from my parents' house, and I rented a flat in an old converted matchstick factory in Bow, in inner East London, where all the Grime MCs came from, and I took Harry Sambhi, who was about to turn nineteen, over there and he lived with me. After that, we were a team.

Then I had to learn how to cook.

But none of that matters. None of any of all of that matters. I knew that the moment I stepped back on the desk. I was embarrassed that I'd shown my emotions, and I was embarrassed that Billy had seen. When I got myself up off of that little patch of grass in Canary Wharf, that day back then after that bonus, and marched myself back onto the trading floor, I knew Billy was looking at me on my right side, and over on my left side JB and Snoopy were probably looking at me too. Billy stood up and walked round to my left, again shielding me from the rest of the desk, as he had done before. He leaned in and asked,

"Are you all right Gal?"

I didn't look. I just said to him, "Yeah. I'm all right. What's the trade?"

Because that's what we're doing now. All we're doing now is trading. We gonna make a hundred million dollars, and we're going to be million-aires.

How do we do that?

Now as you know, the trading story thus far has been simple: we lent dollars out long term, using FX swaps, and we borrowed the dollars back every day. That was a very reliable earner. But good trades are like or-anges, even the best ones will run out of juice.

In the aftermath of 2008, everybody needed dollars. Nobody had them and we did, so we made a ton of money. But that money does not last forever. It didn't take long before central banks all over the world realized that a lack of available dollars to borrow was risking the bank-ruptcy of banking systems worldwide, and relatively quickly the US Fed-eral Reserve started to lend US dollars to central banks in other countries. They did that through FX swaps, the exact same product that we were trading on the desk. The international central banks who borrowed those dollars lent them on to the commercial banks in their respective countries, and before long, what was once a life-threatening desperation for US dollars became merely an impending need. That cut into our margins. Not only that, but over the course of 2009 governments and central banks the world over lent so much cheap money, and bought so many of the banking system's bad assets, that it started to become clearer and clearer that the banking system wasn't going to blow up.

On one hand, that was great. That was exactly what we had been bet-ting on and it meant that our bets all paid off. It was one of the reasons that I, like everyone else in STIRT trading, made so much money in 2009. On the other hand, it was bad. It meant the gravy train was no longer running. As the global need for dollars became less and less ur-gent, and it became more and more obvious that the global banking system would survive, more and more traders and banks entered the game of lending dollars, and what was once an extremely lucrative business started to become less and less profitable. No longer could we lend dollars out at 2 percent and borrow them back at zero. We'd be lucky to get 1 percent.

What compounded this misfortune for me, at the beginning of 2010, when I had just decided to become the world's greatest trader, was that I was no longer up twelve million dollars. You see, when the year rolls over, and you've made your bonus on your twelve bucks, that twelve bucks is no longer yours. The clock resets and you are now back to zero.

This is a problem for a trader, and I'll explain to you why.

Trading isn't a free lunch. There's no such thing as a trade that makes you a lot of money without you taking a significant amount of risk. That's another good rule for life—if anyone ever tells you they've got one, cut that person out of your life.

So it was with the lending of dollars. It was risky. Even though it always made a load of money in the long term, it swung around a lot every day. While it was a near-certain winner over six months, you couldn't guarantee to win every week, or even every month.

That's fine when you're on twelve million dollars, but it's a problem when you're on zero, because if you lose money when you are on zero, you can end up in the dreaded place, *in the red*.

Being in the red means you are down money on the year. It means that every day, when that spreadsheet gets sent out to every trader, with every trader's name and PnL on it, your PnL comes up as a little red number (in brackets).

You do not want to be a little red number in brackets. Trust me.

When you are a little red number in brackets, your boss stands behind you. He asks you about every trade you put on. He speaks to his boss about your trades. Everyone wonders if your trades are actually good, or if you just made them up (they are all made up, by the way). You have to send a little email with your trade rationale to your boss, and your boss's boss. You have to tell them how much loss you are willing to take on that trade before you will "stop out" (crystallize the loss by closing the trade). Worst of all, sometimes your boss, or your boss's boss, will actually *stop your trades themselves*. Nobody wants to have their trades stopped by their boss. You might as well have your mum wipe your arse.

So no, being in the red was not an option, and that limited your moves when you're on zero. Billy did not like to be on zero, so Billy was never on zero. Now, I am not going to point any fingers, and I am not going to make any insinuations, but what I will say is that Billy always made ten million dollars in the first week of every year. I don't know how that happened and I don't want to know. All I know is I didn't know how to do that, so I started every year on zero, like normal human beings.

Starting every year on zero means you have to start small. This was a problem for me because in the coming year, 2010, I wanted to make a hundred million dollars. It was also a problem because my one big trade, lending dollars, was now considerably less profitable and more risky than it had been in the whole of 2009. That was not just a problem because it made it harder for me to make money—after all, if the trade was less profitable, I could always just double the size of the trade—it was a problem because it made it considerably harder for me, for us all, to take massive trades.

The trade that I had taken in 2009 was enormous for a first-year trader. It definitely should not have been allowed. I had gotten away with it through some combination of negligence, goodwill, and the fact that my boss spent most of his time stacking coins into neat piles. More than anything, it had been because the traders around me had been taking so much risk, and making so much money, that I'd managed to slip under the radar.

But at this point, people would have noticed. Firstly, in order to make PnL even at the same rate of the previous year, I would have had to double the size of what was already an enormous trade for a trader of twenty-three. Secondly, *all of us* now had to cut our risks. That meant smaller trades, and smaller PnLs all round. I couldn't hide in their shadows anymore.

And that is why at the beginning of 2010, having swallowed my tears on the green grass of Canary Wharf's Canada Square, and sitting back on my trading desk with the new ambition of becoming Citi's top trader, I stared into my screens and asked Bill to tell me, "What's the trade?"

Because Billy always made money, and Billy always had a trade.

The rest of us, I'll be honest, we were monkeys, we were philistines. We lent dollars and we took in the profits and we went out and bought apartments that didn't have no doors.

But Billy was different. Billy was an artist. He was an artist and he was an addict.

By the beginning of 2010 I had sat next to Billy for nearly a year, and I'd started to appreciate what he did.

Billy lent dollars. Of course Billy lent dollars. Lending dollars was a great trade and if there was a great trade anywhere on the table, Billy took it. But Billy didn't just lend dollars, he'd lend pounds as well. Billy knew everything about pounds. Billy knew the personalities and habits of every single member of the Bank of England Monetary Policy Committee, the "bunch of knobheads" (Billy's own words) who set the UK interest rates. Billy knew everything about them. He probably knew what times they went to bed.

Billy lent other things too, but he didn't lend everything. Lending everything, Billy said, was "pig on pork." Let's talk about what "pig on pork" is.

When you lend a currency, you are betting that the interest rate will go down. The way it works is this: when you get a loan, you go to the bank and you ask for a loan for, let's say, the next five years. Now, at this point in time, the bank does not actually know what the market interest is going to be over the next five years. That is because the interest rate is set every single month by the Central Bank, and your bank does not at this point know what they are going to do. Your bank will then come to someone like us, the traders, the risk takers, and ask us to take the risk, the gamble, on what the interest rate is going to be.

At that time, at the beginning of 2010, interest rates all over the world, including in the UK, were pretty much 0%. But everyone thought (incorrectly) that they were going to go up. Let's say that the traders think rates will go up gradually over the next five years from 0% to 5%, meaning the average rate over the period will be 2.5%. They might offer to lend your bank money at 2.55%, who will turn round and lend you money at 2.8%. Everyone's taking their little bit of cut.

But once the trader has promised to lend your bank money at 2.55%, in what situation does he make money?

The answer is that the trader makes money if interest rates go up less than expected. If rates don't actually go up, but stay at 0%, the trader—who has agreed to lend money at 2.55%—can ultimately fund your five-year, 2.8% mortgage by borrowing cash every day at 0%. He makes himself the 2.55%, and your bank takes its 0.25% cut. Magic—free money!

Of course, it's never really free money. If rates were to go up much quicker than expected—say for example up to 5% instantly and then staying there for the whole five years—the trader could be stuck funding his 2.55% loan at 5%, and taking the hit.

The lesson here is that *lending money is betting that rates will stay low.*

And when do rates stay low? In general, they stay low if the economy is weak. This is because of the way that central banks set rates. They cut rates when they think that the economy is weak, and they raise them when they think that the economy is strengthening or inflation is over-heating. They cut rates to try and get you to spend money, and they raise them to try and get you to stop.

This is why Bill didn't lend everything. Economies are very connected: they tend to be strong or weak at the same time. If US rates stayed low, that meant the US economy was weak, which meant the UK and European economies would probably also be weak, which meant that UK and European rates would also stay low. Lending dollars, and lending pounds and lending euros were, to some degree, the same trade. Or, rather, they were highly correlated trades. If you did all those trades together, you might think that you have three different trades. In reality you kind of have the same trade three times. This is what Bill called "pig on pork."

Billy never had "pig on pork." Bill built palaces of culinary balance. First, he would start with his favorite trade, the best trade in the market at the time. That's the base of the palace. Then Bill would ask himself, what's the risk to this trade? As an example, Bill knew that the risk to lending dollars was further collapse in the global banking system. He would then look at all the trades that would do well if the banking system collapsed, and pick which one of them was likely to do well even if the banking system didn't collapse. He'd add that trade to his portfolio, and then he'd make money either way.

He'd continue building his portfolio up like this. What real-world situation is a risk to my bundle of trades? What good trades are there that would do really well in that scenario? In that way he built up a palace of trades in which every risk was covered. That's why Billy always made money. Whatever tragedy struck, whatever the shock to the system, Bill had some sort of ace to cover it. He seemed to make money whatever way.

Doing this was not easy. I tried to do it, but you needed to know everything about everything. I couldn't do it. I couldn't be Bill.

Snoopy knew Billy was the best. Snoopy was a smart cat. Snoopy tried to be Bill but he couldn't do it either. Bill had been getting into work at 6 a.m. and curling up into a little gray ball and speaking through his hand on the phone for eleven hours whilst betting on the horses on his ninth screen for twenty-five years. We were still trying to figure out how to take that place over, me and Snoopy, and we spoke for hours about how to be Bill. But we couldn't. We were Snoopy and me.

We settled on a second-best strategy: lend as many dollars as we could get away with and piggyback on Bill for every trade we could catch.

Bill's big bets were always on the Monetary Policy Committee. The bunch of knobheads at the Bank of England. Billy hated and he loved those people. He viewed them as everything he wasn't: privileged, self-important, well-educated, prestigious, powerful and, ultimately, stupid. If they sneezed, Billy knew before they did. He made a ton of money from it. And he fucking loved that.

You could make money betting on individual MPC meetings. Bill always did. Every time. Let's say the UK interest rate is 1% and there's a meeting coming up. Everyone thinks they will cut to 0.75%, but Bill somehow knows they'll cut to 0.5%. You go out and lend a load of cash at 0.75% for the exact set of dates relevant to the meeting, then you borrow it back at 0.5%. Easy cash. What is great about this money is you don't even have to wait for it. You make a ton of money, easily, on the day. Billy would dust his hands loudly and quietly say, "Bing bang bosh." Or he'd turn to me and say, "Get up them stairs!" I used to love it when he said that, because usually I'd be on the trade too. I'd turn to Snoopy, and he'd be smiling like a kid.

So that was the plan, and it worked pretty well. Do that to build up a little bit of money and grow my reputation, and then use *that* money to amp up the dollar trade. Grow that trade slowly at first, and then quickly, and by the end of the year, make some *big* cash. Simple plan.

In the afternoons, when the trading would die down, I would go over to Waitrose and I'd buy some ingredients, and I'd go home and I'd try and cook dinner for me and Harry. It was going pretty well. I did a good pork stir-fry with plum sauce. We'd play football once a week, I'd go to the gym. It was nice, it was like having a little family.

3

BUT THEN, THIS CRAZY THING HAPPENED.

I'd been working the PnL up very gently for the first few months of the year, and by the middle of April I was up nearly four bucks. That was a rate of a buck a month. Not so exceptional compared to the twelve bucks off the back half of 2009, but it was pretty much the run rate I was shooting for. All of the traders were making way less money that year, so four bucks in April put me, for the first time, right in the middle of the pack, instead of at the bottom.

With four bucks in the bank, I was teasing the risk up just a little. Lending a little more dollars, nothing big though, very gentle. I was saving the big risk for later in the year.

One evening, I cooked a Bolognese for me and Harry, and we cracked some ciders and put the Champions League semi-final on, just as the sun was setting. We had a nice flat back there in Bow. The old factory was enormous and sprawling, a huge red-brick block dropped right from the sky, with soaring high red-brick towers and smokestack chimneys that hadn't been used for about a hundred years. Back in Victorian days, that factory had made more matchsticks than the rest of the world put together. We were slung down on the first floor, which meant the whole factory soared up and surrounded us with its bricks and its windows and its gardens, and we were level with the branches of the trees, which around us were starting to bloom.

Me and Harry were in the same line of work now, so we'd both be up before the sun. From Bow, I was close enough to the office that I could cycle to work, down the veins of East London every morning in a blue ski jacket and Onitsuka Tigers, past the huge puppy dog mural of Chrisp Street Market, past the old-fashioned, yellow, low-slung warehouse of

Billingsgate Fish Market, and up the steep ramp that takes you into Canary Wharf.

On the days that Harry didn't have to go out drinking after work, which was a little less than half the time, we'd both get home at around five thirty. When there was football on TV, we'd watch it together. Otherwise, we'd watch *The Only Way Is Essex*. I'd go to bed at nine thirty. Sometimes, in the morning, Harry would be hungover, and I'd have to drop him to the station on this little black Vespa I bought with my bonus money.

That evening, just as the game was starting, I got a call. It was from an American number. I picked it up. It was the Frog.

The Frog, in case you don't remember, was the most senior trader on the New York STIRT desk. He traded Swiss francs as well. Swiss francs and Japanese yen. I reached out for the remote and muted the telly and signaled to Harry to shut the fuck up.

The Frog was super excited, talking real quickly. I'd still never met the guy, but he was being real personable, calling me Gazza, like Caleb used to.

Apparently, he'd been to see the SNB: the Swiss National Bank, the Central Bank for Switzerland. I was surprised by this because I didn't even know that the Frog was in Europe, but he didn't stop talking, so I didn't get time to ask.

The Frog said that the SNB was gonna do something big, they were gonna keep the Swiss interest rates high. This was news to me; it would have been news to everyone. The economic carnage of the time had led to a huge increase in the value of the Swiss currency, which has been viewed as a safe haven at least since the Second World War, and everybody thought that the SNB would push rates aggressively lower, even negative, to discourage people from buying too many Swiss francs and pushing their value up.

The Frog said that wasn't gonna happen. The Frog said that rates were gonna stay high. The Frog was gonna make a big pile of cash, and he wanted me to make some cash too.

At least that's what the Frog told me.

The Frog had gone and borrowed a ton of francs. He'd done it in the Swiss FX swap. Now, remember, when you borrow one currency in an FX Swap you lend the other, so this was the "lending dollars" trade that

I'd been doing for nearly a year now—the trade that had made my career so far, and the trade that I'd wanted to ramp up. The Frog said that he'd done an absolute ton of the one-year trade. The Frog said that I should take some.

Now, if I had been older at that time, or wiser, or maybe just less greedy, the following thought would probably have passed through my mind:

"Am I, Gary Stevenson, twenty-three years old, wearing Leyton Orient shorts with a small Bolognese stain on them, drinking cider and watching the Champions League semi-final with a nineteen-year-old burgeoning alcoholic, the kind of person who receives absolute gold dust, monetizable information on my mobile phone, from a person that I have never met?"

But alas, I was neither older nor wiser.

"All right, I'll do two hundred bucks."

The Frog was real happy about that. I unmuted the telly, and we watched the rest of the game.

Two hundred million dollars is not a massive trade. I'd done bigger trades in the past. When it comes to interest rates—that is, when it comes to borrowing and lending—what matters is not only the size of the loan, but also the length of it, and the Frog had sold me in for $200 million of one-year loans. One year is quite a long time, but still $200 million's not massive. The thing is, I'd already had this trade on, in decent size, and I'd been pushing it bigger and bigger as the year was going on. I'd been very methodical about that, very gradual, I had it in the size that I wanted. When I took the Frog's $200 million, it made the trade a big chunk bigger. Bigger than it should really have been.

Thing is, you know, it was a guaranteed winner. Lending dollars paid out every time. Snoopy once told it to me like this: "When it comes to trading interest rates, only two things matter. The interest rate now, in the market, and what the interest rate is actually going to be, when the time comes. If the interest rate in the market is higher than the real interest rate is going to be, you lend it, it's as simple as that, easy money."

We all knew that the dollar rates in the FX swaps were too high. With this Frog trade, I had also borrowed some Swiss francs, but at a super super low rate, and the Frog was sure that that rate would go up.

Something didn't feel right about it. But I let it run for a week or so. I shouldn't have.

It was about a week after the Frog Trade. It was May now. I was on the desk. It was the afternoon.

As usual, it was a quiet time on the London STIRT desk. By the afternoon, the US team are at their desks in New York, and most of the prices get asked to them instead of us. We loll about. Billy makes bets on the horses. JB slouches deep in his chair and tells stories while chewing on toothpicks. Chuck stares into the mid distance. Maybe he's meditating. Me and Snoopy mine Billy for trades, Spengler's on the phone to his mum. Nothing much happens. By May, the sun's shining high through the windows right up until the time we go home. I sit right by the window now, so it's warm. When you're up four bucks and looking up to five, it can feel pretty idyllic.

During those afternoons, I would just flick through my positions and trades. I was still using Spengler's spreadsheets, trying to work out what days were cheap and what days were expensive, making sure my positions lined up. Sometimes sales guys would try and book trades into your book at the wrong price, to steal a bit of money, so I'd scroll through all my individual trades and try to find any bad ones. I learned that from Rupert.

That day I was up $70,000, so it was a good day. I hadn't done anything special. I had the big dollar position and, as usual, it was slowly just grinding my way.

I was on autopilot, checking the trade blotter, refreshing it, checking my position, refreshing it, checking my daily PnL, refreshing it.

The PnL showed down $300K.

That wasn't a problem, that happened sometimes. Gremlins in the system. I refreshed it again. It was still there. Down $300K.

The PnL calculation needed a source feed to value your position. It needed to know what the market prices were at all times, so that it could calculate what your position was worth. As a source, it would use the "broker screens"—a list of the current prices of all the different FX swaps of all the different maturity lengths kept constantly updated by the brokers. It made sense to feed from the brokers, because the brokers were constantly hearing prices from all of the traders. They were the best placed to know what the prices were at any point in time.

The brokers had to constantly update these screens whenever the market moved, and sometimes they fat fingered one of the numbers and put in a typo, and it would throw your whole PnL off. I figured that must have happened. The particular broker feed that was used to value my Swiss FX swaps position was Morley's screen, the broker I'd used to put on that big Swiss trade back in 2009. I pulled his screen up.

His one-year price had jumped massively to the left—higher dollar rates, lower franc rates. I saw this and thought it must be the typo. Then I scrolled through the other maturities—the three months, the six months, the nine months. He'd moved them all massively to the left. You wouldn't expect that for a typo. I flicked up the switch to Morley.

"What's going on Morley? Why you moved your one year down to minus forty? What's going on?"

There was a bit of a delay before Morley answered, which was unusual. When he did answer, he was trying to sound casual, but I could tell he was flustered. The gaps between his sentences were too short.

"You all right, Gal yeah I can't seem to get any prices I'm not sure what's happening I can't seem to get no left-hand sides."

I flicked Morley's switch down and flicked up the next switch, a different Swiss franc broker at a different company.

"Where's one year?"

Another unusually long pause. Then a long sound of cockney prevarication.

"Ayyeeeyaaaeeyeeeeaah we can't seem to get no left-hand side mate. We probably get minus fifty."

This was bad.

FX swaps get quoted as a "left" and a "right" price, rather than a "buy" and a "sell" price. That's because in both cases you are lending one currency and borrowing another, so there's not really a "buy" and a "sell." In US Dollar/Swiss Franc FX swaps, the left-hand side was the lending of dollars and the borrowing of francs. There were no left-hand sides. That meant nobody wanted to lend dollars. I had lent an awful lot of dollars and, over time, would need to borrow them back. Morley had moved his screen down to minus forty-five. I refreshed my PnL again. It was now minus $600K. That was more than I'd ever lost in a day. Much more.

"Morley, what the fuck's going on?"

Another long pause. At least it felt long to me.

"All right mate, mate, I think I've worked it out. The SNB's put something up on their website. Something about a trade in the three months. Here, I'll send you a link on the IB chat."

IB chat is like an internet messaging service for dickheads. The message popped up on my screen and I clicked the link. The link took me, as promised, to the Swiss National Bank's website. It was a simple, clean, minimalist page, with a short paragraph of text written at first in, presumably, Swiss-German and then in English. In the bottom corner was the SNB's simple, clean, minimalist logo.

The English said something along the lines of, "The Swiss National Bank will be offering Swiss francs via the three-month USDCHF FX swap at a rate of minus 35. For transactions, please call this number."

I sat and looked at the website for a bit. It was like some sort of practical joke. Central Bank monetary policy was not normally conducted like this. Usually, Central Banks announce policies at meetings, they hold press conferences. They don't just fucking upload it to their website like it's a fucking MySpace.

I pulled up Spengler's spreadsheet. The price of an FX swap is determined from the interest rate differential between two currencies. So, if you stick in the price and one of the interest rates, you can back out the implied interest rate for the other currency. The implied rate at which the Swiss National Bank was lending Swiss francs was minus 4.5%. NEGATIVE FOUR POINT FIVE PERCENT.

I turned to my right and looked at Bill. He had his feet propped up on the bin and was reading a copy of the *Racing Post*. I looked over my shoulder at Chuck. He was staring through his screens with platonic indifference. I picked up my big brown handphone that was wired into the terminal and I called up the number.

A very polite-sounding woman said something in what I suppose must have been German.

"Hi, my name's Gary Stevenson, I'm the Swiss franc FX swaps trader at Citibank in London. Is this the line for the three-month FX swaps?"

I was covering my mouth with my hand so that no one would notice.

"Yes, this is the line for the three-month FX swaps, would you like to do some FX swaps?"

"Erm . . . Is the price minus thirty-five?"

"Yes, the price is minus thirty-five. How much would you like to do?"

"I don't know, how much can I do?"

"There is no limit as to the size."

I looked round at Chuck again.

"Erm . . . I'll call you back."

I hung up.

Negative 4.5% is a very low interest rate. No country has ever had negative 4.5% interest rates before. No country has ever had them since.

I pulled a piece of paper from my desk drawer. Important maths like this has to be done by hand. When I lent the dollars out, and borrowed the francs, the expected interest rate on both had been pretty much zero. But I was still getting about 1.1% premium on the dollars. Remember it's the *differential* that matters—I've lent dollars out for 1.1% MORE than I've borrowed the francs. To cover the trade, I need to borrow those dollars back (and lend those francs back out) at a *lower differential*. I make money if the dollar interest rate goes *down* (as of course, it always did) or if the Swiss rate went *up*.

OK, let's be optimistic. Let's assume that I can borrow the dollars back at zero, like I'd expected. What does it mean if I need to lend the Swiss out at minus 4.5? That's a differential of 4.5%. I got in at 1.1, so I'm losing 3.4. I had, at that point, something equivalent to about 1.2 billion dollars in the one-year trade. Losing 3.4% on 1.2 billion dollars of one year, that was . . . $40,800,000. That was the most I could lose on the trade, realistically. Yeah, that would be bad though. That would be really bad.

You might be thinking, "Well, just call the SNB back and get the fuck out of the trade," but if you think that, you don't understand what's happening. I've lent dollars and borrowed francs, and the SNB are offering to borrow dollars and lend francs, at a much *much* cheaper rate than I ever paid to borrow them. In unlimited size. I can't get out of the trade with them. They're trying to do the same trade that I need to do. At the moment, there's no left-hand sides in the market.

I can't get out of the trade with anyone.

I can't lie. There was a moment here where my heart tightened in my chest and all the hairs on my arms stood on end.

I know there are guys, like my best friends, who would have panicked and scrambled and gotten out of there the minute they realized that they could lose forty million dollars.

But I didn't.

I got to admit the truth. It turned me on.

You can't keep rates at negative 4.5%. It's not possible. It's too low.

The thing about money is, you can take it out of the bank. You can hide it under your bed. You can bury it in the garden. And when you do that, you get 0%. Why the fuck you gonna take negative 4.5 when you can get 0 with it under your pillow?

Of course, you are not a bank. Banks themselves do not have regular bank accounts. They can't withdraw their cash and hide it under their beds. Commercial banks themselves have accounts with the Central Banks, and, if the SNB had wanted to, they could have cut the interest rate on those accounts to negative 4.5.

But they hadn't done that. The SNB were still paying 0 on any cash held by commercial banks, whilst simultaneously offering to lend Swiss francs out at negative 4.5 via the three-month FX swap.

What that meant was, I didn't have to take the loss. Surely. Swiss francs had become unbelievably negative in the three-month swap, and they were getting negative in the longer-term swaps, but day to day I could still lend the francs out at 0.

I remembered what Snoopy taught me: all that matters is the rate now and the rate at the end. In the gap between those two things is where you make money. I had bet on a difference of 1.1 falling to zero, and it was expanding now to 4.5. But all I had to do was wait and it would come back to zero. It had to. Didn't it?

I wanted to do more.

I looked again at Bill. He was on the phone to the bookies. I got out of my chair and I turned round to Chuck.

"Chuck, I'm down six hundred grand."

Chuck emerged from his meditation slowly, and he greeted me with a warm smile.

"What happened?"

"The SNB put something up on their website, they're lending Swiss out in the three-month FX swap at negative 4.5."

"Negative 4.5!?!?!"

That wasn't Chuck who answered, it was Snoopy. He'd been booking a holiday to the Maldives, but it seemed I'd caught his attention.

Chuck was stroking his chin. He hadn't gotten out of his chair but he'd swung it round to face me.

"What are you gonna do?"

"I wanna do more."

Chuck thought that was real funny. Billy had finished his gambling and was looking straight through me, and JB was watching as well. Spengler had his phone to his ear but was quietly staring my way, and in the silence of Chuck's contemplation I could hear the faint voice of Spengler's mother speaking Flemish.

"Why?"

"They haven't done anything to the overnight market. We can still place Swiss francs at o percent. Even if the three-month market stays at negative four and a half, we can just roll them down and lend them out every day."

"I wanna do some."

That was Snoopy. Snoopy was in.

"What if they cut the overnight rate?"

"There's no way. They can't cut the overnight rate to negative 4.5. The banking system would collapse."

"I'm in."

That was JB. He was still eating a toothpick. With that he turned back to his screens.

Chuck was still thinking. He didn't look at me and he thought for a long time. "OK. You can do it. Good luck."

So Snoopy was in, JB was in, I was in.

I had about twenty times as much as anyone else.

Billy wasn't in.

So what the fuck was happening here?

The Swiss National Bank were taking action to protect their currency. Not to stop their currency from going down, but to stop it from going up. If your currency goes up everything gets too expensive for foreigners. Your exports become non-competitive and your exporting businesses can struggle. The SNB had already brought their official interest rate down to zero and they wanted to try something flash. For some reason, and I'll never know the real reason, they chose this crazy move in the FX swap market.

Lending Swiss francs for minus 4.5% in the three-month FX swap is basically cutting the interest rate on three-month loans to minus 4.5%. But they were still accepting daily deposits from commercial banks at 0%. This seemingly created an opportunity for "arb." Arbitrage is when you can do a set of different trades that cancel each other out and make a free profit at the end. In this case, you borrow a load of dollars, at 1% or whatever, exchange them for Swiss francs with the SNB at a 4.5% differential, and then leave the Swiss francs with the SNB every day for 0%. That leaves you with 3.5%.

The problem with arbitrage is that it's almost never risk free. If it was risk free, then it wouldn't exist. Someone would do it and keep doing it until the prices moved back into line and all the profits disappeared. The second problem is that arb requires you to do a lot of different trades, and on the STIRT desk we were only allowed to do the FX swaps. We weren't allowed to just go out and borrow dollars, we weren't allowed to lend francs to the SNB. Trades like that were managed on another desk.

So I had to just do the FX swaps for longer periods, like three months and one year, and hope that I could lend the Swiss francs out every day, for a day at a time, at zero. Hopefully other traders, who were actually able to actually leave the francs with the SNB for 0, would pay me something close to zero for them.

The risk to that trade was so obvious that even Chuck had noticed it. What if the SNB were to slash the rate that they paid on overnight deposits of Swiss francs? They had already done something totally mental to the three-month FX swap market—what if they were to do something crazy to the daily interest rate too?

The reason that I gave to Chuck was that it would cause the banking system to collapse. My logic behind it was this:

Minus 4.5% is an extremely negative rate. If the SNB were to force Swiss Commercial banks to pay 4.5% on all their Swiss franc deposits, the banks would have to pass that on to customers. But there was no way customers would accept taking a 4.5% annual cut from all of their savings. They'd take all their cash out of the banks. If everyone takes their money out of the bank simultaneously, it causes a bank run. The banking system would collapse.

At least I hoped it would. Otherwise I was gonna be fucked.

Looking back, I honestly don't know if my logic was good. Since then, negative interest rates have become common in most of Western Europe, although never anything close to negative 4.5. Maybe I was right that negative 4.5% *is* an impossible interest rate. Maybe I just wanted to believe that because I wanted to make my money back.

Anyway, here's what happened.

By the time I got back to my seat I was already down $800,000. But I'd gotten myself into the mindset that that was actually a good thing. Better entry levels for me to lend even more dollars, and it meant I could get Snoopy and JB in at good levels as well.

I went home that day and I didn't say nothing to no one. I went swimming for a long time.

The next day the markets edged against me, but only a little. I lost just over $200,000. That brought my total losses up to just over a million and brought my PnL for the year down to just over $3,000,000. I felt that the relatively calmer markets were a good sign, vaguely reassuring. I reported that to Chuck and to Snoop and JB. I went home and I started looking through my old LSE textbooks to see if there were any sections about negative interest rates. There weren't.

The next day was not calm. The market fell through the floor. I lost two and a half million dollars. $2,500,000. In a single day. Snoopy and JB maybe lost a couple hundred grand between them. My total PnL was under one million dollars now. Chuck didn't say much, but he started standing behind me a lot.

"What do you think's going to happen?"

"It will come back. It's gonna come back."

I put on more.

That evening Harry had invited some of my mates over for pizza and beers and Pro Evo. I had lost 3.5 million dollars in the previous three days. There were about six or seven of my good friends from high school there. Busting jokes. Passing around slices of pizza and PlayStation controllers. And I wasn't there.

I was there, I mean, but I wasn't there. I was down three point five million dollars, nought point six million dollars left. How much of a percentage move can you take before that will hit zero? What will change if you go into the red? What team you gonna play as? Classic England. I always played as Classic England. Bobby Charlton, he could score from anywhere.

Is it really true that minus 4.5% interest rates are impossible? Is it really true? Don't say that to your friends. Ask Andreas if he wants another beer. Of course he does. He always does. I'll get in early tomorrow. Before Billy. I wish everyone would go home.

Do you think they'll stop my trade out if I go into the red? What if they don't? How far could my PnL go down? I won't lose the job. I never thought about losing the job.

I wish everyone would go home.

The next day I lost two million dollars again. I was in the red now. Down 1.5. Chuck didn't say anything. He just kept on standing behind me. Snoopy came over once. He'd lost maybe $300K by now.

"What do you think's going to happen?"

"It will come back. It has to come back. Minus four point five percent rates are impossible. Unsustainable. The banking system would collapse."

"Yeah, you're right. It'll come back."

We both did a little bit more.

That was Friday. I didn't do much on the weekend. I didn't go out. I texted my ex-girlfriend. I can't remember what I said to her.

What a pathetic thing to have done.

. . .

On Monday I lost another 2.3 million dollars. That brought my overall loss to nearly 8 million dollars. In less than a week. My yearly PnL was now 3.8 million dollars in the red.

In the afternoon, Chuck was off the desk for a bit, about half an hour. When he came back he just put his hand on my shoulder and said, "That was senior management. You know what it means."

"Yeah. I know what it means."

Chuck kept his hand on my shoulder when he said, "I know that you'll learn from this."

It took me two days to close the trade out. By the end I was down 4.2. And then the fucker came all the way back.

So what's the lesson here? Is there a lesson? There's always a lesson.

The lesson is that Snoopy was wrong. The price now and the price at the end are not the only two things that matter. You must also be there at the end.

The trade was good. It was the right trade. Snoopy and JB didn't get stopped out and they both made a ton of money on it. That's because it was a good trade. JB didn't even really know what the trade was, but he made a ton of money on it while he ate toothpicks.

Having the right trade is not all that matters. It's also important *that you survive*.

Every trader has a pain threshold. Every trader has an amount they can lose. You could have the best trade in the world, but if you hit your pain threshold, it doesn't matter, you'll lose all your cash.

The lesson, then, is *never hit your pain threshold*. And since that trade, I never have done. Every time you put a trade on, you must ask yourself: What is the worst possible thing that can happen to this trade in between now and me being right? Is that realistic? Am I lying to myself? Could it go a lot more? Take your worst-case scenario, and double it.

Me, I know what I'm like. When a trade kicks my arse, I'm gonna do more. If it kicks my arse more I will do more again. I don't know why I'm like that. Maybe because fuck you that's why. All I know is if a trade's gonna fuck me then I'm gonna fuck the trade back and I'll keep fucking it until I win. But if I'm gonna do that, then sure as hell I had better be able to afford it. And sure as hell I had better be right in the end.

Two rules for life:

1. Be right in the end.

2. Be alive at the end.

Write them down.

And what else? Any other lessons?

Yeah, a couple. Number one, when Billy said you don't fuck with a trade without knowing the risks, I should have listened to him, and I didn't. That's OK. We all make mistakes. Just don't make them twice.

Number two, fuck the Frog. Three days into my losing streak it suddenly occurred to me that a big chunk of my trade had come from the Frog. What was the Frog doing? He must have had a fucking lot too, he must have been getting his arse whooped. I pulled up the Frog's position.

What did he have?

He had nothing. Of course he fucking had nothing. The fucking Frog had had nothing for more than a week. Where the fuck had his position gone? He'd given it to me. He'd dumped a load out on the market and he'd used me as the dustbin for the rest that he couldn't get rid of.

Cunt.

Fuck the Frog.

4

SO. WHAT DO YOU DO NOW? YOU ARE TWENTY-THREE AND A HALF years old. You are down 4.2 million dollars. What do you do?

Well what the fuck else can you do?

You work.

The mad thing about this next part of my life, the rest of 2010, is that I can remember almost nothing about it, almost nothing at all.

There are a few things that I know did happen.

I started getting in early. Real early. I was getting in before Bill. I would cycle in as the early summer sun was rising and as soon as I hit the trading floor I would stick my little headset on and plug myself into the machine. No one was in so I didn't even used to get changed, and I would spend the first hour or two of the day reading and talking and trading in the gray Primark hoody and busted Onitsuka Tigers that I used to wear to cycle into work.

I was riding the market like a hustler in that time, which, to be honest, other than in that short period of my career, was never something that I was very good at. I'm not a very sociable person. I'm not like Spengler. I can't know what everybody's doing and when they are doing it. But at that point in my life, I had to.

I started looking a lot at US dollars and the US economy. Since everyone on the desk was trading their particular currency *against* the US dollar, we didn't really have anyone looking at US dollars specifically. We hired some guy to do it, actually, but he wasn't making any money, so I decided to take it for myself. I wanted to know the US Federal Reserve as well as Billy knew the Bank of England.

I scraped through every inch of my Swiss franc position. I'd been stopped out of the position, but you can't really stop an entire book of

FX forwards. We do like a hundred trades every day, so you end up with a huge amount of money going in and out every single day in the future and the amount of money is different each day. You can't really "stop out" of a position when you have separate cashflows on a thousand different days.

That meant that when I stopped out, I had a choice: which days do you stop out, which days do you keep? I stopped out of all the least risky days. I kept all the risky days. In effect, that meant I kept a lot of the risk. Some may argue that that is not really stopping out. For my part, I am not a moral philosopher, I am a trader. Did you think I was gonna let that trade kick the shit out of me and not make a little bit back on the comeback?

Nah, not me.

That's all I can seem to remember of that part of my life. Eight fucking months. Trades and positions, trades and positions. Little green lines on little orange screens. Bleeps and numbers. Positions and trades. I dream about them sometimes.

Who am I kidding, I dream about them every fucking night.

By the end of the year. I was back in the black. Positive four point five million dollars.

Job fucking done.

There is one thing I remember though, from that time. It is a brief conversation. Actually, more of a monologue. It happened very, very soon after I lost that eight million dollars, and I remember it because it is probably the most important conversation I have ever had in my life.

In the immediate aftermath of that huge loss, I became obsessed with understanding why it was that I had lost that money, and whether and how I would make it all back.

One thing that I did, as part of that obsession, and as the obedient and well-disciplined former LSE student that I was at the time, was I went back to the books.

I started to read through all of my old textbooks to try to understand what had happened. Why was the Swiss franc appreciating? Why had the SNB acted as they had? Was the minus 4.5% rate sustainable? Were the FX swap prices really arbable? I stuffed my old textbooks into my work bag, and in the afternoons when trading slowed down, into the evenings when everyone had gone home, I would read through them while sitting on the desk.

That lasted for two days.

Billy did not accept the third day.

I was deep into a chapter on the mathematical nuances of forward interest-rate parity when the book was slapped powerfully from between my hands, straight into the bin at my feet. In its place was thrust a perfectly round, frosty white-tipped, deep-red Liverpudlian face.

"What the fuck are you fucking doing you fuckin cunt!? How old are you mate!?!"

Billy swore a lot, but he wasn't usually so red when he did it. I had to think for a moment because I hadn't been in the mental space for taking personal questions.

"Erm . . . I'm twenty-three."

"So why the fuck are you in here reading fuckin books mate? Does this look like fuckin *Jackanory*!?"

Bill was standing but bent ninety degrees at the waist like a maniac, and he gestured wildly toward the trading floor with his left hand. I wasn't sure if I was supposed to look round, but I decided that it was probably best not to.

"No. It doesn't."

Bill sighed and placed both of his hands deep into his white hair then wiped them all the way down his red face. He looked tired. He sat down.

"Listen, you're not a fuckin kid anymore. I know you've lost a lot of fuckin money. But you're not gonna find a penny of it there in them books. You wanna know what's happening in the world, you go take a fucking look at the world. You wanna know what's happening in the economy? It's fucked. And you can see it everywhere you fucking go mate. Go take a walk down the high street. See all the fucking shops closed down. See the fucking homeless people under the fuckin bridge. Go look at the ads on the tube. Debt relief, home equity release, debt relief. People losing their fucking homes just to pay for the kids. Go home and ask your mum about her financial situation. Ask your friends. Ask your friends' mums. The time for books is fucking over mate. You're not a fucking kid. You're here now. You're in the big leagues. Look at the world with your fucking eyes."

And that was it.

The most important thing I ever heard.

A few more things happened that year. Spengler went back to America. Billy became the most profitable trader in the bank for the third consecutive year.

It made sense for Spengler to go back to America. He'd been nearly three years without his mum by that time. It was starting to get hard for him. He left me with his Swedish and Norwegian trading books, as well as his spreadsheet, which I'd continue to use for the rest of my career. The Danish book went to Snoopy. We'd still never been to Scandinavia.

At the end of the year, to recognize the ungodly amounts of money he had made for the bank, senior management made Billy MD. MD, or Managing Director, is a big deal in the banking world, and the bigwigs probably didn't wanna give it to Billy, on account of the fact that he obviously hated them, but they didn't have much of a choice.

They announce the names of the new MDs on the loudspeaker, at the beginning of December. They don't say "these guys have all made MD," they just say "can this guy and this guy and this guy and this guy all come to the office," and everybody knows what it means.

We cheered and clapped when Billy's name got called out, but he didn't say nothing. He just put his newspaper down and walked off.

He came back to the desk one hour later, holding some kind of heavy glass object in his hand. He looked angry. He sat down in his seat and dropped it into the bin, which clanged and fell over, pouring a small pile of used tissues onto my shoes.

I was about to say something, but Bill cut me off.

"Shut the fuck up Gal, you cockney twat."

I waited for him to go to the toilet, and then I pulled the object out of the bin. It was some kind of molded trophy—a globe made out of thousands of tiny bubbles blown into the inside of a big block of glass. At the bottom, Bill's own name had been bubbled in:

"WILLIAM   DOUGLAS   ANTHONY   GARY   THOMAS—MANAGING DIRECTOR 2010"

I put the bin back into its upright position, and placed the trophy gently inside.

. . .

Just after that, toward the end of the year, Chuck called me into his office. I figured he was going to do some kind of "end-of-year-review."

Since I'd made so much less that year than the previous year, I was pretty disappointed with my own performance. But I'd clawed my way back from more than four bucks in the red, so I figured the review wouldn't be bad.

As soon as we sat down, Chuck looked me right in the face and apologized.

"Listen, I just wanted to tell you that I'm really sorry. I'm really sorry. I should have known earlier, but, honestly, I didn't realize until now."

I looked at Chuck. I had not the slightest idea what he was talking about. His face was not registering a joke. His brow was furrowed, so I furrowed my brow.

"There's nothing I can do. There's really nothing I can do. I've spoken to HR and I've spoken to management. But they both say there's nothing that can be done. It's a company-wide policy."

I was starting to get a little worried now, and was running through a list in my head of all the things this could possibly be. I was coming up blank.

"Look, I'm really sorry that I can't do anything about it. But I just want to know, are you OK?"

I looked at Chuck and Chuck spoke with the cosmos. I tried to read his eyes for some kind of extra information. I gave up.

"I'm sorry Chuck, but, could you tell me what this is about?"

Chuck spread his huge hands and laughed at me incredulously.

"I mean, of course Gary, of course it's your salary. But, you know, there's nothing we can do. It's a company-wide salary freeze!"

I slowly started to realize what was happening here. Chuck was worried about me and my salary. His concern was, it seemed, on a basic humanitarian level. My salary was £36,000. Plus the £400K bonus, of course.

"I just want to know that you are OK."

I stared for a while at Chuck's face. I thought about what this all meant. The guy was not joking. I sighed and looked down at my feet. I reached up and knuckled my brow.

"To be honest Chuck, it's pretty hard."

I raised my face up from my hands. Chuck was nodding. It was obvious he really cared.

Chuck placed his hand on my shoulder as I stared out the window.

"Don't worry Gary, we'll see what we can do."

And so Chuck went and spoke to senior management, and they booked me a trip round the world.

5

THUS, I SPENT THE JANUARY OF 2011 IN SYDNEY'S SUMMER, AND TO-
kyo's Winter, and I received my bonus on the eighteenth floor of a huge
hotel in Singapore, overlooking the Marina Bay.

Rupert was happy to see me. He was living a great life over in Oz. He
had a beautiful apartment and a beautiful boat and a beautiful girlfriend, and he was kind enough to line them up sequentially, so I could
appreciate them one at a time. We went on a cruise down to Botany Bay,
during which Rupert explained in great detail the costs of boat mainte-
nance and I spent the entire time putting on sunblock and then got
burnt on the backs of my hands.

Tokyo was cold cold in January. A gray Lego city of bright lights and
strong winds. I met the prosaic Hisa Watanabe and the irrepressible Joey
Kanazawa. You'll hear more of them later on.

There was no reason for me to go to Singapore. None at all. There
wasn't even a STIRT desk out there. But Chuck had asked me one time
where in the world I'd like to go to, and I had just said to him "Singapore," without really knowing where it was. So Chuck added it to the
tour. It was a bit like when I told my nan I liked Lion bars, and then she
got me them for Christmas every year till she died.

Singapore was beautiful. I had friends from LSE there, so I spent the
time hanging out with them. And when Chuck called about my bonus
on the phone in my hotel room, I was sitting on a bed, high, high up in
the sky.

Over the phone, Chuck told me how proud he was about the way I
clawed my way back from four bucks in the red. He said everyone had
noticed. Not just everyone on the desk, but everyone on the whole floor.
I hadn't realized. Maybe he was just blowing smoke up my arse. He told

me that he really believed in me. That he thought I would be something big. That he really wanted me to hit it the next year and he knew that I would. Then he gave me £420,000.

I looked out over the marina. The sun was so bright it was blinding, and it reflected off of everything. The water, the skyscrapers, the gardens, the little lion that shoots water from its mouth.

It wasn't my sun, it was another man's sun. I wondered what all of it meant.

OK, I thought, time to go home then. Time to be the best trader in the world.

Part Four

THERMOSTAT

1

WHEN I GOT BACK TO LONDON THE WHOLE FUCKING DESK WAS gone. I mean that—the desk wasn't there. Over by the window were a bunch of fucking sales guys, and we'd been moved right into the middle of the floor. We were making too much money to be hidden in the corner. They wanted us where they could see us.

I was sad about losing my seat by the window, but worst of all, I lost my seat next to Bill.

Chuck pulled me into an office before I could say anything. Billy was going into semi-retirement. He was going to stop quoting the Sterling FX swap book. He was just going to sit in the corner, taking massive bets on the UK economy, while Snoopy sat next to him and quoted the book.

Motherfuckers. I'd been covering Bill for a whole year at that point, all the while digging myself out of the grave, and now the fuckers had given the book to Snoopy without even telling me. Motherfuckers.

They had a plan that was supposed to appease me. Snoopy taking the Sterling book meant a space was opened up on the euro book, working with JB. They wanted me to be the junior euro trader. I didn't wanna be the euro trader, I wanted to be the sterling trader. Yes, I know this place is a shithole, but it's *my* shithole. I told that to Chuck. He was stroking his chin.

I didn't speak to Billy for two days. I didn't speak to no one. I think it was then that I started breaking pens. Snoopy quoted both the sterling and the euros for two days before Billy took me into a room and told me to stop being a cunt.

So that's how I became the junior euro trader.

Junior euro trader is a good job. The only trader who ever made a hundred bucks in a year other than Bill was Hongo, and he did that because he was the junior euro trader. That raises the question—if junior euro trader was such a good job, then why the fuck was it given to me?

The answer is that junior euro trader was a fucking lot of work.

This is how it works. Junior euro trader only quotes very short-term euro FX swaps, one month or less. Senior trader gets everything else. Short-term FX swaps are low on risk, low on profit and low on excitement. But there's a fucking lot of them.

As we've discussed, corporations and pension funds and hedge funds use FX swaps to borrow money. But FX swaps are primarily short-term instruments, mainly one year or less—and companies need to borrow money for longer than that. That's not really a problem, because you can just borrow money for three months at a time and come back again every three months. Some companies choose to do it like that, quarterly, others choose yearly or six monthly, whereas others choose to roll those trades every week or even every day. If you borrow money six months at a time, you only need to do two trades a year, but if you are borrowing that money daily, you need to do *two hundred and fifty trades a year* (we are closed on holidays and weekends). That is why the junior euro trader has a lot of fucking work. The amount of risk that might take JB two or four trades a year, is going to take me *two hundred and fifty* trades a year. The end result is, with no exaggeration, that the junior euro trader does more trades than *all of the other traders on the desk put together.* If you can hold it together, you can make a lot of money. *If* you can hold it together. There was a reason that both Snoopy and Hongo had given the book up.

So just like that, I was the euro dealer. But I wasn't there to get business cards made. I was there to be the best trader in the world. So what was the plan?

For starters, I *had* to move seats. The new seat I had been given was between JB and Chuck. I loved JB and I loved Chuck. I still do. But JB never stopped talking my ear off and Chuck had this whole "communing with other worlds" vibe going on that was kind of messing with my hustle. I told Chuck that I needed my own junior, and that I was going to sit with him on the end of the desk.

The kid that I wanted was Titzy Lazzari.

Titzy Lazzari's real name was Fabrizio. I called him Titzy because he hated it.

Titzy turned up on the desk in 2009 as a twenty-two-year-old summer intern wearing the world's shiniest silver suit, and he refused to shave off his scruffy designer stubble when Chuck had demanded it. I knew right then I wanted him as my junior.

Titzy was bristly and wiry in both physique and temperament. He had a mousey look, although not without being handsome, and he argued with me and Snoopy incessantly.

Titzy used to drink single espressos. Snoopy told him, not incorrectly, that a double espresso only cost ten pence more. Titzy had replied that he'd known that, but a single was all that he wanted. Snoopy told him that if he liked single espressos, he could buy a double and pour half of it into a separate cup, and that way get two for 65 pence each, instead of paying £1.20 at a time. Titzy acknowledged the math, but affirmed that, for him, one was enough. Snoopy wasn't happy. It didn't make sense, he had said, as he'd seen Titzy drink four single espressos the previous day. "Yes," replied Titzy, "but if I keep it on the side for two hours, it will get cold, won't it?" Snoopy said he could microwave it. They argued like that for an hour.

With me, it was economics. We argued about economics constantly. Titzy graduated from Bocconi. That's basically just LSE for Italians. But if Titzy was anything to go by, Bocconi had not yet gotten round to communicating LSE's core central message: that economics degrees are raffle tickets for banking jobs. Titzy still cared about the theory, about the ideas!

Can you imagine that! Poor Titzy. No one had cared about that shit for twenty years.

So why did I want this scruffy, silver-suited Italian who went around overpaying for his coffee? The truth is, I liked arguing with the guy. I've got Italians in my family, I've always liked winding them up. What can I say, it's a weakness of mine. I liked the way he'd get mad about the nature of the causes of inflation, or storm off in the middle of a football game, shouting (probably correctly, in fairness) that we weren't fit to polish his boots.

But those weren't the main reasons that I wanted Titzy. I wanted Titzy coz he was the voice of the street.

I'm not talking about the back streets of Naples here. Titzy was more of a Lake Como type. I'm talking about Wall Street.

Titzy always thought that the market was right. Always. Just like he always thought the textbooks were right. I think the guy had some sort of deeply laid innate desire to believe in a kind of higher wisdom. To trust that the guys upstairs had it under control. Bless him, his dad must have been a nice guy.

That was exactly what I wanted. I wanted a kid who read the *Financial Times* in the morning and then spent the whole day on the phone to his business school mates.

Let me explain to you why.

When I lost that eight million dollars I realized something. You don't become the best at anything by copying people. I wasn't going to get better than Bill by copying Bill. And I wasn't going to get better than Spengler by copying Spengler. Ultimately, when the shit hit the fan, it took me out and nobody else. Billy and Spengler didn't come to save me. That's what you get from copying people. Second-hand tactics, second-hand skills. It's not good enough.

I needed something that was mine.

And when Bill slapped those textbooks out of my hand and into the bin, I realized what it was.

See, Billy was right about those textbooks. They were bullshit. Textbooks are for kids. If you want to understand the real world, the time comes when you have to go and look at it. That time had come for me.

Rich daddy. Private school. Princeton Finance Society. Citibank.

Algebra. Calculus. Lagrangians. Proofs.

Most of those dicks on the trading floor, they're still living in their daddies' pockets. They believed everything they read and sucked up every word they got told. Why the fuck wouldn't they? It gets everyone paid. That's why Billy beat them year after year.

But when Billy threw my books in the bin, there was something else. I could see it in his eyes.

See, when we were memorizing algebra in castles, and lining up in queues for Finance Society events, little teenage Billy wasn't doing that. He was sitting down behind a sheet of glass, in the middle of buttfuck nowhere in Yorkshire somewhere, handing out wads of cash to punters. He was a cashier. A checkout boy.

Billy never had those books.

And I could see it then: Billy was jealous.

Now, I'm going to tell you a secret about trading. Making money trading is not about being right. It's about being right when everyone's wrong.

Billy was right. Billy was right year after year after year after year. But when did he make his big money? He made his money when something happened that no one else had foreseen, when the global banking system collapsed.

When people are wrong, their predictions are wrong. When people's predictions are wrong, their prices are wrong. And when prices are wrong, we make millions.

The reason Billy was right, year after year, when everyone else wasn't, was because Billy knew that the economy was a real thing. The economy is people, it's houses, it's businesses, it's loans. The rest of us had all been trained to see it as numbers, and besides that, barely any of the traders knew a single person who wasn't rich, if you don't count their cleaners. What did they know about the real world?

That was one advantage that both Billy and I had over them. We didn't have to strike up conversations with our cleaners.

But I had something else, too, something that Billy never had. Billy knew he was surrounded by idiots. But I'd been inside the universities. I'd taken the courses. I'd memorized the book. I'd seen the dark heart of the idiocy. I knew it. Its flavors. Its taste.

The best trading, you do it with your nose. It smells like stupidity.

And back then, at the beginning of 2011, the whole place was stinking of it.

See, something happened in 2010 that I couldn't get out of my head.

Interest rates stayed zero, all year.

That probably means nothing to you. You saw interest rates stay zero for nearly fifteen years. Zero interest rates were normal for you.

They weren't normal back then.

More importantly, they hadn't been predicted.

In the beginning of 2010, everybody thought that interest rates would go back up that year. Everyone had thought the same in 2009.

But it hadn't happened. Everyone had been wrong, two years in a row.

Why?

Well I've read the textbooks, just like Titzy, and every other pink-shirted dickhead on Wall Street. Let me tell you the story they tell.

Interest rates control the economy. If you control the interest rates, you control the economy. We are good at this. We have this well under control.

Sometimes people lose confidence and they stop spending money. When people stop spending money businesses lose customers and they go out of business. That means that people lose their jobs, and they spend even less money. That means more businesses shut down. That can lead to a spiral of rapidly increasing unemployment and poverty. It can cause your economy to collapse. That's what happened in the Great Depression in the 1930s leading, ultimately, to fascism in Europe and the Second World War.

That could have happened again in 2008, but it didn't because we've got it under control. We know how to deal with this problem. When this happens, we cut interest rates. Cutting interest rates is great because it makes saving less attractive, and borrowing cheap, so people and businesses will save less, and they'll borrow and spend. This perfectly counteracts the root cause of the problem—people stopping spending money. Through diligent management of interest rates, a tweak here and a tweak there, we can always reach the *first-best-optimal-outcome-for-the-economy*. The best of all possible worlds.

Back in 2008, economists were very confident in their ability to achieve this. The previous two decades had seen a golden age of success for economists, during which they successfully

1. Conquered Inflation

2. Ended Boom and Bust

3. Achieved Sustained Economic Growth

All through the miracle of interest-rate management.

Given the generally accepted wonderfulness of the strategy, it is no surprise that when the massive (and unforeseen) banking crisis of 2008 dropped, there was uniform nodding of heads within the economist community that the correct response was to slash interest rates. Interest rates were, accordingly, slashed enormously. Whereas previously central bankers would do things like pruning interest rates from 5.75% to 5.5%, suddenly they were slashing them from 5.5% to zero. And this happened across the rich world.

Everyone was very confident it would work.

I won't bore you with the technical details, but slashing interest rates is printing money. The way a central bank lowers interest rates is that it prints a fuckton of money, and then it lends it out to banks super-duper cheap.

Everyone was very confident it would work.

The level of confidence in this plan is probably best summed up by a quote from Ben Bernanke at about the same time. Ben Bernanke (ex-Princeton, ex-Harvard, ex-MIT) was at that time the head of the US Federal Reserve, on paper the most powerful and smartest economist in the world. Here's what he said:

"The US government has a technology, called a printing press, that allows it to produce as many dollars as it wishes at essentially no cost . . . Under a paper-money system, a determined government can *always* generate higher spending."

Everyone was very confident it would work.

It didn't work.

That's why I wanted to sit next to Titzy Lazzari. I wanted to sit next to Titzy Lazzari *because Titzy was wrong.*

OK. This is not about Titzy Lazzari personally, this is about the whole market. By the beginning of 2011, it had started to become clear to me that *the market was wrong.* Not just the market, but the economists, the universities, the fucking Monetary Policy Committee in the Bank of England, the dickheads on the news, the whole fucking shitshow.

These fuckers had been wrong about everything. Every single fucking thing since the day I showed up. When I showed up everybody thought that the pink-shirt dickheads were one step down from God. Next thing those guys blew the world up using nothing but mathematics, idiocy and hubris. After that, every economist in the whole world had spent two and a half years constantly predicting a recovery that never happened. One day I sat down and looked through some historic interest-rate predictions. Every single one was a mile too high. They were wrong about everything. We were wrong about everything.

I needed to know why.

That's why I needed Titzy. I needed to measure the distance between the real economy and the universities, between the real world and the markets. For that reason, I needed someone beside me who was fresh out of university, fully plugged into the matrix. Someone who knew every economic theory, who read every business paper. Someone whose friends were all fresh out of business school, and whose father messaged him asking for stock trading tips from a yacht. Someone whose silver suit was pumped full to bursting with Kool-Aid.

Yep, I needed Titzy. I needed Titzy because he was wrong.

2

SO WHY *WERE* PEOPLE NOT SPENDING MONEY? IN 2009, IN 2010, IN
2011?

Titzy saw it as a crisis of confidence. 2008 was a big shock to the system. The consumer had been badly rocked. Now, by the beginning of
2011, confidence is coming back, more than two years have passed, people are ready to go out spending again.

It's an opinion, I guess.

What did Bill think?

The banking system got fucked. People got fucked over. People lost
their homes and their jobs. But those homes are owned by new people
now, and unemployment is coming down and inflation's going up. Now
that the banking system is repaired, it's only a matter of time before the
economy, and interest rates, bounce back.

It's an opinion, I guess.

What did Antonio Mancini, the wealthy, snakeskin-belted Oxford
macroeconomics professor think, when I asked him seven years later, in
2018? "We always knew rates would stay zero! People had had a shock to
their consumption-savings preferences!"

Well . . . It's an opinion, I guess.

JB used to have a saying about opinions. "Opinions are like arseholes.
Everyone's got one."

I asked Harry Sambhi. Harry was still just a kid. Harry had holes in
his shoes and was jumping over the barriers on the tube to save costs.
That's why he didn't spend money. I asked Asad. Asad said his mum had
sold the family home to support him and his sisters and now he was
sleeping on the sofa to try and save up a deposit. That's why they didn't
spend money. I asked Aidan. Aidan's mum had lost her job and hadn't

been able to get a new rate on the mortgage. Now the monthly payments were sky high, and Aidan was having to pay them himself. That's why they didn't spend money.

They were losing their homes. I hadn't even noticed.

Opinions are like arseholes, I guess. Everyone's got one.

I was sitting on the desk one afternoon in February and I tried it out on Titz.

"Titzy. Do you think the reason no one is spending money is because no one's got any money?"

"What the fuck are you talkin' about, *geeza*? How can no one have any money?"

His accent is deeply Italian. "Geeza" is a new word that he's recently learned and he's trying it out.

"Well, you know, I been askin' people and that's all they keep saying. 'I don't have no fuckin money.'"

"'*I don ava no fuckina money.*'" Titzy tries to copy my accent and somehow comes off sounding even more Italian. "Come on geeza. It's a monetary system. It's not possible for no one to have any money. The whole thing has got to add up." He tries to lean over to pick a newspaper up off of the floor while his feet are resting on the table, and he nearly falls off of his chair.

Immediately after that, Citibank hires a huge estate in the countryside somewhere outside London and invites all the global traders for a conference and a piss-up. The Slug is there and I realize why they call him the Slug. The Frog is there and I realize why they call him the Frog.

The big boss, the Slug's boss, gives a big speech where he tells us all to take much, much more risk.

"If you are happy to risk it in one million dollars, then why shouldn't you risk it in ten!"

They give us all army camo baseball caps with "Go Big or Go Home" printed on the front.

I didn't stay for the party. I put the cap on and climbed into my little Peugeot 106 and I just drove it all the way home.

. . .

Back on the desk, everyone put massive bets on, just like the Big Boss Man told them to. Big bets on recovery. Billy was in, Snoopy was in, JB was in, Chuck was in. Fuck, even Hongo was in, and he never bet on anything. It wasn't just the STIRT desk, everyone was doing it. Spot desk, Options desk, Emerging Markets desks. I waited though. I didn't like the smell. I wasn't in, so Titzy wasn't in.

The next week I got called into a meeting. There used to be a fortnightly meeting between all the heads of the different desks on the floor. Back when Caleb was the boss, I had to go to every meeting to carry the sandwiches. When Chuck came in, I never told him about the meeting and I just kept on going myself. I don't know why, I thought it might be useful one day.

That week's meeting was held by one of the only economists in the whole bank that I actually respected. He was from the Credit department, and I remembered him from my internship. His name was Timothy Prince.

Timothy had a bunch of charts. He went through them one at a time. On each one was the fiscal situation of a single country. Italy. Spain. Greece. Portugal. Ireland. Also the United Kingdom, the US, Japan.

They were all variations on the same story. All these governments were spending more than their income year after year and their debts were growing. If things kept going in the same direction, the interest rates on their debts would start rising. People would stop lending to them, and they'd have to sell their assets. That would be bad.

I packed all the leftover sandwiches into a brown paper bag and I carried them back to the desk.

I couldn't get it out of my head. Not the collapse of western welfare states, no, I wasn't too worried about that. What I couldn't get out of my head was this sense of similarity. It was the same. The government of Spain, the government of America, the government of Japan. The situation was just like Asad's mum, it was just like Aidan's mum. Outgoings more than their income. Losing the ability to borrow money. More and more income going into servicing debt. Losing their assets. The situation was the same. It wasn't just Harry with holes in his shoes, it was the world.

But it came up against the economics though, Titzy's wisdom. We're in a monetary system. The whole thing always has to be in balance. For everyone who's in debt, there's someone who's in credit. For everybody losing money, there's somebody who's gaining. The whole system is designed to be in balance. Not only that, but what about the houses? What about the stock market that was rising and rising? These assets weren't disappearing. But if we didn't own them, if the people didn't own them, and the governments didn't own them . . . Then who did?

And that was it, I think, that was the moment that it hit me, surrounded by millionaires and sandwiches.

I looked to the left of me. Pink shirt, pink shirt, white, sky blue. I looked to the right of me. White shirt, white shirt, pink, ooh, pinstripes, don't see much of that nowadays. There, in string, sewn into a collar, four letters: "A.I.E.Q." Who the fuck's surname begins with a Q?

Millionaires. Every single one of them.

And me, too. What about me? I'd be a millionaire, before long.

It was us. It was us, wasn't it? We were the balance. We were the boys who'd be richer than our fathers, in a world of children who'd be poor. We were the ones with the growing bank balances that balanced the Italian's debt. We were the ones receiving the interest on Aidan's mum's mortgage, that Aidan himself was now having to pay, to us. And our children. Maybe my children. Maybe they would own the house that Asad's mum sold. And the rent from that house, and the interest from the Italian government: maybe our children could lend that back out to Asad's own children, and then we'd own the houses and the debt, as well. And it would grow, that's what compound interest does. We would use the money from the assets to buy the rest of the assets. You'd sell your assets to us, to pay your mortgage, to pay your rent. To pay it to us. That's how it would go. It would get worse and worse. It would grow, it would grow out of control. It wasn't a crisis of confidence. It wasn't the fucking of the banking system. It wasn't an "exogenous shock to consumption savings preferences." It was inequality. Inequality that would grow and grow, and get worse and get worse until it dominated and killed the economy that contained it. It wasn't temporary, it was terminal. It was the end of the economy. It was cancer.

And I knew what that meant.

It meant I had to buy green Eurodollars.

.   .   .

A green Eurodollar is a bet. A nice, clean bet on what American interest rates will be in two and a half years' time. None of this complicated "lend one currency borrow another" bullshit that you get in FX swaps. None of this having to borrow the money back every day. We are talking pure betting now. Casino stuff. We loved it. Billy loved it, Snoopy loved it, I loved it.

Our job was not *supposed* to be betting. We were supposed to provide FX swaps to customers. But we were given access to products like Eurodollars (and their equivalents in all the other currencies) so that we could "hedge our risks." We hedged a fucking lot of risks, often risks we didn't have. I was about to take the hedge of my life.

See what I had realized, at that moment, was exactly, precisely why we were all wrong. We had been diagnosing a terminal cancer as a series of seasonal colds. We thought the banking system was broken, but fixable. We thought confidence had collapsed, but would recover. But what was really happening was that the wealth of the middle class—of ordinary, hardworking families like Aidan's and like Asad's, and also of almost all the world's largest governments—was being sucked away from them and into the hands of the rich. Ordinary families were losing their assets and going into debt. So were governments. As ordinary families and governments got poorer, and the rich got richer, that would increase flows of interest, rent and profit from the middle class to the rich, compounding the problem. The problem would not solve itself. In fact, it would accelerate, it would get worse. The reason economists didn't realize this is because almost *no* economists look in their models at how wealth is distributed. They spend ten years memorizing "representative agent" models—models that view the whole economy as one single "average" or "representative" person. As a result, for them the economy is only ever about averages, about aggregates. They ignore the distribution. For them, it's nothing more than an afterthought. Moralist window dressing. Finally, my degree was useful for something after all. It showed me exactly how everyone was wrong.

If I was right, this was a big deal. It meant that markets were horribly, horribly mispriced. The recovery would never happen and the normalization of interest rates would never happen. At that point, the beginning of 2011, markets were pricing nearly 6 full hikes of 0.25% each from the US Federal Reserve in the following twelve months alone. They were going to be wrong. Everyone was going to be wrong. Those rate hikes weren't going to happen. They would never happen. I would be able to make money off this year, after year, after year, as the interest predictions got pushed back and back. These idiots never even looked at inequality. It would be a decade before they caught on, at least.

There was an alternative to doing green Eurodollars. I could bet with something called "OIS." Eurodollars were machine-traded and you had to fiddle about with them, whereas with an OIS you could get another bank to quote you a price for a single massive trade, and you could do the whole thing in one drop. Plus, guess who brokes US dollar OIS? That's right, Harry Sambhi. I wanted Harry to see.

I pushed Harry's button. I'd never traded through Harry before. I asked him to get me a price on 700 million dollars of one-year OIS starting in the spring of the following year, 2012. That was a big trade, especially for me since I wasn't officially a dollar trader. Harry was shocked. I think he might have thought I was doing him a favor. He went out and got me a price from Deutsche Bank and I hit it. It felt good. Every single other fucker on the desk was betting on recovery and now I was clean betting against them. Let's see who's right then. Me, or everyone. Yeah, I liked that. Time to play with the big boys. Game on.

Then the earthquake happened.

How would you feel if an earthquake happened and twenty thousand people died and you made eleven million dollars?

That's five hundred and fifty dollars per person.

I didn't know there was going to be an earthquake. I ain't a fucking magician.

When I got to my desk I had hundreds of emails. One of them was from the Citi Macroeconomics department. It said: "We anticipate the earthquake to be strongly positive for 2011 Japanese GDP growth."

I opened my desk and I pulled out a blue ballpoint pen and I quietly snapped it in half and I dropped both halves into the bin. I took my second pen and I did the same thing. Then I went to the stationery cupboard to get more pens.

The junior on the Tokyo desk had sent Titzy a video of our Tokyo STIRT trader, Hisa Watanabe, on the trading floor during the earthquake. He was crouched under his desk and gripping onto something under there, but his little head kept popping up in a little yellow hard hat and he was trying to grab his mouse and do some trading while Tokyo swayed wildly through the windows in the background.

Titzy forwarded the video to the desk, but no one found it funny. Do you know why they didn't find it funny? Because earthquakes make interest rates go down.

It's weird isn't it? You spend three years of your life studying economics, then another three trading on it. You wake up at 5 a.m. and you read a hundred emails. Every day. You hire a kid fresh out of university so he can talk to you nonstop about economic theory. You finally come up with your grand idea and you bet your arse on it. Then you make 2.5 million dollars, in a single day, because of an earthquake, and twenty thousand people die, and all of the people who you are closest to, the people who you spend every single day of your life with, the people who taught you to trade, the people who taught you everything, all of them get smashed.

What does it mean?

Titzy kept looking at me like I was a fucking genius, like I knew the earthquake was going to happen. As if I caused it or something.

Billy lost the most, of course, because Billy was the biggest. I think he lost 5 or 6 million dollars. He had it to lose. Snoopy lost 1.5 or 2. That was a lot for him. Pretty much his whole PnL for the year. JB tried to hold on and fight it and he ended up losing nearly 4, in the end. That dropped him into the red. Hongo tapped out immediately and only lost $500K. Chuck is some kind of Teflon Buddha and he barely lost anything. I don't know how he did it, sometimes I'm not even sure he really existed. I didn't say nothing. Just waited and watched, breaking pens.

There was a nuclear disaster. You probably know about it. They evacuated 154,000 people from the prefecture of Fukushima and people thought the nuclear plant might blow up. That was good for my position. Up three and a half million dollars. Up four and a half million dollars.

By a week in I was up six million and JB was absolutely choking. It was hard to watch. Then I did something a little bit crazy which, as a trader, I probably wouldn't do nowadays.

There was a sales guy on the floor on the desk next to ours. I liked him. He was a nice guy, but he wasn't the smartest. A crisp, clean cut, nicely raised Englishman in his mid-forties. His name was Stanley Palmer. One day, in the midst of the nuclear panic, Stanley Palmer went crazy. He stood up, at 11 a.m., in the middle of the trading floor, and he screamed out, "THE NUKE RODS ARE EXPOSED!!!"

The words echoed around me as desk juniors across the floor repeated them loudly to their own desks. Titzy stood up beside me and shouted, "THE NUKE RODS ARE EXPOSED!!!," his hands around his mouth.

There was a chaos of noise and activity as people ran back to their seats and shouted at their brokers and each other. Stanley was still standing and repeating the words, "THE NUKE RODS ARE EXPOSED!!! THE NUKE RODS ARE EXPOSED!!!!"

Titzy was echoing it like a clown.

I told Titzy to shut the fuck up.

Titzy spread his hands real wide and shrugged wildly as if I was the mad one.

"Titzy, what the fuck is a nuke rod?"

Titzy did that thing that Italians do with their hands.

I turned back to Stanley, he was still shouting and shouting.

What did I know about Stanley? I was pretty sure he had graduated from Oxford. What was it he had studied? Was it History? Or was it Classics? Could it have been PPE?

"Titzy there's no way. There's no fucking way Stanley knows what a nuke rod is."

Titzy wasn't listening. He was deep in his screens. JB was screaming down his broker lines. He was finally stopping out of his position.

I picked up the heavy brown telephone and I pressed the button to my Eurodollar broker. I covered my mouth with my hand, and I sold a fucking ton of Eurodollar futures. That flipped my whole position. I wasn't betting on a disaster any longer, I was betting on rates going up.

You shouldn't do that. You shouldn't flip your whole position on a feeling, on a whim. You shouldn't play God, you are not invincible. But what am I gonna tell you? I was twenty-four years old and I did it.

The nuclear plant never exploded. Thank God.

I made another five million on the way back up.

The best trading, you do it with your nose. It smells like stupidity.

3

AFTER THAT EVERYONE WAS FUCKED. EVERYBODY GOT STOPPED out of their positions. JB had stopped out at the worst possible moment, at the very peak of the carnage, the exact point when I was going the other way.

Once everybody calmed down, I took profit on all of the Eurodollars, flipping myself back into predicting disaster. There may not have been a nuclear explosion in 2011, but there was going to be an explosion. I could smell it. By the middle of April, I was up over 11 million dollars. The desk as a whole was up less than ten. JB was 1.7 in the red.

Being in the red isn't fun. It is not fun for anyone, but it was definitely not fun for JB.

JB was from another generation. He was a good man: a sportsman, a talker, a charmer. He would have been a lawyer if he hadn't dropped out of Oxford. But he wasn't a numbers guy, or a details man. The ground moved from under his feet.

In 2011, Europe collapsed. First it was Greece. Then it was Spain, and then Italy, Portugal, Ireland. Dropping like dominoes, just like the Prince had predicted. Nobody would buy the bonds of any of these governments, nobody would lend to them. It was good for me. I made a lot of money.

Who lends money to national governments? Largely, it is the banks of the countries themselves. Ultimately, it's you, if you're a bank depositor. The bank takes your deposits and it lends them to governments. That's totally fine, because, prior to 2011, economists had considered lending money to governments to be "risk-free."

They were wrong.

Why is lending to governments risk-free? Theoretically, it is because governments have the ability, in the case of emergency, to print their own money. If they get into big trouble, and they owe you a lot of money, they can print the money and use that to pay you back.

The trouble with that is that Italy can't do it. Nor can Spain. Nor can Greece. Nor can Portugal. A consequence of the creation of the euro was that European countries lost their legal ability to print their own money. Nobody really worried much about that because these countries were always considered to be super-safe credits. Until they weren't.

In 2011, when people realized that these countries were bankrupt, questions were quickly raised over whether the banks, who had lent to them and were owed huge amounts of money by their governments, were bankrupt as well. This was less than three years after the Lehman crisis. Nobody wanted any more banks to go bankrupt. The European Central Bank had to act.

What the ECB did next was highly unconventional. They offered all European banks unlimited loans at 1% interest.

This is not how Central Banking usually works. Setting the interest rate is a big deal for central banks; they like to get microscopic on the detail. Usually, they would monitor closely the interest rates at which banks were lending to each other. If the rates were too high, they'd inject a little bit of cheap money into the system, pushing the rate down. If rates were too low, they'd do the opposite, lending less money or borrowing it back, bringing the market rate up. The way that central banks controlled interest rates was thus by manipulating the quantity of loans in the system. If you control the quantity, you can control the price. Just like iPhones and Nike trainers.

But once you offer *unlimited* loans, you can't control the quantity anymore. And if you don't control the quantity, then you don't control the price. The ECB must have felt that they had to do it to guarantee that no bank would go under, but the result was madness in the markets.

A stupid game played out between the ECB and the commercial banks. The ECB offered unlimited 1% loans in what it called "auctions" — although they weren't really auctions, since everyone got exactly whatever they asked for, without limit. As it became clear that the Greek government was going under, banks swarmed into the auctions to bid for the loans. They borrowed so much that there was an absolute flood of money into the system, and European interest rates collapsed to zero, even to less than zero on some days, a full percentage point below the ECB's "official" interest rate of 1%, which was the cost of the loans. Seeing that interest rates had collapsed to zero, hardly anyone bid for ECB loans at the next auction. That led to a huge lack of money in the market, and rates shot up to above 2%. Every week it would be like this, with each bank trying to work out how much money the other banks would borrow. If you knew everyone would borrow, you'd try not to borrow yourself, anticipating cheap money in the market. If you thought other banks *wouldn't* borrow, you'd get in as much cash as you could. Everyone was trying to do what everyone else didn't do. The end result was nothing but carnage.

Sometimes there were multiple auctions in a week. There was no way of knowing what the interest rate would be on any given day. It could be anything from sub 0% to above 2%. It would swing wildly between those two extremes on consecutive days. To be honest, I had no idea what was happening. But that was OK, because I had Titzy. Titzy tracked that shit like a bloodhound, all day, every single day.

JB didn't have Titzy. JB didn't have nothing. JB was becoming an old man by then. Interest rates never used to be like that. In his day, the Central Bank would set them once a month and then they'd stay where they fucking were. All of our valuation systems and pricing systems were set up for that kind of world. JB couldn't adapt. My job was only to price the front month—that's about twenty-six or twenty-seven business days. It was only possible with Titzy constantly updating every single day manually. There was no other way to do it. JB had the following twenty-three months to deal with. That was about six hundred days. He was out of his depth.

He was getting smashed day after day. His prices were wrong and I knew they were wrong. Simon Chang, the HSBC trader, had also been promoted to euros, and he'd hit me up on the IB chat every day asking me why I was showing wrong prices.

"It's not me," I would type. "It's JB."

"Well why the fuck is JB showing wrong prices? He's going to get steamrolled. Why don't you tell him!?"

Good question. Why didn't I tell him?

.   .   .

You know what, the truth is, it never occurred to me. I'm not sure why, maybe that's just the kind of person I am.

JB was flailing. He was struggling for air. He was losing money day after day. I was killing it. I was creaming it. I was making money on all of Titzy's prices and my disaster position was just pouring cash in every time I stepped onto the floor. JB never once turned round and asked me why.

The truth is, he was hardly ever there.

The last few years had been good to JB. They had been good to everyone on that desk. Everyone had made a lot of money. So had I. JB had done his share of living the dream. He might have done your share as well.

JB had bought a string of luxury apartments overlooking the Thames. He'd gotten one of the secretaries pregnant. She was about to bear him his first child.

He was off the desk a lot now. He'd go on long broker lunches. When he'd come back he'd be bright red all over, and then he'd smear himself onto the markets like bugs on a windscreen. It was painful to watch.

I told Snoopy I was worried.

"Don't worry about JB," Snoopy said with a smile. "He's the wealthiest man I personally know."

So it goes, I guess. So it goes.

When JB was off the desk I had to cover for him. He was off the desk more than he was on it. My book, remember, the short-dated euros book, was the busiest book on the desk by a mile even *before* the euro market went insane. Now it had become a nonstop, manic rollercoaster, and I was doing more than half of JB's job, too. It was intense.

But what do you do, you know? What else can you do? You work. As Europe collapsed my PnL exploded, and I went through 22 million dollars in June. I was the top trader on the whole floor by that time, and by a bit. This was my big moment, I was killing it, and I weren't going to let no Queensland alcoholic get in my way.

I did my job and I did JB's job as well. I got into work early every day and I made Titzy get in early too. I jumped straight off of my bicycle and onto the trading floor. I locked myself into the screens, the speaker-boxes, the headsets, the beeps and the dings and before long I was dominating the market. I was trading over half a trillion euros every day. I don't really know how these things rank globally, but I would guess that must have made me one of the biggest traders in the world. There was no other way to trade it really, that market, it was insane.

I started forgetting to change out of my cycling clothes, and before long, I didn't even care. I stopped even bringing my work clothes into the office. I traded in a gray hoody, black fingerless gloves, and old, faded Onitsuka Tigers, all day, every day. I set up sound alerts so that my computer would warn me whenever certain things happened. My station became a riot of noise, and it would scream out loud "Ka-Ching" sounds whenever my PnL went through another half a million dollars. It would make them a lot. On big win days, in the afternoons when the trading got quiet, I would bang out reggae tunes from my speakers on maximum volume and me and Titzy would put our feet up on the desks and drink single espressos two at a time and jam out. Liquidator, Return of Django, 54–46. I was the number one trader in that whole place, the King of the Trading Floor, and Titzy was my right-hand man. Titzy wasn't making any money himself, of course, but he was just a kid, he was happy to be along for the ride. Fuck, what do I mean he was a kid? Titzy's older than me. We were both twenty-four. I went home and I dreamed about markets, every night.

"Has anyone ever called you . . . arrogant?"

JB had just come back from the bathroom. JB always wanted to ramp when he came back from the bathroom.

I'd had just about enough of JB's shit. Man's never here, making wrong prices, losing money day after day. What little money he *does* make he gives it all to the brokers, now he wants to call me fucking arrogant.

I didn't look at him. I could feel his eyes burning into my left cheek but I just stared forward with my hand on my mouse. I was wearing my little Bluetooth headset and I shifted the left earphone off of my ear as a sign of respect.

"No. Never. No one ever."

"Well. I must say I find that highly surprising. Don't you think that's quite an arrogant thing to say?"

I took a blue ballpoint pen out of my drawer and I tapped the tip of it a few times on the plasticky desk. I thought about snapping it in half but I decided not to. I put it down and I turned to JB.

"JB, when are you gonna get yourself out of the red?"

Our faces were less than a foot from one another. The broken blood vessels of his nose were spreading across his face like an illness, and I suddenly remembered how much the man had helped me and I felt bad for saying what I'd said. But I didn't let it show on my face.

"Don't you worry about that. I've done it before and I'll do it again. I know what I'm doing."

"What's the trade then? Come on JB. What's the trade?"

JB looked into my eyes and I looked into his. Our faces were even closer now, almost touching, and I could hear his slow, measured breathing. I noticed how blue his eyes were, the pale blueness of the eyes of an old man that have seeped their blue into the world for many years. There was a long pause. I wasn't sure if he was reading me or if he was thinking. I wasn't sure if I was reading him.

"Stocks."

"Stocks?"

"Stocks," JB repeated, decisively.

"Stocks are the trade?"

"Stocks. They're too high."

"What do you mean stocks are too high?"

"Look at them! They're too fucking high! They've barely fallen and the economy's going to shit! They've got to go down."

I turned away from JB and I picked up the pen again and I tapped it onto the bare desk about twenty times.

"JB, you don't get it do you? It don't work like that. Stocks never go down. Stocks only go up. When the economy is good stocks go up, and when the economy is shit, they print so much money stocks go up even more. Same with fucking houses. Everything goes up. The asset holders never lose. The rich never lose. The rich only win. Buy the fucking stocks mate. They'll go to the moon. And you will be fucking fine mate. Don't you worry."

And I went and bought four single espressos.

.   .   .

I've got to be honest. When JB was off the desk, and I was quoting his prices as well as my own, I didn't put as much effort into his as I did into mine. His prices went into his book and his PnL. My prices went into my book and mine. I had my priorities. I'm sorry, but I did.

JB knew it. It was bound to blow up.

You may remember that, as market makers, we take the spread. Say the real price is 71. I quote you 70–72, you buy at 72, I look for someone to sell to me at 71, and we're done. You got to buy the thing you wanted, I got my profit. Everyone's happy.

The problem is, the real price doesn't exist. Or perhaps it's fairer to say, it's moving all the time. And what happens if it's moving and you didn't see it?

Let's say that it's 74 now. Some shit happened when I was taking a piss. Morley hasn't shifted the price on his screen yet because he's busy and it's only just happened. You call me up and you ask me for a price. I look at the screen and it's 70–72. I tell you 70–72. You lift me at 72 and I wanna buy now at 71.

I ask Morley for a price and it's 73–75.5.

Fuck.

I can't get out of it now without taking a 3.5 loss.

Tell Morley I'll pay 73.

"Too late. Someone else is already bidding 74."

"OK fuck it, do you still have the 75.5 offer? Tell them I'll pay 75."

Two minutes of silence.

"Sorry mate 75.5 is gone. Best I've got now is 77."

See market-making isn't so easy. You've got to think long and hard about when you take your pisses.

JB was off desk. He was out drinking God knows where filling himself with beer and sake and raw fish and God knows what the fuck else.

Someone called me on a price for JB and I was pretty busy. What was I doing? I don't know. Maybe I was deciding what to cook for dinner that evening. I was trying to perfect my duck à l'orange.

Put your cookbook to the side of the table quickly, pull up your price screen. Ask a broker:

"Where's three months?"

"34–37."

34–37, yeah that sounds about right, repeat it to the salesman.

"34–37."

"37 mine, 2 yards."

A short crackle of radio fuzz on the speakerbox as the salesman hangs up.

Two yards. That's quite a lot. We should probably cover some right away. Flick the switch up to the broker.

"Marco. You still there in the three months?"

"Still there. 34–37."

"Mine. One yard."

Crackle. Two and a half minutes of silence. You're watching price screens on your computer and you can see they're being adjusted. 35–38. 36–39. Fucking Marco, he never had a 37 offer. Fucking bullshit.

"Marco, where's my fucking three months."

"Mate I'm really sorry it's gone, best I got is 39."

"Fuck! Why the Fuck did you tell me you had 37 then!?"

"Mate I had it, I had it, I been fucking let down."

Fuck him, he never had it. I knew straight away it was gone.

I refreshed JB's PnL. He was down 100K. He had only just scraped himself back into the black. That would be nearly enough to put him in the red again. I lean over to Titzy.

"Titzy!"

"Hmph!?"

Titzy was eating lasagne from a cardboard box with a plastic fork.

"Titzy, I got hit in three months for JB and it's already fucking gone. He's down 100. What should we do?"

"Ah fuck, he only just got above zero. Can you cover it?"

"If we cover it now, he'll lose two hundred and he'll be back in the red. What do you think?"

"You should text him."

I wrote out a text to JB.

"You got hit in the three months. It's down 100K."

Before I sent the text I refreshed his PnL. It was down 200 now. I deleted "It's down 100K," and replaced it with "It's not looking good."

I sent the text.

. . .

By the time JB got back to the desk it was 4 p.m. and the trade was down 400K. JB was looking simultaneously delighted and like he may well at any point fall over. I knew straight away he hadn't read the text. I looked to my right at Titzy, who was looking at me. I did up two of the three open buttons on my shirt. Titzy did the same. I muted my computer. This would be a bad time for a ka-ching.

"All right fuckers, how's the world looking?"

JB settled himself in his chair. He refreshed his PnL. I was trying my best not to look at him but in my peripheral vision I saw the blood drop from his face. He pushed Marco's button as if reflexive instinct.

"Marco where's three months?"

Crackle. Pause. "41–44."

"What the fuck is this?"

I didn't look at JB, I looked at his speakerbox. Marco's light wasn't on. That meant he was talking to me.

"It's the three months mate. You got hit in the three months. I told you about it—it's in the text! Didn't you see the text!?"

I had him here. He hadn't seen the text. We both knew he hadn't seen the text. We both knew he should have done.

JB slowly stood up and put his hand to his pocket. He pulled his phone out as if it was a gun. He read the text out slowly, one word at a time.

"You. Got. Hit. In. The three months. It's. Not . . . Looking . . . Good."

JB put down his phone and stayed standing, and so I stood myself up as well. He turned to face me and now we were squared. JB repeated the last three words straight into my face.

"Not looking good. Not . . . looking . . . good."

I chewed on that for a second.

"Well . . . I mean . . . It's not really . . . Is it?"

JB pursed his lips and started nodding quickly, almost imperceptibly.

"What are you gonna do?"

It was obvious what he was saying. I was up over twenty-four million dollars. That trade dropped JB in the red. I have no doubt, I am absolutely certain, that JB himself would have taken the trade.

I remembered the first time I'd met JB. How he'd taken me in. How he'd been the first trader on the desk to talk to me, how he'd given me my first book. I remember how he'd comforted me when I'd lost eight million dollars. I remembered the exact words that he'd said to me — "tough times don't last, tough people do." Then I looked into his red face and I saw four luxury flats, overlooking Big Ben.

I stuck my tongue deep into my cheek and bit down on it hard.

"Tough times don't last JB. Tough people do."

JB blew up. He picked up his heavy brown handphone and launched it full speed into his screens. The phone hit his central screen squarely in the middle, which buckled and splintered, and the phone bounced harmlessly back onto his desk. Nothing shattered. Screens aren't what they used to be, I suppose. I distinctly remember thinking that the whole action, which had itself been swift, decisive and athletic, had made disappointingly little sound.

JB was clearly as disappointed as I was. He picked up the phone and smashed it, full strength, onto his desk at least seven or eight times, each strike punctuated with a distinctively Australian "fuck."

This was much more effective with regards to noise output.

There was a brief moment of calm during which everyone looked at JB and JB looked into the future. He still had the phone in his right hand. Again, almost as if physical reflex, his left hand reached out to his speakerbox, and his right hand brought the phone to his ear.

"Robbie where's three months?"

He'd pressed the button for another broker.

"ROBBIE WHERE'S THREE MONTHS!?!?"

A short pause, and then a FUCK and a BANG simultaneously as the phone came down hard on the desk. It was gratifying.

"Timmie where's three months? FUCK!" Bang!

"Millzy where's three months? FUCK!" Bang!

He was going down the broker lines one at a time. There was a real musicality to it, a beauty.

"JB WHAT'S GOING ON?"

Chuck had his hands around his mouth and was calling out to JB in a perfectly natural manner, as if the commotion were entirely external. JB was very busy so he didn't reply.

"GARY WHAT'S GOING ON?"

It was not a simple question to answer. I reeled through a few possible responses in my mind. Eventually I settled on: "I THINK JB'S PHONE IS BROKEN."

Which I assumed to be factually correct.

Chuck nodded with a great deal of understanding, as if JB's behavior was the only natural response to being a trader who has a broken phone, and he hauled himself out of his chair. He walked slowly to the opposite end of the desk, past JB and past me, where there was a small cabinet of supplies. He leaned himself with great difficulty down to the bottom draw, from which he pulled a replacement large, heavy brown hand-phone, with a long, curled, dangling wire attached.

What Chuck did next I will never understand. Rather than walking down across the desk, like a sensible human being, and handing the phone to JB, he shouted,

"HERE YOU GO JB."

And he threw the phone into the air.

It seemed to me to travel in slow motion. It was a high, arcing throw that scraped the trading floor's high ceiling. It reached its apex above Titzy's head, to my right. Titzy was looking directly upward. It started to come down above my head, and I ducked and stepped back.

I needn't have, because Chuck never missed. The phone landed per-fectly, squarely, in the center of JB's bald head.

I waited. Everyone waited. For a moment the trading floor was per-fectly silent. I wondered if JB would kill Chuck.

But he didn't. He just stopped. He did nothing. He stopped pressing the buttons. He stopped smashing his phone. He gently lowered himself down into his chair and he seemed to think very, very deeply. He flicked up one of the switches to one of his brokers instead of using the buttons, which allowed him to communicate without having to use his broken phone and had, in fact, always been an option.

"Where's three months?"

"41–44."

"Can you get me two yards at 44?"

A brief pause and then: "Yes, do you want it?"

"Mine 2 yards. 44."

After that JB did nothing. He just sat and breathed deeply for about five minutes. At one point he reached up with his right hand and touched the top of his head and then looked at his fingers, as if checking for blood. After that he stood up and went home.

I didn't think you could knock sense into people by hitting them on the head. I thought that only happened in cartoons. But who knows, maybe you can.

That was the third last thing that Chuck ever did.

Back at home, Harry was getting worried. I wasn't going out. All I did was cook food and make money.

Word of me was going around the market and Harry had heard it. It was clear I was becoming a big deal. Harry couldn't understand why I didn't want to enjoy it. Neither could I, to be honest. He used to invite my mates round to drink up and try to convince me to go clubbing. On my birthday he threw a big surprise party and invited everyone to an expensive VIP table at Cargo. I pretended to go to the bathroom and then I snuck out and I took the bus home.

Harry kept going on and on at me, and I could see that it came from a good place. So eventually I told him, OK, we can go to one party. There was going to be some kind of Summer Event at the Matchstick Factory where we lived. Some girl had been smiling at me at the gym down there, so I figured she'd go. I just wanted to show the kid that I still had it in me.

We went there and she was there with her friend. I'd brought along a one-liter bottle of Bacardi and I asked them if they wanted to drink. Turned out they did. I ain't really much of a charmer, but I can drop a move if I have to.

The four of us went out to a bar until the early hours, way past my usual bedtime. My eyes were drooping and I thought Harry liked her, so I figured I would just let it go. I asked the friend, who turned out to be her flatmate, if she wanted to go to McDonald's, and then we got a night bus home. I fell asleep the moment I sat down on the bus, and when I woke up she was stroking my hair.

.   .   .

Snoopy got married that summer. He didn't invite none of us to the wedding except Bill.

Snoopy was still betting on economic recovery, and I was over in the corner trying to convince him that weren't going to happen, when Chuck came over and said: "How's married life treating ya!?"

Snoopy was sitting down and Chuck was standing directly behind him, so he had to kind of twist and arch his neck.

"Ermmm . . . It's all right Chuck, yeah. It's all right, it's all right . . . It's good!"

"Ah come on, what do you mean it's good!? Gimme some details!!"

"I don't know Chuck, what do you want me to say? It's nice! I work all day, I get home, she's cooked dinner . . . It's nice!"

Chuck wasn't happy with that.

"Well, what does she cook you?"

"What do you mean what does she cook me? Every day she cooks something different!"

"Well . . . What did she cook you last night?"

Snoop thought for a bit.

"Last night . . . last night she cooked . . . pasta bake."

Chuck's face creased and his forehead wrinkled. He scratched his head and looked off to the side.

"Pasta?," he asked, with incredulity. And then: "Pasta!?," once again.

He leaned his heavy weight down into the desk so that he could look Snoopy in the eye, and asked with the earnestness of a child, "Pasta . . . with *curry*?!?"

Me and Snoopy laughed about that for a long time, we had to take a bit of time away from the desk.

That was the second last thing Chuck ever did.

"There's something about her. I think she's a wizard."

That's how Harry described her once, when he was drunk. The girl from the party, the one who took me home on the bus. After that she was always called Wizard.

Wizard had this white skin and these huge green eyes and this long, straight, blond hair. In the moonlight she was all a pale blue.

I tried to explain what my job was.

"It doesn't sound like you like it much," she'd said to me.

"What do you mean I don't like it? Of course I like it!"

"If you don't like it, you know, you should just quit. That's what I'd do."

And then I said: "Look, I ain't looking for nothing serious, you know. I don't think I'll be around for that long. I've gotta go somewhere, and I don't really know where that place is. I think you should find someone else."

Chuck called us all into a room. I was allowed to be in the room this time because I was no longer the desk junior. It was Titzy sat out on the desk.

The room was flooded with sunlight. Chuck always managed to get the best rooms. There was a long table and Chuck was at the head of it with the window behind him. I was standing next to JB. Across from us, Bill sat with Snoopy. The other traders were dotted around.

Chuck said that a couple of weeks previously he had gotten lost on the way home. Chuck said that that was not the first time he had gotten lost. But it was the first time his wife had found out, and she'd sent him to the hospital. Chuck had a tumor in his brain the size of a tennis ball.

"So I've got to take some time off from work."

I looked across at Billy and his eyes were already on me, and he kept looking at me for some time, and JB dug his elbow into my upper arm and I could feel the warmth of his skin through my sleeve.

"But it's OK. The doctors say they can remove it. So I shouldn't be off the desk that long."

With that, my eyes were brought back to the dark shadow of Chuck outlined by the window, and his thick glasses, and his broad smile, and his haircut that was the same as my father's.

And that was the last thing that Chuck ever did. I never saw Chuck again.

4

WIZARD'S BEDROOM WAS ACROSS THE GARDEN FROM MINE AND three floors up, and I could see her curtains move when I lay in my bed. We used to go to Greenwich Park and watch the sun go down across the skyscrapers, from the top of a hill, in the middle of the world.

"When you say you've gotta go somewhere, what do you mean?"

"I dunno. I just mean, I've gotta go somewhere. I can't stay in this place my whole life."

"Where will you go?"

"I don't know. Japan? Sail to Chile? Somewhere far away. Somewhere not here."

"This is about that job, isn't it? You hate that job. Why don't you just quit it?"

She didn't understand. Inside of me were twenty-nine million dollars, and each one screaming, "You can't quit."

We begged Billy to do it, me and Snoopy. We knew if it wasn't him, it was gonna be the Frog. We didn't think he'd actually do it though, but he did. Billy became the head of the desk.

I don't know why he said yes, Billy hated managing. He swore at the sales guys and the traders on the other desks, and when the phone used to ring and me or Titzy used to answer it, he'd slice his hand across his throat wildly as if to say, "Tell him I'm not here."

Nobody wanted to speak to the Slug when he rang. Bill wouldn't speak to him, JB wouldn't speak to him. Nobody was making any money, and nobody was expecting a bonus, so nobody gave a shit. Nobody except me of course, I gave a lot of shits.

So it was me who spoke to the Slug when he called. I'd say to him, "Billy's off desk boss, but listen, is there anything that I can do for you?"

And the Slug told me he wanted Citibank to become the biggest foreign exchange bank in the whole world by traded volume, so I started trading almost a trillion a day.

Harry was trying to get with Wizard's flatmate, but I don't think he was making any cut through. He started asking me to arrange outings for the four of us more and more, and before long we were out every other weekend.

Harry and me never really used to go out together, when we were kids. It was more of a football and PlayStation relationship. It had only been a couple years that he had even been allowed to drink legally, so I'd never really been out drinking with him. As a result, this was the first time in my life that I realized the guy was a fiend. He could drink more than my body weight. Lesser men would have been killed.

Once he'd filled himself to the nostrils with alcohol his left eye would go wonky and instead of talking to you he'd lean right through you and talk one foot behind you, his forehead pushing deep into yours, and then he'd lurch and paw at Wizard's flatmate on the dance floor and she'd push him away and grimace.

I didn't care. I was only for numbers. Trade volumes and PnL numbers and central bank auctions and seven hundred, eight hundred, nine hundred billion dollars of single-day loans every day. Kids from the internship or the grad scheme used to come and sit behind me in twos and threes and they'd say, "How did you figure that trade out, Gary? What's your entry level?"

And I'd say, "Who the fuck cares about my entry level? Entry levels are in the past man. All I care about is today and tomorrow, I don't keep numbers I don't need in my head."

Then the interns would get scared and they'd shuffle off for lunch.

Titzy said, "You shouldn't be so mean to the interns. They call you The Legend, you know."

I knew. I just didn't give a shit.

"Listen, you're a good trader. Maybe more than good, maybe you're great. But you're not as smart as you think you are. I see you pick out the highs and the lows, but it isn't from genius. It's out of instinct for you. For you it's a game."

I didn't say nothing. That didn't deserve a response.

"You've got a big problem Gary, and you've got to fix it."

Here we fucking go.

"What's that then Titzy?"

"You are, how we say, *Homo Homini Lupus*."

This guy, man.

"What the fuck is *Homo Homini Lupus*?"

"It's Latin, Gary. It means 'Man is Wolf to Man.'"

I'd had enough of this shit.

"Titzy, stand up, look around you."

I stood up and I spread my arms wide.

"Look at these guys. Every single one of these motherfuckers. Every single one of them's got their hand in my pocket. Every one of them is stealing my cash. So don't talk about homo homini lupus to me, son, we are both of us surrounded by wolves."

At the time, I felt that that was a compelling argument. I guess that means Titzy was probably right.

I did have a point though. Suddenly, I was one of the biggest traders in the whole world, and the world sure wanted a piece of the action. Kids would turn up on the trading floor patting me on the back, talking about what a great time we'd had back at LSE, and I wouldn't even recognize their faces. When the Slug came over, I had to have lunch with him one on one. It was disgusting.

More than anyone else though, the brokers went crazy. It was impossible to get them off of me. They were growing up my skin like a rash. One company hired some Z-list celebrity to cover my line in an attempt to win my business. When I googled him there was a picture of him on a beach somewhere, drinking a cocktail out of a pineapple with a straw. Another company hired a kid from my old high school just because he said that he knew me. Every single one of them was taking me out. Restaurants, football games, holidays. It started to make me so sick I brought in a "Nando's Only" rule. You wanna meet me? We go to Canary Wharf Nando's—you pay for you, I pay for me. But eventually I was eating too much Nando's so I had to can that as well, and then I didn't meet anyone at all.

The Bosses sent the Frog over to replace Bill. It was bound to happen eventually. Billy was still holding on to this idea that the economy was going to recover, and he was barely keeping his own head above water. Between him and JB they had managed to piss off just about everyone on the floor. Nobody was managing the desk and I still needed to get paid so I had pretty much taken over. They weren't going to let a twenty-four-year-old manage the desk forever.

For me, the Frog's simple presence was physically unbearable. He made me feel sick. I never forgot the way that guy fucked me over, and I itched when he spoke. The first thing he did was he hauled me into a meeting room and said he was thinking about taking JB's job. He didn't tell JB, he told me, which meant that I had to sit next to JB for a whole month without telling him he was about to be axed.

It wasn't just me the brokers were trying to take out, they were taking Harry out too. I don't know if they were using him to get to me or if they just liked him, but Harry and the brokers were a match made in heaven. You see, brokers mine you for vices. They feel you all over with their dirty hands till they notice a weak spot, then they cram their fat fingers inside of it and they fill you right up with whatever you need. Harry had a lot of weak spots. He was everywhere—pubs, restaurants, clubs, brasshouses, and he was taking drugs I'd never even heard of. I knew when he was on the meow meow because I'd wake up in the morning with forty-seven indecipherable text messages and he'd be standing, tweaking, in his room.

Should I have defended JB? Probably. Would he have defended me? 100% yes. But I was up over thirty-one million dollars by that point and

I was keen to get paid on them. I'd have probably let the Frog take my mum's job if he'd asked nice enough.

So the Frog took JB's job on the euro book. That made him my partner, which meant that I had to sit next to him every day. He sent JB to go sit in the corner and trade Aussie until he could find a good reason to fire him.

As soon as he had JB out the way, he came for me.

"Listen Gary, we've got a problem. You know, you're a great trader, and you're having a great year, but the desk's really struggling . . . And the bank's really struggling . . . I'm not sure we're going to be able to pay you."

I felt the blood rush to my hands and my head and I felt a bit dizzy. I wanted to spit on the floor.

I looked at the Frog. Everything he wore was sticking to him and falling off of him, as if his body was made of the wrong Lego pieces. The fucker was smiling.

Who the Fuck was this guy? Wide-mouth, shabby-haired, baggy-faced-looking motherfucker coming over here and telling me he can't pay me. Does he know what I've been through for this? No he doesn't, to him it's a game. This amount of money is more than my family made in twenty-five fucking generations and for this guy it's nothing but a game.

Well I'll tell you, it weren't a game to me.

There's a lesson in here somewhere. Something like, protect the people around you when they are getting fucked over, or else there'll be no one there when they come to fuck you.

Na, fuck that, I ain't here for lessons and I don't protect no one. I protect myself. I always have.

Harry was never home anymore, and when he was, he was dribbling on the floor.

I had the flat to myself in the evenings, me and Wizard, cooking pasta and watching movies. It was the first time I'd ever watched movies, to be honest.

I told her that some Fat-Frog-Looking-Motherfucker was trying to fuck me over and not pay me but I wasn't gonna take it, and she said to me,

"Those guys, they just don't understand you. No one understands you but me. Listen, I've bought some brown paint and I'm going to paint one of the walls in my living room. Do you want to come over and paint it together?"

I used to get called by headhunters all the time back then. Every week, a few times a week. Previously, I'd been cutting them off but I started to answer. I asked them to email me on my personal email address which, at the time, was "Thegazman1000@hotmail.com," and they'd ask me to spell it out for them and then they'd be like, "Thegazman1000@hotmail .com?"

And I'd be like, "Yeah, that's right, Thegazman1000@hotmail.com. Is there something wrong with Thegazman1000@hotmail.com?"

And then they'd say, "No no no, no no no. That's fine."

Then they'd get me interviews.

I interviewed with Barclays. I interviewed with Bank of America. I interviewed with Goldman. For the interview with Goldman I turned up in my hoodie and trainers and I told them that I definitely didn't want the job. They put me through to the second round after that.

At every interview I made sure to get a business card from the managing director. I'd take a photo of it, then bring it into the office, and leave it on the Frog's desk in the morning. He needed to know there'd be consequences if I didn't get my cut.

I asked the headhunters what a fair cut was. They said 7 percent. Seven percent of thirty-two million dollars. It had to be mine.

5

I CLOSED OUT THAT BIG US DOLLAR OIS TRADE I'D DONE THROUGH Harry earlier in the year. I made nine million dollars on that one single trade. I made sure to close it through Harry, with the Deutsche Bank trader, the exact trader with whom I'd put it on. Then I got Harry to calculate the PnL to see how much I'd made in that one trade from just that one guy. I'd like to tell you I did it because I wanted to give the kid something to look up to. The truth is probably that I knew he was singing my praises in every bar in the Square Mile, and I wanted to build up my reputation before bonus day.

Things were getting tetchy with Harry. He was fucked pretty much all of the time. He'd come home at midnight all wild-eyed and it'd wake me up and I'd say to him, "Bruv are you on cocaine?"

And he'd say, "Na, I don't take cocaine."

And I'd say, "Yes you fuckin do mate, you're on it right fuckin now. What would your mum say if she knew you were taking cocaine?"

And then he'd change the subject and he'd stumble and he'd say, "Mate, how much money are you gonna get paid this year?"

And I'd say, "I don't know mate, two million dollars?"

Then he'd laugh and poke me in the chest and say, "Why the fuck do you get paid so much money? I work ten times harder than you!"

And I'd say, "It ain't about how hard you work mate, never has been," and I'd go back to bed and leave him to fall over his shoes.

Things were getting tetchy in the office as well. Sitting next to the Frog was making me sick. He'd tell these horrible jokes and I'd have no choice but to laugh at them and every time I did I'd get this sharp twinge of acidic bile shoot up from my stomach and through my heart and into my throat and there was nothing to do with it but swallow it down. We were coming into December now and I was nearly up thirty-five million dollars. I couldn't let one single thing go wrong.

JB was still sitting over there in the corner where the Frog had sent him and there was something wrong with him. He'd lost a lot of weight and he was getting real skinny now, and when I looked round at him his mouth was moving slightly as if he was talking real quiet, and he started doing this twitchy kind of thing with his eye.

I weren't sleeping that much.

One night I got woken up at 1:30 a.m. There was some sort of commotion in the living room. I opened my door and what was I confronted with but Harry and a bunch of Clapham-looking dickheads that I hadn't never before seen snorting cocaine off my dining-room table.

Harry looked up at me gormlessly, beaming.

"You all right Gal!"

I was wearing nothing but a pair of underpants. The other brokers (because they had to be brokers) were less fucked than Harry and they kind of nodded awkwardly and looked round the room.

I stood in the doorway for a moment. Then I walked through them and into the kitchen. I took a glass out of the cabinet and I slammed it down on the counter, and I filled it up with milk. I took it back into the center of the living room, drinking it, slowly, in my underpants, and I stood there, right in the middle of all of them, staring each of those cunts in the face, one by one.

They started looking around for their jackets and putting their shoes on and saying things like,

"Anyway Harry mate, I think I gotta go."

And Harry was saying, "Oh don't go mate, we only just started!"

But within a minute they had all disappeared, and I was going back to bed, and Harry was shouting after me, "Why you always got to ruin my fun!?"

.   .   .

The Frog was away the next day, so I was covering the whole euro book by myself. I was pissed and I weren't talking to no one, not even Titzy. Just sitting there and doing my job.

About 2 p.m. a message from the IB chat dinged up on my screen. It said, "Met your bird last night mate. She's pretty fit mate. Well done."

The name next to it was "Quentin Benting."

I didn't know no stupid fucks called Quentin Benting.

I must have been staring daggers into the screen or something because JB walked past and he noticed and he said, "Fucking hell mate. What's wrong?"

I didn't say nothing, I just pointed to the message on the screen and JB squinted his old eyes and he looked at it and he said, "Fuuuuuuuuck-ing hell mate! Who the fuck's Quentin Benting?"

I was shaking my head, "I don't fucking know mate," and I opened the message. It showed his company in brackets in big capital letters after his name: (ICAP PLC).

Neither of us said anything for a moment. We just stood side by side with our hands on our chins and we thought about what should be done. Then JB leaned over and pressed my switch down to ICAP: "All business from Citibank to ICAP is off, permanently. If you wanna know why, ask Quentin Benting."

Then he turned round and announced to the desk: "Everyone go down your ICAP lines and tell them no business from Citi. If they wanna know why, tell 'em ask Quentin Benting."

Then he reached his hands to his mouth and shouted out loud across the floor,

"ALL LINES ARE OFF FROM CITI TO ICAP. IF ANYONE WANTS TO KNOW WHY, TELL THEM TO ASK QUENTIN BENTING."

IB chat requests were already cascading down the side of my screen. The dings were bouncing in before the last one could finish. JB patted me a few times on the back of the neck, and then he went off to the bathroom and snorted cocaine.

ICAP was a big broking company. It was one of the two biggest broking companies in London. They had brokers in every single prod-uct, meaning every single trader on the whole floor had at least one

ICAP broker. At that exact moment, every single one of those fat bastards was putting down their cheeseburgers in a wild apoplexy and marching across the broking floor to the seat of one Quentin Benting, a seat that sat immediately next to a very young, very hungover, and very nervous Harry Sambhi.

I messaged Wizard. Apparently she had been out with her flatmate when Harry and a bunch of drunk, coked-up brokers had turned up in the bar. The girls tried to leave, but since the girls and Harry all lived in the same development the guys kind of followed them home, and they all ended up in my flat. The girls didn't stick around long, so, when I woke up, all I saw was a bunch of coked-up fat lads. I guess one of them must have been Quentin Benting.

When I got home, Harry was disconsolate. He was pacing the flat with his oversized shoes on, sobbing hoarsely with his head in his hands.

"What the fuck are you doing? What the fuck are you doing!? We're gonna get fired! We're both gonna get fired!!"

"What the fuck do you mean what am I doing, what the fuck are you doing!? Who the fuck's this fucking cunt Quentin Benting? And it wasn't me anyway it was fucking JB!"

"Yeah but you can fucking stop it. Fucking stop it, you can stop it! Put the lines back in, open them up!"

"Why the fuck should I put the fucking lines back in!? That fucking dickhead's gotta learn a fucking lesson and so should you mate. What the fuck are you doing!?"

"What do you mean what am I doing? I didn't do anything! What the fuck have I done?"

"Listen you fucking idiot," and I was right into his face now, "I'm fucking one month away from being a fucking multimillionaire mate. And I can't afford to make no fucking mistakes and what the fuck are you doing? You are bringing four fat fucking cunts, who are in the fucking MARKET, into my fucking HOUSE at one fucking a.m. on a fucking worknight, and you are snorting cocaine off of my fucking placemats that's what the fuck you are doing. Are you fucking stupid or what!?"

Harry didn't say nothing. We just stood there with our noses touching.

"What would your mum think? What would your mum think if she knew what you were doing? Don't think I don't know what you're doing because I fucking know. I know where you go at nights, I know what you do. What would she think? What would she think if she could see you now and if she could see me now? Would she be proud of us? If she knew how you lived?"

Harry pushed me hard in the chest and it was all I could do just to stay on my feet.

"Don't talk about my fucking mum you're not my fucking dad mate! It's not your fucking job to look after me I look after myself!"

"Oh yeah and how is that going? How the fuck are you doing? Where the fuck is your dad? Who the fuck is looking after you? Who cooks your fucking dinners? Who pays your fucking bills? Who the fuck got you your fucking job and who the fuck takes you to work when you're too fucked to get yourself out of bed? That's fucking right I fucking do. I'm the one who fucking looks after you and I'm the one who's making this money and all you're doing is fucking it up!"

"Yeah and why though Gary? Why Gary? Why? Why the fuck are you making this money Gary, you never fucking spend it! You never fucking enjoy it! You never fucking go anywhere, you never fucking do any-thing, you never even talk to your fucking mum! When was the last time we went fucking Orient with your dad mate? Fucking never! We never fucking go mate, we never do anything! You never even fucking talk to your friends! What the fuck are you doing? What the fuck is it all for? You talk about Ilford like it fucking matters to you, like it fucking means something like you're doing it for them. You never even fucking GO to fucking Ilford! When was the last time you've been? You never talk to anyone from Ilford, you never talk to anyone at all! What the fuck is it for Gary? What the fuck is it for?"

There was nothing to say to that, so I left him. I walked out the flat and I went to the gym. When I came back he was passed out on the sofa, and his dribble had pooled on the floor.

The next day I arranged a meeting on the quayside. Me, Quentin Bent-ing, his boss. I arranged it with the boss, not with Quentin. I didn't want to talk with that cock.

Quentin was in his mid-thirties. His boss was in his forties. They knew, I know that they knew. They knew about the kid's situation, that he didn't have no family, they knew they should have taken better care.

I told them. I told them that I'd promised his mum I'd look after him and I'd be fucked if I was gonna let those two fat fuckers wash his life down a drainhole of pussy and drugs. I asked them what they thought of themselves, fucking grown men and what they'd done with a twenty-year-old kid.

They promised me they'd take better care of him. I don't know if they ever did. I walked back onto the floor and I shouted: "LINES ARE BACK ON WITH ICAP."

6

THEN IT WAS BONUS DAY.

Of the day itself, I remember only numbers. My PnL was just over thirty-five million dollars. The fair rate for my work was 7 percent. That is pretty much it. I don't remember the room. I don't remember receiving the bonus. I don't remember the Frog's ugly face.

I remember that I knew exactly, to the dollar, the amount that I wanted. I don't remember now what that number was, but it was 7 percent of just over thirty-five million dollars, so it must have been something like 2.45 million dollars.

As soon as the number turned over, I forgot it. It was another dead number from the past. I don't keep numbers I don't need in my head. Thirty-five times nought point zero seven. That was what I got. That was what I deserved.

Everyone was happy.

Job done.

When I cycled home that evening, in the dark and the cold and the white breath of an East London January night, I cut through Chrisp Street Market, like I always did. There's a huge mural there, it's my favorite graffiti. An enormous, six-story Chihuahua, up on its hind legs, with its tongue out, and there, at the bottom, is a halal fried chicken shop. I looked at the fried chicken shop, sweating and glowing red in the darkness, and there, tucked down the side of it, was an old gray man who was tucking a mattress cover around the edges of a large, beaten-up mattress. The mattress cover was luminescent. It was a gleaming, sparkling white, or rather a bright blue in the moonlight. It simply must have been fresh out the packet. I wondered how such an old, gray man, tucked down an alleyway beside a fried chicken shop could possibly have gotten such a brand new, sparkling white mattress cover. And then, suddenly, for the first time in twenty-five years in the city, when I breathed in, I felt the cold air of London come into me, come inside of me, and it filled up my lungs, and it burnt them, and I just couldn't understand why.

When I got home, I was doing my investments, in a small office area I had in the corner of my living room. It was a lot of money: I had to invest it.

Wizard came round. I looked at her as she came in and I noticed that when she saw me her face caught a pale shadow of worry. I turned back to my screen. She came over and she stroked my hair.

"How was it? Are you happy?"

"It was good. It was great. It was what I deserved."

"You don't seem very happy."

"Well, you know, it's a lot of money, I've got to invest it. It's stressful."

Wizard paused then for only a moment. Her hand was still resting on my hair.

"You know, if I'd made as much money as you just have, the last thing I'd be doing is sitting down, all alone, in the corner of my living room stressing out."

As soon as she said that, I knew she was right, and I really fucking hated her for that.

The next day, in the office, it was all the same.

Same people, same noises, same pink and white shirts.

Same economy, same fucking trade.

I'd cleaned the book out by the end of the year, but it was a new year now, so I needed a new trade.

No, actually, I didn't need a new trade. I didn't need a new trade because nothing had changed.

Same inequality, still growing and growing, same families losing the same homes. Same inability to spend. Same fucking nothing. No growth, no fucking improvement. I picked up my phone and I put it back on, the disaster trade second year running.

You know what? It made me a ton.

. . .

Part of my grand thesis about the economy had been that the rich would get richer and richer and everyone else would get poorer and poorer and that would mean that interest rates would stay zero forever because there would never be enough spending power in the economy to ever drive prices seriously up.

But that didn't refer to *all* prices. The reason prices struggle to rise when inequality rises is because the rich spend a way lower proportion of their income on goods and services than ordinary people. But the flip of that is that they spend way way *more* on assets. The rich were accumulating money at an ever-increasing pace, and would also now have access to super-low interest rate loans. Those two things were inevitably going to combine to push asset prices up massively, including stock prices and house prices.

That worried me, because I had just been given a shit ton of money, and I didn't have a house, so I went and viewed some fancy apartment on some fancy marina just down the road from the office and I bid 5 percent through the asking price and I went and bought it just like that.

I took Harry down to see it one night and we were standing on the balcony looking out at the boats, and he was smoking and I wasn't and I said to him, "I'm buying this place, Harry. You know what that means, right?"

And he said to me, "Yeah man, it's gonna be great! We're gonna have a great time! It's so big, I can't wait!"

And I said to him, "No, Harry, I'm buying this place. Me. Not you. I'm buying this place and you're gonna go home."

I still remember how the moon looked in his eyes.

I no longer gave one single shit in the office. I didn't talk to no one, I barely even talked to Titzy. Titzy and my brokers did the bare minimum trading for me that was needed and the whole thing just poured money in. All I did was sit there with my headphones in, reading the paper. By the end of March I was up another nine million dollars.

The Frog never once asked me how I was making so much money. Neither did the Slug. I think they preferred not to know, just in case.

But I wasn't laughing at the Frog's jokes anymore. In fact, I'd stopped talking to him at all unless it was absolutely necessary, so he hauled me into an office and he said to me, "We're worried about you Gary. We're worried you might not be a team player. We want you to be one of us."

I hadn't really been listening, but that last bit caught my attention so I asked him, "What do you mean, 'one of us'?"

The Frog dropped his oblong head and leaned it into me conspiratorially and he said, "Listen Gary, you're a great trader, you're super smart, you've got a bright future. You could be like us, you could be in management. But, I don't know . . . There is some sort of problem. We don't really know what you want."

"What do you mean, what I want?"

"Well . . . You don't seem to be motivated by money and . . . I'm not sure I really understand you. Me, and the rest of senior management . . . We want to know . . . What do you want?"

I was looking at the guy and obviously I was thinking, "Well, it would be nice for you to stop being such an unbearable prick."

But I was tired. I was real, real tired. And even though I wasn't laughing at the jokes anymore I was still getting that acidic pain in my chest, and it was really bad right at that moment, so I just kneaded my heart hard with my fist and I said to him, "Frog, I just want to be more of a team player. I want to be a team player and make more for the bank."

A bunch of big-shot traders from other banks wanted to meet me, so they got Billy's brokers to ask him if he would bring me out. I wasn't going out much, at that point in my life, but it was Billy, so I went.

It was a cavernous room, low and dark, lit with candles, and a long straight table had been set up, all laden with food, stretching out lengthwise across the back of the room.

Traders lined up on both sides of the table, and when Bill and I walked in they were already eating. I could see the backs of the traders facing away from us, hunched over and bulging through their white shirts as they lent over and into their food.

An enormous man stood up and reached over the table, the two brokers opposite him parting like the Red Sea as he lent me his hand.

"Carlo Lengua, Senior Sterling trader, Credit Suisse."

"Gary, Gary Stevenson," I told him, and Bill said nothing and we went to our chairs.

Our seats were on the end, on the right side, and from there I could see the whole table and the two lines of men.

What I remember most about them was their physicality. Muscle and fat in perfect harmony, in abundance, marbled together as in Japanese cows. And mirroring the abundance of their bodies, the abundance of the table, plate upon plate of meat, ever-flowing wine topped up by invisible waiters.

It became clear very quickly that this was Carlo's party. Carlo sat at the center of the table and spoke loudly, picking men at intervals and bringing them into the conversation. He ate and he drank as he spoke and held court, and there was nothing to do but behold. Billy went to the bar and he bought us two beers.

Carlo had made a lot of money. A *lot* of money. That dripped from all that was said and was done. He wanted to be surrounded by the best traders, all, in the world, and he went round and he spoke of each one of us, in turn.

He knew about me, and he knew about Billy. Even though I had no idea who he was. He spoke of how great we were, as traders, quite loudly since we were all the way down the end of the table. Billy and I nodded and we held up our beers.

Billy drank quickly. Very quickly. Within less than an hour he was gone and he stood up and he Scousely slurred something, and I quickly stood up and said something more polite and more comprehensible than he had said and then I helped him get to the front door.

"FOKKKIN . . . Carl . . . Fokkin . . . CARL LENGUA!!"

I'd called Bill's taxi driver from Bill's phone, and Bill had chosen to use our waiting time to point wildly and dance. He grabbed me by both sides of my shirt collar and decided to repeat once more, for emphasis, in my face.

"FUCKIN CARL LENGUA! FUCK HIM! FUCK FUCKIN CARL LENGUA! HE LOOKS LIKE A FUCKING FAT ROMAN EMPEROR! FUCK THAT FUCKING . . . FUCKin . . . Dickhead . . . Fuckin . . . Cunt?"

He had gotten distracted halfway through that last sentence because he had seen a fox scuffling away in the darkness, and that had unfortunately compromised somewhat the emphasis of his swearing. He was still holding my collar though, so I slapped him a little and said, "Bill!"

And that managed to get him back.

"Listen. Gal. If you ever, fuckin ever. End up like that Fat Roman Cunt. I will fucking, fucking kill you myself. With these hands!"

And then he pulled his two little hobbit dukes away from my collar and he waved them about wildly and I thought, "Well, I'd better be careful then," and then Bill's taxi driver finally turned up and I roly-polyed him head first into the back of the taxi and he rumbled off to piss on the Bank of England.

I went back downstairs so we could eat a fuck-ton of food and talk about how great we all were.

Maybe that sounds terrible to you. Maybe that sounds disgusting. But it wasn't really that disgusting. By then, I didn't get disgusted by anything, anymore. By then, it was just fucking boring. Boring, boring, boring, boring, boring. I wished that Billy were still there. I wanted to go home to Wizard.

Eventually it got to 10 p.m. and I felt like that was an acceptable time to leave.

"Oh, DON'T go!" screamed Carl. He was nicely reddened and fattened by now, ready to be removed from the spit.

"I'm sorry Carl. I've really got to go. Work in the morning, you know?"

Carl was not happy with that, and he extricated himself from the table, and he lurched to me across piles of food, and before long I was enmeshed in his deep wagyu beef and I remember being surprised about how warm and how soft he all was.

"Don't go Gary." I could feel his breath, wet, on my ear.

"Listen, I wasn't going to tell you this," quietly, intimately now, "but me and some of the lads are going out after this. We are going to Dover Street Wine Bar. Have you been to Dover Street Wine Bar?"

I hadn't.

"Listen. It's bloody brilliant. You've got to come. Jam full of fit birds. Eight out of tens, eight *and a half* out of tens."

And then he stopped me and he flipped me so that we were now facing one another and he added, with a fatherly air of correction, while looking unhesitatingly into my eyes,

"You know, I'm talking about a *serious* one-to-ten scale here."

I didn't go.

I took the train straight home to Bow. And on the walk home from the station, in the middle of the night, I grabbed hold of the wing mirror of a car, and I ripped it right off, for absolutely no reason at all.

7

I TOLD HARRY WE COULD HAVE ONE FINAL BLOW-OUT PARTY ON
our last night together in the flat. He was delighted and he invited
everyone—kids from home, kids from the City. He got a little over-
excited and invited the girls who worked at the Pret A Manger down the
street.

Titzy came, some other kids from Citi came, a couple others who
said they were from Citi but to be honest I didn't know their names.
Asad from Ilford came. Jalpesh and Aiden and Mashfique all came.
Wizard's little sister came down all the way from Norwich. My older
brother came and spent the whole evening in the kitchen drinking tea.
We opened all the doors and windows and we blasted music into the
late hours and we got a ton of complaints but I didn't care because I'd
already moved all my stuff out and we were gonna be gone the next
day.

There was a moment there, in the middle of that party, when it all
seemed all right, when it all seemed OK. When people from home, and
people from work were all talking and drinking and it all just seemed
normal. Asad's avant-garde Ukrainian fashion student friends were dancing and taking drugs and I was leaning out over the balcony with Wizard in the cold night and looking up at the tall red-brick cylinders of the
two-hundred-year-old matchstick factory chimneys and wondering if
we'd ever be there, together, again.

But I could see it though, deep in the late-night, just before it happened. I could see his eyes going and his words start to stumble and I
could see his feet losing their grip on the floor. I knew I was going to lose
him. I knew he was gone, to be honest. I knew he was gone. He held up

his whisky bottle high in the air and then the both of them down to the ground. Bottle and boy crashing down to the floor and the brown shards of glass in his hand.

And the blood on the carpet, and it was Wizard who went to him, not me, and him pawing and lurching all over her as she tried to wrap his hand in a kitchen towel. And when she'd done just enough to stop the bleeding, I grabbed her hand and I went and grabbed her sister's hand and I said, "Come on. Let's get the fuck out of here."

And I didn't speak to Harry for eight years.

I moved into the new flat and ripped everything out. Walls, floors, lights, toilets, kitchen sinks. I cleaned it all out till there was nothing there left, just a clean gray-white, concrete-plaster box.

Gray concrete floors, white plaster walls.

After that, I was supposed to call builders, get all new things. New kitchens, new floors.

But I didn't. I don't know why. I couldn't.

I put a TV down there on the bare concrete of the floor, and a mattress in the bedroom as well. And every day I'd wake up at 5:30 a.m., and then I'd read five hundred emails, right there, on the floor.

One day Wizard came round and said, "What are you doing!? You can't live like this!"

And I laughed and said, "Looks like I can."

So she opened up her laptop and went onto some website called "Freecycle," and she somehow arranged for some old, broken, tatty, red corduroy sofa to get delivered into my living room, opposite the TV, and I'd come home from work every day at 5:30 p.m. and pass out straight onto it, and I'd wake up every day in the middle of the night at one or two in the morning, and the curtains would all be wide open, and the moonlight would be flooding into the wide empty room, and she'd be there, with me, curled up into a little ball next to me on that tatty red sofa, and I'd stroke her hair and wake her up and I'd take her to bed.

· · ·

HR used to get me to do all kinds of shit. Giving speeches. Talking to new graduates. Fuck knows why, maybe they think I'm approachable.

One time, they arranged for a big group of local schoolkids from the area to come into the building, and they asked me if I could take them up to the top floor and give them a speech.

Of course I said "Sure, why not." That's the kind of shit guys like me do.

It was only a couple of days before the event that I realized it coincided with a European Central Bank meeting.

European Central Bank meetings are probably the biggest things that happen for a euro STIRT trader. You probably shouldn't spend them telling local schoolkids about your life. But, you know, fuck it. I'd already promised.

To be honest, I probably would have gotten away with it, but as you know euro trading on the STIRT desk was a two-man job, me and the Frog, so when I was on my way to provide the schoolchildren of Poplar with a positive male role model, the Frog was loudly screaming, "WHERE THE FUCK IS GARY?" across the trading floor—an exclamation which soon found its way to my phone in a text.

I replied to the Frog in the politest way I could think: "I'm really sorry, I promised HR that I would provide support for local underprivileged school kids today."

To which the Frog responded himself rather impolitely, "GET THE FUCK BACK TO THE DESK!!!"

Which was both rude *and* insensitive to the high levels of social deprivation that were manifest in the locality of our workplace, but was also a relatively clear instruction, so it left me with little choice but to abandon my civic responsibilities and turn round and head back to the floor.

Nothing fucking happened during the fucking ECB meeting, so I spent it writing the following apology email to HR:

Dear *name omitted*

Please accept my apologies for my inability to attend, at short notice, the event that you had kindly arranged.

This happened because my manager *real name omitted* (cc'd) has decided that talking to local, underprivileged schoolchildren is not a valid use of my energy nor time.

All the best,
Kind Regards,
Gary

The Frog was shouting. Shouting and screaming. All up and down and wailing and arching and leaning and pacing and waving his arms.

I wasn't really listening. Every now and again I would give him a nice thoughtful look, and a nod. Just to be respectful, you know, to let him know I was with him. But really, I didn't give a shit.

He'd hauled me off into a little box room to shout at me and it was just like I was back at school.

I used to get shouted at a lot at school. Being late, not doing my homework, talking back to teachers. Selling drugs, also, although that only happened the once.

The reason I used to be late so much was that I used to have to do my paper round and then sprint for one and a half miles to try to get to school on time, and the reason that I didn't do a lot of my homework was, well, to be honest because I never really had a safe place to do it.

But, you know, they didn't really give a shit about stuff like that, did they, so I used to just let them shout. And I'd look up at them compassionately sometimes, and I'd nod, and I'd think, well, you know, maybe it's good for them. Maybe they're letting something out.

But mostly I'd sit, with my hands on my chin and my elbows on my knees, looking down at the floor, and I'd just let them shout till they ran out of shouting, just like I was doing right then, in that office, with the Frog.

And he was shouting and screaming and wailing, and there I was with my gaze to the floor.

And that's when I noticed something for the first time.

That I also had holes in my shoes.

There, at the outside corners of my Onitsuka Tigers, perfectly symmetrically, exactly where my two little toes were, were two torn holes, about two centimeters wide each, and there, flashing through them, two bright screams of color, my two little toes, in my red Leyton Orient socks.

Fuck man! How long have I had these trainers? Since the first year of university. Fuck man! How long have these holes been there? Fuck man . . . I didn't even know.

Then I looked up and I remembered the Frog was still shouting, and I looked him in the eyes and I said: "Boss, I don't think I can do it anymore . . . Boss, I think I need to quit."

And that hit the Frog sharply, like a phone to the head, and the suddenness of that made me laugh.

"What did you say?"

8

I NEVER THOUGHT THAT I'D SEE HIM AGAIN, BUT THERE THE MAN was.

Big fucking head. Big fucking shoulders. Big fucking fingers on big fucking hands.

He stood, as he always stood, backlit by the sun, though the window was more distant now. Caleb Zucman.

I hadn't seen him come in or walk round to the desk because, as was my wont at that time in my life, I had been trading with my hood up and my earphones in. Titzy, who was young and impressionable, had adopted the earphones, but had not felt quite confident enough for the hood, so he had noticed when JB, the Frog, Snoopy and Billy all stood up and mobbed the man on the end of the desk.

He tugged at my sleeve, and I pulled out an earbud and he said to me, "Hey! Who's that guy?"

It was then that I turned and I saw them. An orgy of back pats at the end of the desk. It had been three years since I saw the man last. He looked the same, just a little bit smaller, in the same way that your grandad does after you've had a growth spurt.

All the traders had left their seats and gone to him, except Titzy, who'd never met him before, and me.

I didn't stand up though. I turned my chair and I looked at him. The acid was riddling my heart.

I needed to ask the man, "Why?"

You can't just ask a man, "Why did you come back?"

It's disrespectful.

To do so would be to imply that the venture upon which the man departed had been a failure. You don't do such a thing to a man such as Caleb. You must artfully disguise your question.

Likewise, Caleb, who had himself always been a master of the art of conversation, recognized the impropriety of asking me, now Citibank's most profitable trader, directly why it was that I, only a week earlier, had told the Frog that I wanted to quit trading, and then, when pressed on my reason for such a weighty decision, had pointed to the holes in my shoes (a justification rather generally considered somewhat unsatisfactory) before rapidly de-escalating my demands from my own summary dismissal to merely a long-term sabbatical, a request which was still formally under consideration.

For these reasons, as Caleb, JB and Billy and I sat on the veranda of a Japanese restaurant a few hours later on that warm, summer day, drinking many drinks deep into the late evening, and looking out at the moon rising over the Thames, the truest questions in the hearts of all four of us men were never to be heard by the air.

Would you believe that the Japanese drink rice wine from a wooden box? They really do. They place a glass inside of a square wooden box, and then they slowly fill your glass with rice wine until it is full to the very brim. At that point, they do not stop pouring. They continue to pour and the rice wine overflows and it flows down the side of the glass and begins to fill up the wooden box. They continue to pour into the glass until both the glass and the wooden box are both full. Only then do they stop. I've always liked it. I suppose it's supposed to represent an overabundance of hospitality, or something. But, for me, who first witnessed the act on that evening, the practice has always reminded me of the questions that do not overflow from men's hearts.

The three men who wanted to know why Caleb was back, and the four who wanted to know why I was leaving, never gave voice to those thoughts. Instead we spoke of Caleb's life in California, and of the trading heroics of Billy and I; of JB's newborn child and the Frog's dastardly overthrowing of the man and, of course, JB's future revenge.

We didn't speak, though, of his failing marriage or the cocaine that at that moment surged through his veins. We didn't speak of the changes in our faces, of how both JB and I had grown gaunt. We didn't speak of the glimmer that was missing from Caleb's eyes, or of how that absence reminded me of a younger, happier me.

On that warm night, in the sparkling lights of the city that reflected to us from the Thames, those things were not ours. We basked in our glories, not our failures. We left those to sink into the river, unheard.

But still, though, the pain in my heart.

We all knew, then, that Caleb would take me. It was obvious then that that's what he would do. Wherever he went—Citi, or Deutsche, or anywhere—he would take me. That was what he'd come back for. He was there to take me from the Frog.

But I couldn't go, not without asking, and so I waited for my time.

Then suddenly there was the opportunity, when JB and Billy were both deeply embezzled, in their drinks and in one another's eyes, and I pressed my face into Caleb's and I asked him.

"Tell me, what was life in California really like?"

And it was just the two of us for a moment, and he told me, "It was beautiful, Gary. We had this huge, beautiful house, the front all held up by huge columns. We had the thing specially made, out in the countryside. And from the inside it opened up, outwards, into this huge, beautiful garden that spread for miles out the back, far deep into these huge trees. You don't get trees like that over here. And the kids would play together in the garden all day out into the late evening and Florence would cook dinner for the four of us and I'd go out there and I'd call them in. It was beautiful, warm all year round."

There was a pause, and, for an instant, he faltered. And I met those huge eyes and that huge smile, and I caught them and held them and I didn't back down.

"But there was a problem. The guys who built the house, you know . . . I'm not sure they were the best guys. They were friends of my wife's family, you know? There were a few little things . . . With the design . . . Of that place . . . I'm not sure, you know? I think they weren't great . . ."

Another pause, and he looked away, and I pressed him for more.

"Like what Caleb? What do you mean?"

"Well, I mean, for example . . . The thermostat. They put the thermostat too close to the fire. When you put the fire on, in winter, the thermostat would trip. And the heating would go off upstairs, and it would get cold."

Keep the eyes. Don't let them evade you.

"We got them to come back. And to move the thermostat. But the problem, it kept coming back. No matter where we put the thermostat, we couldn't get it right."

Caleb kept talking then, but I wasn't listening. All I saw then was a vision. A huge, beautiful house, a huge, beautiful kitchen. Opening out to a beautiful garden. Two beautiful, blonde-headed boys, full of life, play around as the golden sun sets over them, casting them into the shadows of huge, alien trees. The beautiful mother heads into the garden.

"Timothy! Jacob! Dinner's ready! Come on in!"

And there, adjacent to the huge room of the kitchen, a huge dining table, and beyond it, a huge living room.

And in the center of that living room, beneath a shimmering chandelier, a huge luxury armchair, and in it a huge, wealthy, large-headed man.

And his eyes fix on something small, there, on the wall. Above the fireplace, up, to the left.

He watches and he watches and he watches, like a wolf. Then one fat finger twitches, on the arm of the chair.

The thermostat.

And I knew then why Caleb came back to the trading floor.

He came because he had to be here.

"I want to tell you something."

The sharpness of my sudden exclamation alerted JB and Billy, and brought them back into our space.

"Do you remember when I told you that I left my grammar school because I thought it would give me a better chance to get into LSE?"

The three men nodded.

"It was a lie, it never happened. I left because I got expelled. I got expelled for selling drugs."

Slowly, slowly, JB and Caleb started to smile. And their faces lit up, with a fire.

But Billy wasn't smiling, he was looking deep into me, and when I looked into his eyes I could see he was scared.

9

WHEN I WAS A LITTLE KID, I MEAN REALLY LITTLE, I HAD A FRIEND ON the street. His name was Jamie Silverman.

Jamie was the best at everything—football, throwing, climbing, cycling, spitting. He could almost piss over the street's far wall into the recycling center. He was good at school stuff too, always getting the best grades. Everyone loved him, and because my older brother was kind of weird and he used to get picked on, and I was too small and scrawny and young to protect him, Jamie used to protect the both of us. I looked up to him a lot, growing up.

As we got older, whenever new stuff came in—a new sport or a new competition, a new school subject or a new trend, like rollerskating—Jamie always had to be the best at it, and, effortlessly, he always was. Nothing was too hard for him. He'd get into the regional teams for school stuff and sports stuff, especially throwing, and he never even seemed to try hard.

When girls became a thing, he was the best at girls, when drugs became a thing, he was the best at drugs.

He never left me out either, always brought me along, always taught me to do what he did.

When I got expelled from school, at sixteen, for drugs, I stopped doing them, forever. Jamie didn't. He just did more, and more and more and more. That kid was really good at drugs. Really was.

Came a point I couldn't see him no more. He was losing weight more by the day. Every time I saw him he was taller and skinnier than the last time, smoking up in some trainyard, on somebody's roof.

Time come I just thought, I ain't gonna see that kid no more. I loved him of course, but I just didn't like to see him. Every time I did, hurt my heart.

Years later, kid got emphysema, which is when your lungs break down from smoking too much, and I went to see him in the hospital and I brought him grapes and fucking flowers and the guy looked like a skeleton and had tubes in his nose.

Still wanted to laugh about the old times though. Still does, every time I see him. As if nothing ain't changed.

All I could think when I saw him there, skinny as fuck in the hospital, all tubes and all yellow, was that he used to be the best thrower in the whole fucking borough.

Fucking waste.

10

THE FROG SAT ME DOWN IN THE ROOM.

"The Slug says you can't have the sabbatical."

Don't reply. Just nod.

"He said the last time he gave someone a sabbatical they never came back. He doesn't want that to happen with you."

Nod again.

"But there's another option. Caleb's coming back. He's going to be the Head of STIRT in Tokyo. He wants to have you over there."

One more nod.

"Well, what do you think?"

Sigh deeply. Think for a little.

"To be honest, Frog, I don't think it's a good idea. I'm fucked. I can't do it anymore."

Now it was the Frog's turn to sigh. He looked down and pretended to think for himself, and while he was doing it he was cracking his knuckles. Then, after a while, he looked back up at me, with a grimace bigger than his ugly face.

"You don't understand, Gary. You have to go."

OK.

No problem.

So it goes.

I took my parents out to a fancy Japanese restaurant in the City to let them know I'd be moving to Japan.

They both dressed as if they were going to church and shuffled around endlessly in the stool-like high chairs.

"Are you going to be OK out there?"

That was my mum.

"Of course I will. I'm always OK."

They couldn't seem to destarch themselves the whole time, and I guessed it was because they didn't know how to use chopsticks.

"It's all right," I told them, "you're allowed to eat sushi with your hands."

I picked one up and I popped it into my mouth to show them that it was allowed. But my dad was doing something weird with the soy sauce bottle so he didn't catch it.

I called the waiter over and asked for two forks. But it didn't seem to help.

It was only a couple weeks before it was my time to leave, and the plan was to tell Wizard that we needed to break up.

It was deep in the blue of the night when I chose to speak about it, and we were both in bed.

"Hey . . . You know I'm going to Japan, right?"

"Yeah, of course, I know you're going."

She was lying in bed and I was sitting up over her. And all the curtains were open and the room was totally flooded with blue. Her words hung in the air and it was like I could see them and I was trying to catch them. And I remembered that there was something that I was supposed to be saying, something that I was supposed to be *doing*, but I couldn't for the life of me remember what on earth it could possibly have been, and she stepped in and she filled up the space.

"You know I'm going to go as well, don't you? You know that I'll go to Japan?"

And I heard that from another room, as if from a dream, and it awoke me, and I looked down at her and what I thought was,

"You know I don't deserve you. You should go find somebody else."

But what I said was,

"I think that . . . I need . . . you to come."

And I don't know why I said that, because it hadn't been what I had planned. I guess I said it because it was true.

.   .   .

My last day ever on the Citibank London trading floor was in late September, 2012. Pack your bag. Pat a few backs. It was JB that went down the hoot and shouted out, "Gary Stevenson is leaving the building!" as I walked off the desk.

I knew they were all standing up and cheering and clapping as I walked out the room. I could hear them, and I could see them all in my peripheral vision, down every aisle, both sides. White shirt, white shirt, pink shirt, blue.

But I didn't turn and look, I just walked out the door.

Part Five

東京
GOING
DOWN

1

TOKYO IS A WONDERFUL PLACE TO BE DEPRESSED. ESPECIALLY IN the autumn.

The banks congregate in an area of the city that is called "Marunou-chi," which means "inside the circle," and that name derives from the fact that the area, at some point, fell within the confines of the outer moat of the Emperor's palace, although where that moat is now, I have no idea. I was never able to find it.

For a long time, it was illegal to build high buildings in Marunouchi, because they would be able to overlook the palace, and, I don't know, someone could try to shoot the Emperor with a crossbow or something. But eventually, in the 1980s, the land value of the area became so high that exceptions were made, and, by the time I arrived there, the whole area was fifty floors high. Tradition and the Emperor are important, of course, but then, so is money, I guess.

If I left the Citi office building, the dark gray and metal Shin-Marubiru, and walked west, I could enter the Outer Garden of the palace itself, "Koukyogaien." This garden is nothing but an enormous and perfectly manicured field, split into three sections by two busy roads, and planted with nothing but a million unique but identical trees, each perfectly spaced at intervals of seven or eight meters.

Each tree is small, not too much taller than the height of a man, and intricate, of a type which I have never seen in England. When I first walked in the garden, I assumed they were bonsai trees, but I later learned that bonsai is actually a kind of Japanese artform of tiny-tree growing, and not in fact a type of tree at all, so I suppose they must be some other kind of Japanese tree.

If you walk through the gardens, for ten minutes or so, past the million unique, identical trees, you can reach an old, stone bridge, which crosses the inner moat and leads to the inner part of the Imperial Palace complex. There is a gate there, that is always closed, and you cannot go in.

I would often go there, and I would sit down, on a little step on the ground in the gravel, and I'd turn around and I'd watch Marunouchi. From there, you get a little bit of perspective. You can see the huge block of skyscrapers surging up into the blue sky of Tokyo, and, in the foreground, the green field and trees of the Koukyogaien.

Marunouchi is not like Canary Wharf. Canary Wharf doesn't have so many skyscrapers, and I saw them rise one at a time. To me, they exist as individuals, especially those central three that I watched go up as a child—the Citibank Tower, the HSBC Tower, and that middle one, the pyramid one. In Marunouchi there are so many skyscrapers that the whole place is more skyscraper than not skyscraper. There must have been at least thirty, or forty, or fifty, all forty stories or more, and the whole place rises as one, as a block. Even though the weather in Tokyo varies hugely from summer to winter, the sky in my memory is always warm, and always blue. Perhaps that is because that's how it was when I first arrived, at the end of September in 2012.

When I sat there, on that small step outside the Emperor's Palace, and watched Marunouchi, I would always think the same thing.

"My God," I would think, "there are so many windows."

So many skyscrapers, with so many floors, and with so many windows. And behind each of those windows, rows and rows of men and women working day after day on rows and rows of computers, from the early morning deep into the night.

How on earth have they not solved the world's problems?

Then I would get up, and I would dust the white gravel dirt from the seat of my trousers, and I'd walk back to my office, and then, when I got to the office, I would bet on the end of the world.

2

AT THE TIME I MOVED TO TOKYO, I REALLY SHOULDN'T HAVE BEEN moving anywhere. The weight had been dropping off me for some months by then, and by that point I was down to under 60 kilograms, which is about nine and a half stone. Even for me, that's not a lot.

I'm not sure I knew I had a problem. There was a point where it had occurred to me that it was probably not normal to be pathologically unable to buy sofas, or, in fact, any item of household furniture. But I allowed that moment to pass, as I had done with so many doubting moments. If I hadn't have done that, maybe things wouldn't have gotten so much worse, so quickly. But there were other pressing issues at hand, like interest rates.

The pain in my heart was being medicated by these pills called "PPIs," which stop the acid in your stomach from being acidic, which is what it's supposed to be. The first time I went on them, about a year previously, they were pretty effective, calmed the pain right down. By the time I moved to Japan I was on my third course, and they weren't working quite as well anymore. I had asked the doctor at the time, "Is that it then? I just take these pills for the rest of my life?"

He had smiled as he handed me the prescription and said, "Probably."

Through it all, though, I had the trading. The trading, the trading, the trading. The only true friend I had left. Objective, impassive, secure.

The thing about trading is, it's always there. The markets, you know, they don't stop.

Well, they do stop, I guess, on the weekends, but even then, there's the economy.

The economy had become an obsession, it spread like an oil spill through the acid of my heart.

It was true that I didn't give a shit about the office anymore. But the economy? That love never died.

When I first had my realization that the economy was broken, that it would get worse and worse, year after year, I didn't think about it that much. I mean, I did think about it, of course I did. But I never asked myself what did it *mean*.

It was my job, you know? You look at the economy and you say—OK, what is it gonna be this year? Is the economy strong, or is it weak? What about next year? That's simplifying it, just a little bit, but when it comes down to it, that's pretty much what interest rates trading is. That was my job.

Say your job was measuring the depth of swimming pools. You wouldn't go around measuring the swimming pools and then asking yourself, "What does this *mean*?," would you? Say it was your job to fix sofas. You don't ask your friends, "What does this sofa *mean*?"

At the time that I realized that the economy would get worse forever, I was confident. I was confident enough to bet big on it. I could see the mechanism by which it would happen, and I could see exactly why most trained economists would miss it. I could see that clearly. I can still see it now. But I never asked myself, "What does it mean?"

I just put the trade on. I just did my job.

But as that trade started to make me the most profitable trader in the whole of Citi Global Foreign Exchange, there was a growing, dawning realization that this was not just a theory. This was a thing that was real.

And then I got paid a ton of money for doing that, and then I invested that money. There was a point, when I was doing the investing, that I asked myself, "What am I investing this money for? Will I ever spend it? Probably not."

And I thought then, "Well, in that case, I'm investing it for my kids."

And then, just very fleetingly, "But then, what if I'm right? What kind of world will my kids live in?"

But I squashed that thought, and I moved on very quickly, back to the investments, because investments and numbers are things that I like. Numbers are a place where I'm safe.

There were moments though. Little, brief moments. Where the thick canopy of trees opened up above me, and I caught just a glimpse of a dark, starry sky. And in those moments, I did dream of quitting. I think that's what had happened that day in the office with the Frog. I had had one searing moment of lucidity, and, in that moment, I saw the sky, and I realized that it wasn't really right for a millionaire twenty-five-year-old to be working with holes in his shoes, to be living in a house with no floors. To be sleeping in the evenings on a broken red sofa and to wake up cold, in the middle of the night, dreaming of numbers. To have such shooting pains in his heart and at times to be unable to eat. That's probably why, in that moment, I had said that I wanted to quit.

But the problem with quitting was—I couldn't. You see, I was handcuffed right in. When Citibank paid me that huge bonus, the bonus that I can't remember, at the beginning of 2012, they took care to tie me tight to my screens. Some of the bonus was to be paid up front, which was the money I was investing. The rest was to be paid with a significant delay. A quarter in 2013, a quarter in 2014, a quarter in 2015, a quarter in 2016. So you see, at that point, I could not really leave. The bank owed me over a million pounds. If I quit, I'd lose it all.

So that is probably why, as I sat there that day in that office, with my broken shoes and my broken stomach and the acid shooting through my heart; feeling low, on the ground, like a rat, when the Frog told me that I had to move to Tokyo, I said yes. Even though I knew I didn't have the energy to do it. I had nothing. No strength to say no with. I was shackled.

But rats have teeth too, you know, and so do I. In my spare time I did my research.

Because if traders are shackled in, and can't leave, then how did Caleb leave back in 2009? How had Caleb been able to build it? His wonderful house in the wonderful trees?

I poked around, I asked a few people. OK, I admit, I just went and asked Bill.

Bill told me there was a clause in the contract, a way to get out and keep all your cash. You had to leave and go to work for charity. Not many people knew about it, but Caleb did, and somehow he'd triggered that clause. He'd never gone to work for charity, everyone knew it, but for some reason the Slug let him go anyway. Nobody knew exactly why. Nobody was quite sure. Maybe Caleb had shit on the Slug.

This was the slender escape rope I carried, on that long flight, alone, to Tokyo. If Caleb had gone, with his money, then surely I could go as well. Not only that, but I was going to work for Caleb. If it all went terribly, if it all went tits up, I'd wait for the next bonus and then I'd leave and I'd go work for charity. Caleb would understand that, surely, wouldn't he?

Of course he would. Caleb would understand.

And I was, indeed, alone on that flight over to Tokyo. Wizard was not there with me. Wizard would move to Japan, like she promised she would, but she didn't go when I did. She went on her own ticket, and she arranged her own job, not in Tokyo, for some reason, and that job didn't start till January 2013.

So what I did take with me was almost nothing. The bank gave me eight cubic meters of air freight in which I was supposed to bring, I don't know, my favorite furniture? But I barely had anything that I couldn't fit in a backpack, so I asked them to just send my bike. My bike took two weeks to arrive though, so when I got there, it was just me, my backpack, and the markets.

At that time in my life, and still now, when I looked at markets I no longer saw a set of numbers. What I saw was a set of predictions for the world, the same way you might look at the weather forecast and understand that it's telling you what will happen. The interest rate predictions were a neat map of exactly when and how quickly each economy would recover, and they were moving around every day. If the rates move down, that could mean that economic prospects have weakened, or it *could* mean that the central bank has come out and said they're not going to hike rates. Which is it? If you look at the stock market, you can probably see—the first reason will probably push stocks down, the second, probably push them up.

Real traders don't watch the news, they watch the markets. Fuck *The Economist*, fuck the *Financial Times*, fuck *The Wall Street Journal*. The only thing you need is the markets. They'll tell you something that is real.

But it's wrong though. It's real. But it's wrong. And I was working out exactly why. At that point, I'd only been right on the economy for a year and a half. I needed to watch it more, to challenge my theories. I needed confirmation. I needed to watch the economy die.

So that was my plan. Even though I had nothing left, just a half-empty backpack, I knew that, always, always, I could trade, and I knew I'd make money. I wanted to watch my predictions be right again, for another year. I wanted God to reveal his truth.

That's all I wanted. Nothing else, just the markets.

3

PINK SHIRTS ARE NOT POPULAR IN TOKYO, AT LEAST THEY WEREN'T
when I was there. Blue shirts neither. It is very much a white shirt, white
shirt culture. And the white shirts, neatly bordered by black trousers and
slim, black suit jackets, cascade out of the exits of the underground stations at 8 a.m. and 9 a.m. like waterfalls flowing upward, into the real
world, and the individual men and women inside of that flow are carp
fighting upstream, opening umbrellas, checking their phones, carrying
neat, prim, rectangular suitcases, mopping their brows with small white
handkerchiefs.

I was among them.

Citibank had taken care of everything. A crisp, cream and white
apartment had been allocated to me on the thirtieth floor of the Prudential Building, which is a skyscraper in which people should not live, but
in which insurance should be sold, the top corner of which has been
delineated for human habitation. In that top corner, brave adventurers
such as I go to sleep and wake up every night high, high up, in the sky,
and we see Mount Fuji, each day, in the morning, but we don't breathe
the high air of Tokyo, because the windows are designed to stay closed.

The Prudential Building locks directly into the vast, sprawling, and
unerringly efficient Tokyo subway system at Akasaka Mitsuke station,
which itself lies in the heart of Akasaka, an upmarket commercial district in the center of Tokyo, all old-fashioned sushi shops and narrow
paved alleys and soaring rents.

The connection to the subway was, indeed, so direct, that I could
take an elevator from the hallway outside my bedroom all the way down
into the station, from where I could take the Marunouchi line in just
eight minutes to Tokyo Station, from which I could take another eleva-

tor directly into my office. All the way from my bed to the trading floor, without ever once seeing the sky. Convenient, don't you think? Or, as the Japanese would say, "便利ですね?"

The Tokyo trading floor, on the twenty-fourth floor of the Shin-Maru-Biru, meaning "New Marunouchi Building," was not small. But to me, it was small. If you stood at the entrance door with your back held up straight and against it, and the back of your head touching it, you could see the back of the room, and both its right and its left side, all at the same time. For me, that meant that it was small.

In reality, that sense of smallness probably came not from a lack of actual size, but from its lowness of ceilings, and its quietness. The altitude of the room also created a vastness of great distance through the windows, on the two sides that did not face the rest of the Marunouchi skyscrapers. I'm not sure why, but from the very first day I spent in the office, I got the sense that the sky in Tokyo was unusually high.

Unusually high, and unusually quiet. With those impressions I was overwhelmed. You could not, of course, have really heard a pin drop, if for no other reason than that the floor was expensively carpeted. But I always got the sense that you could.

On the trading floor itself, there were a few pink shirts, and this provided a little comfort, a little familiarity. The reason for this was not that the traders of Japan were atypically adventurous in their fashion sense, it was because the trading floor had a lot of *gaijin*. *Gaijin* means foreigner. It kind of means white person and it kind of means American. Usually it's not derogative. Sometimes it is.

About a third of the trading floor were *gaijin*, and about two thirds of those were Americans. The rest were Europeans who'd gotten lost at some point. People like me. The only people I knew on the whole trading floor were Caleb and, vaguely, two Japanese traders called Hisa Watanabe and Joey Kanazawa, who I'd met on my world tour nearly two years previously.

The STIRT desk was at the very back of the trading floor, by the far window, which meant that, if I wanted, I could wander over to that window and peek over at the palace. I don't own a crossbow, so it's not a big deal. To call it a desk was something of a misnomer, because there were only three traders there, including myself, and only one of us ever did any trading.

At that time, Citi STIRT in Asia was split between Tokyo and Sydney. Every single currency was traded out of Sydney, with the single exception of the Japanese yen, which was traded from Japan. This meant that there was only need for one single trader in Tokyo, the Japanese yen trader, and yet, there we were, three of us, in a little line: Hisa Watanabe, Arthur Kapowski, and, stuffed between the two of them, me.

Hisa Watanabe had been the yen trader for as long as anyone could remember. He was a small, mousy man, who had inexplicably chosen to speak his English with the accent of a 1920s New York gangster, and he was a very, very bad trader. No, that's unfair. He wasn't a trader at all. He was a shopkeeper, an accountant, a paper-shuffly sort of a man.

Hisa should have been fired when his job was given to me. He wasn't. He was promoted sideways in the most literal way possible: his chair was given to me, and he was moved into the chair to the right of it and declared to be "my manager." The manager of literally only one person: me. Hisa came to meet me at the airport with his wife and crying baby when I landed in Tokyo. I should probably have recognized what that meant when it happened—I didn't. That guy would back-seat drive my trading unerringly and incessantly, stuck right up my fucking arsehole like a hemorrhoid for the next fucking six months of my life.

To my left, was Arthur Kapowski. Arthur was Australian and his dad was some mining magnate or celebrity plastic surgeon or newspaper tycoon or something. I don't know exactly what, something anonymously rich and influential, and it looked as if he had raised his son to be the next clean-cut leader of whatever the fuck the Australian equivalent of the Republican Party is. He had the air of the world's tallest and most prestigious fifteen-year-old, but I suppose he must have been at least twenty-five. Think Jared Kushner with a much better personal trainer. Arthur was the most right-wing person I have ever known personally. Arthur was great. He was a real hoot.

There was absolutely no reason for Arthur to be in Tokyo other than the fact that Rupert Hobhouse (yes, him, Clapham's finest, the wolfman) was still head of STIRT in all Asia, and he liked to move people around like pieces on a chessboard. Arthur was possibly put there in an attempt to help me settle in, or he may have been put there so Rupert could show off to Caleb that he had somehow hired a man who was clearly destined to be the future leader of the free world to be his junior trader on STIRT. Arthur himself seemed delighted to be there. He said it was closer to his girlfriend. His girlfriend lived in New York.

So there we were, the three STIRT "traders"—one trader, his boss, and his junior. Three fucking cooks with not much fucking broth.

As if three men for one job was not already overkill, Rupert, who was somehow also "my boss" despite being 5,000 miles away, had insisted on a live video screen between his and my desk. This meant that one of my precious screens was now permanently devoted to a rolling livestream of "Rupert's daily moments," including such unmissable highlights as "Rupert eats noodles too quickly," "Rupert perfects the art of the full windsor necktie" and "Rupert suddenly unmutes his screen to shout at you 'What's Eurozone CPI?' like some fucking horrible recurring dream from childhood which has inexplicably come back to haunt you as an adult."

To the left of us was the rest of the Foreign Exchange department. Since the overall Tokyo FX team was much smaller, we were not big enough to split into separate desks, and so we shared our desk with, firstly, a pair of thoroughly unobjectionable middle-aged Japanese salesmen who, as my Japanese got better, I would gradually come to realize spent their entire day discussing firstly what they would eat for lunch, and then, after they had eaten said lunch, a thorough assessment of how the lunch had been. Past them were a pair of Japanese currency traders, which included the semi-legendary and violently irrepressible Joey Kanazawa, and to their left, on the very end of the desk, the broad and robust Caleb Zucman, who had been made head of the whole foreign-exchange-and-interest-rates department and who, in propping up the desk like the world's largest bookend, brought the number of bosses in my immediate vicinity up to a round total of three. I would be well looked after, no doubt.

4

THERE'S A CONCEPT IN JAPANESE, IT'S CALLED *O-MO-TE-NA-SHI.*
For some reason, Japanese people say it like that, one syllable at a time,
and they do this funny thing with their hands when they say it. It means,
I am told, "the spirit of Japanese hospitality." I think it's something to do
with green tea.

Joey Kanazawa showed me some Japanese hospitality, but I think
that, maybe, it wasn't *O-mo-te-na-shi.* I think it was something different.

Joey Kanazawa was a small man with intense eyes and an economy of
movement. He was a "spot trader," which means he was a pure trader of
currencies. It is the simplest, least complicated kind of trader that you
can possibly be, and they have a reputation for boorishness and stupidity. All traders call FX traders monkeys, and FX traders call spot traders
monkeys. So they are the monkeys of the monkeys. But Joey Kanazawa
was not like that. He was cool, he was slick, he was quiet.

Joey said almost nothing to me, or, indeed, to anyone on my first day
on the trading floor. Then, at the end of the day, at precisely six thirty, in
one sparing, fluid, precise movement, he stood up, slid his chair in, took
three steps to his right, and shouted something in Japanese.

The three Japanese men around me—Hisa Watanabe, and the two
lunch connoisseurs—responded with a loud, militaristic grunt that slid
into a long hiss. They stood up and tucked in their own chairs.

The combined movement of the four men was balletic in its simulta-
neity. Shocked and impressed, I had turned to face Joey, and was staring
the man in the face.

Joey extended his right arm, with perfect straightness, toward me.
With his palm up, and his thumb, index and middle fingers outstretched,
it was clear: the pointing of a gun. He held my gaze for just a moment

in which his eyes blazed with roaring intensity. He ripped the gun into the air.

The gesture was clear and decisive and broke through the language that we did not share. I groped under my desk for my little string backpack, and I followed him into the night.

It is already dark by that time, in Tokyo at the end of September, and the last traces of blue were dying from the air.

The sky becomes black and the streets become neon. The stars fallen down to the ground.

Knowing what I know now, I can see that we must have been walking through the wide streets of Ginza, an area just to the east of Marunouchi, and one of the grandest and most illustrious shopping streets in the whole of Tokyo and, in fact, the world.

But I did not know then what I know now, and all I saw was a grand, wide street, pavements flecked with perfect trees and flanked by tall buildings. Hanging neon signs that I could not read, innumerable, flowing down in towering cascades from the sides of the buildings. Four Japanese men walking in two pairs, all in white shirts and black jackets. Behind them, looking around, looking upward, broken white trainers, thin black Topman peacoat—me.

What was I looking for that first, hot Tokyo evening, following those four white-shirted men into the night? Maybe I was looking for some *omotenashi*. The spirit of Japanese hospitality. Isn't that what every silly little white boy is looking for, when he packs it all in and moves to Japan? To be held in the arms of a new, different place; to be embraced by the warmth of its air.

A sharp right into a tiny alley that had no right to be there, barely wide enough to walk two abreast. Four men at a hot red counter slurping noodles in perfect unison, one boy dropping his on the floor. I asked Hisa how to say "black pepper" in Japanese. He said it was "burakku peppaa." A short walk, a second tiny alley. Five men bundled into a lift. No one had thought to tell me where we'd be going. It was from then that it went downhill.

What can I tell you about hostess bars and about soaplands and about hostess karaoke? Probably far more than either of us would like to know. Just, women. So many women. Did I make it clear I wasn't warned?

There were older women and there were younger women. Girls, really. There were women about Wizard's age. There were huge rooms with ornamentation and smaller, private rooms as well. Allocation. So much allocation. Always one allocated to me.

Cigarettes were lighted and mixed drinks were poured, and jokes were laughed at behind hands. I'm sorry, I don't speak Japanese. A giggle, a touch on my thigh.

What do you do, in that situation? I probably should have gone home. I didn't though. Why didn't I?

I held on and I tried to drink slowly, but the glasses were always full and it was difficult to measure my drinks. The connoisseurs had their ties round their heads now. My *furendo* my *furendo*. *She izu. Adaruto mubii staa.*

It is all blurring now and we are tumbling into taxis and before long on to the next place. Hisa is singing "Wonderwall," and Joey Kanazawa is leaping from his seat, like an animal, and he rips the man's shirt from his chest. The girl next to me is pushing her shoulder into my shoulder. She looks about twenty. She's very pretty. I'm sorry, I don't speak Japanese.

I try to move away from her and she looks nervously to the small porthole in the door and so I look too and there are the eyes of a man watching us, and within minutes the door is opened and my girl leaves and another is sent in, for me.

"Listen, you seem really, really lovely and everything, and I'm really sorry I don't speak Japanese but, I just wanted to tell you that really I'm OK, I don't need anyone, so . . . Yeah I don't know how this works, really, but, like, you can just do what you want or if you want you can go home."

But she can't hear because the music is too loud and because the connoisseurs are screaming some kind of traditional Japanese ballad into the microphone, so I lean in and I say the same thing right into her ear and then I look at her and she smiles and puts her hand on my shoulder and cocks her head, a little, to the side. They replaced her another four times.

My soul died a little, on that carousel, if there was anything left still, to die. Eventually a girl found her way to me who could actually speak a little English. She should definitely have been higher up the list.

"Please, please, please, don't let them replace you."

"Pureezu, pureezu pureezu. Be . . . More . . . Happy."

The thought came to me that I'd never tried that. I wondered if it was too late.

5

"SO. HOW DID YOU MAKE SO MUCH MONEY THEN?"

Arthur wasn't like other traders that I'd worked with, and that was typified in his asking of this question. For nearly two years, by that point, I had been one of Citi's top traders, and no one had asked me that once.

"Easy. I just bet that interest rates would stay zero forever."

"HA!"

Arthur guffawed extremely loudly. One single, extremely pointed, Australian private school guffaw.

"Interest rates can't stay zero forever."

Arthur asked a lot of dumb questions, and made a lot of bold statements. I liked that. The reason that he did this is because he had never studied economics. He studied music. He was a concert pianist or some shit. The best job a concert pianist can get nowadays is trader for Citibank. It pays very well.

Economics nowadays is a subject in which students never really quite understand what they are being taught, because the people teaching them, who are of course former economics students, never quite understood it themselves. Occasionally, experiencing a rare moment of lucidity, a student will be simultaneously intelligent enough to realize their own lack of understanding, and brave enough to ask a professor about it. This will incite a brief twinge of psychological torment in the professor, who will have spent many years trying to suppress his own knowledge that he does not really understand his subject, and will also remind him of the bitter fact that his father has never been proud of him. In order to shut these escaped feelings back up in their safely locked vault of repression, the professor will either shame or bore his interlocutor into submission (which is what intellectually insecure people usually do when questioned). By this process, economists learn to never ask the stupid questions, which are, of course, almost always the most important questions to ask.

Arthur didn't have that, and he was also very good at piano. How lucky. What a fortunate boy.

"Of course interest rates can stay zero forever. Why the fuck can't they?"

"Well . . ." And with this, Arthur pondered a little bit. I liked the boy, you could witness him think.

"Well, because it's only temporary. It's the sovereign debt crisis. The economy's going to recover. And then interest rates will come back."

"Clever boy, where did you read that? The economy's going to hell."

"HA!"

This boy loved to guffaw, and he did it so loudly. He did everything loudly actually. The Tokyo trading floor was the quietest trading floor I have ever been on by about a million miles, and when Arthur spoke everybody could hear him. Arthur didn't care though. Why the fuck should he care? He's the next leader of the free world.

"What do you mean the economy's going to hell?"

"What the fuck do you think I mean? It never gets better. It's not temporary, it's terminal. It goes down from here. Year after year."

"What goes down? Interest rates? The stock market?"

"Fucking stock market, come on Arthur, you're smarter than that, have you been asleep for five fucking years? Shit economy is great for the stock market. Stock market goes to the moon."

That was a good point that I'd made. It was becoming increasingly obvious. Arthur chewed on it a bit.

"But why's the economy fucked though? Nobody's saying that. Why is it fucked?"

"Fucking hell Arthur. If you just believe what everybody else believes you'll never make a pound in your life. You can't beat the market by being the market. You make money when people are wrong."

Arthur looked genuinely baffled, and I wondered if he shouldn't maybe be in a concert hall somewhere instead of sitting here with me.

"OK, go on then. I'll fucking tell you. It's inequality. That's the only thing that matters. Trade on that you'll be a millionaire."

Arthur guffawed for one final time, before quickly realizing I was serious.

"Inequality!?"

"Yes Arthur, yes, inequality. The rich get the assets, the poor get the debt, and then the poor have to pay their whole salary to the rich every year just to live in a house. The rich use that money to buy the rest of the assets from the middle class and then the problem gets worse every year. The middle class disappears, spending power disappears permanently from the economy, the rich becoming much fucking richer and the poor, well, I guess they just die."

That hung in the air for a second and I could see the cogs move in his brain.

"So . . . What about interest rates?"

"Interest rates stay at zero."

"Hmm . . . Do you think we should buy green Eurodollars then?"

Fucking Arthur. Smarter than he looked.

The conversation had attracted the attention of Rupert who was, as always, able to look at the pair of us on his video screen. He unmuted the screen and shouted my name, a habit of which he was unfortunately fond.

"Gary! Glad to see you're getting on with Arthur! What are you talking about?"

At that stage of my life, I was finding it increasingly difficult to separate my contempt for Rupert from my face. I'm sure Rupert never noticed though. He probably thought all faces just looked like that. I was getting a weird twitch in my eye and my lip so I didn't answer and so Arthur filled the gap and shouted,

"Economics!"

"Ahh . . . economics! I love economics! I knew Gary would turn out to be a great economist. That's why I hired him to the bank! Tell me Gary . . . Who do you think is the best economist at Citibank?"

At that point in time, Rupert was one of about seven different people who were claiming that they'd hired me to the bank, but I supposed Rupert's claim was stronger than most. He did take me to Vegas, after all. I'd managed to get my eye under control so I spat out the word, "Bill."

Rupert was shocked.

"Bill is not an economist!" He thought I was joking.

"OK. If it's not Bill, it's me."

Rupert and Arthur both loved that, and they laughed at it gleefully. There was a little inlay of our own camera display in the corner of the screen showing Rupert, so I could see Arthur's beautiful pearly smile. Rupert had had his own teeth done since moving to Australia. They were perfect, like piano keys.

Suddenly, Caleb's face appeared behind mine in the frame of the screen and I felt his heavy hand on my shoulder.

"Rupert! How is it going? What are you guys so happy about?"

"Caleb! How are you? I was just talking with Gary. He says he's the best economist in the bank!"

Caleb found that as funny as everyone else, and they all laughed with their teeth and their cheeks.

"Well, it's true though, he is a good economist. I always knew he would be, even back in the Trading Game. That's why I hired him to the bank." Caleb paused, then, to recalibrate himself physically, so as to continue with a little more gravity.

"You know, I'll always remember giving Gary his first bonus. I knew whatever I gave him would be a huge amount of money to him, but I wanted him to feel appreciated. I'll never forget the way his face looked when we gave him that £50,000."

The three men smiled warmly, and they all gazed at me, while I just looked into the screens. It hadn't been £50,000, it had been £13,000, and I wondered why Caleb would lie so brazenly to a man who knew it was a lie. Three huge smiles, each one so perfect. I wasn't smiling, I looked like a rat.

Around about that time, global interest rates collapsed for me one final time, making me a fair bit of money and winning me Arthur's undying loyalty. It was probably the worst thing that could have happened to me.

You see, once interest rate predictions fall to zero, then everyone's not wrong anymore. Everyone's right. Finally, for the first time in nearly two years since putting on the position, everyone was agreeing with me. The economy *was* fucked forever. There *would* be no recovery. There's nothing worse than being right and everyone agreeing with you. There's no way to make any cash.

Just a few months earlier, I had been one of the biggest traders in the whole world. I had been trading hundreds of billions, every day, in a market that was flying around. That was over now. I was the yen trader. For an American bank. Not a Japanese bank. The Japanese interest rates never fucking moved and the market was deader than dead. Even when I did have prices to make Hisa overruled them and I couldn't be fucked to fight back.

So that was it. No customers to play the trading game with. No economy to bet on the death of. Just me, and Arthur, and Hisa Watanabe, and two men talking about lunch.

No trades. For the first time in a long time for me, no trades. I looked down at my hands, on the mouse and the keyboard, and I realized how empty they'd become.

I looked round to the right of me. There was Hisa Watanabe. He was slurping noodles out of a little cardboard bowl with chopsticks and it sounded disgusting. I don't wanna hate too much on Hisa Watanabe. I know why he did what he did. Backseat driving me and overriding all of my trades. It wasn't good for him, me being there, doing his job, and making more money than he had ever made, without even working. Man had a wife who had married him for his trader salary and he damn sure needed to keep that salary. God knows he weren't the first trader to meet that predicament. Fuck him but good luck to the guy.

I looked to my left. Arthur Kapowski. Kid was so happy about all the money we had made betting on the end of the world. I wondered if it had ever made me happy the way it was making him happy. God knows the people suffering looked like my parents and didn't look like his parents.

I looked into my top left screen. Rupert Hobhouse. By some blessed coincidence the guy was also slurping noodles from a little cardboard bowl, and I thanked fuck that his screen was on mute. For the first time in my life I realized that I hated him. Did I hate him, or did I despise him? I don't fucking know, what's the fucking difference? I wondered if he knew that I hated him and I wondered why I hated him. God knows the guy had done a lot for me, in my career. The more he did for me the more I hated him. So it goes, I guess.

Left again, past Arthur, to the connoisseurs. They were talking about the tempura on rice that they had had for lunch and saying that it had been delicious. I knew that they were right, because they'd bought me some too. No, it wasn't their fault, no one could hate them.

Past them, to Joey Kanazawa. He was taut, with his eyes on his screens. I couldn't blame Joey Kanazawa. He'd tried his best to bring me in.

And there he was, on the end, Caleb Zucman. The first trader I had ever seen. How could he ever have thought I would fit in here? No markets, no customers, no real traders around me. No battles, no victories to win. And for the first time ever a thought flickered into my mind: maybe he hadn't been the first trader I'd seen. Maybe he'd never been a trader at all.

I turned back to my screens and saw that I had pulled my phone out of my pocket and had been flicking through it. No one in there mate. Ex-family, ex-friends and ex-girlfriends, every one of whom you've pushed away. You could always text Wizard, she understands you.

I didn't text her. I put my phone away and I waited. If you wait long enough, another trade will always come. Maybe it was then I started to go mad.

I think someone might have noticed I wasn't quite right, because senior management decided to allocate me a young Japanese kid called Kousuke Tamura to be my junior trader, bringing the number of men on my team doing one man's work up to four, like a set of fucking trading Russian dolls. There was, of course, no work for Kousuke to do, so Kousuke spent all day, every day creating a grand, enormous trading spreadsheet, analyzing all of the markets in STIRT.

One day, in the afternoon, I saw Kousuke select the whole spreadsheet, delete the entire thing, and start from the beginning, afresh. I pulled Kousuke aside the next day, in a moment when Hisa wasn't there, and I asked him very quietly, "Hey listen, did you delete your whole spreadsheet yesterday?"

Without a moment's hesitation, and with his face an Easter Island statue of seriousness, Kousuke nodded. I was baffled.

"What the fuck? What the fuck man . . . Why!?!?"

Kousuke glanced over both shoulders, and then looked me deep in the eyes.

"Don't finish work. Don't ever finish work. You finish work, you get more work to do."

For me, this was a real problem. Because I hadn't done any work in about a year. Even in my last nine months in London, I had barely traded. Titzy had done most of it for me. Now there wasn't even any trading to do.

It wasn't that I was lazy. I had lost the capacity somehow. I had lost the capacity to do work. I had lost the capacity to give a shit. I couldn't even buy a sofa for fuck's sake. I probably would have stopped eating if it weren't for the fact that if I went three hours without a meal my heart started to set itself on fire. It was becoming a serious struggle just to shower every day.

I had still made money though. I had always made money. That was easy. All you had to do was bet on disaster. The end of the economy. The end of the world. That had been the last thread connecting me to humanity. Suddenly I'd lost even that.

I used to get into work at eight in the morning. Everyone got in at eight in the morning, even though there was fuck all to do. All the action in markets happens in London and New York trading hours, which are the Tokyo afternoon and evening into the night. No one in the whole fucking world is awake at fucking 8 a.m. in the Tokyo fucking morning except fish. But still, though, we had to get in.

There was like, the tiniest bit of trading to do. A little business in yen FX swaps. I could have done it in twenty minutes, but if I stretched it to its absolute maximum it could take me up to 10 a.m. After that, what was there to do? Nothing. I'd shoot the breeze about the economy with Arthur and Kousuke, practice my Japanese with the lunch connoisseurs. The truth is, they were all about as busy as I was, but they were great at pretending to work.

I wasn't. After ten I would sleep. I would nap with my feet on the desk. I would nap with my feet on the floor. I would wake up with my insides on fire and I'd run out to buy noodles. I would bring up the PnL sheet from the London desk to see how Titzy was doing now he'd got my old job. I would take 300 one-yen coins that I had been collecting, in a little bag, to the floor cafeteria and use them to buy random Japanese snacks and green tea. There was nothing. Fucking Nothing. To do.

Hisa hated it. Hisa hated all of it.

There is this weird thing in Japanese culture where people won't tell you if they are pissed off with you, at least not directly. What they will often do, instead, is to manifest physical pain in themselves.

Let me give you an example. If you are studying beginners' Japanese, in a textbook, one of the first words you will learn is *iie*, for no. Technically, according to the dictionary, this is the correct word, but no one ever actually uses it. Why? Because no one ever actually *says* no! There's a kind of a wobbly nasal grunt you can do, but that's more an internationally accepted sound for "no," and you can only really use it with your friends. With people you aren't that close with, you just never say no.

So what do you do then if someone asks you to hang out on Saturday, and you have a hot date on Saturday? Do you say no? Of course not. What you do is you tilt your head to the side, and you grimace and you sharply inhale through your teeth, as if afflicted with toothache. The other person, seeing your sudden pain, understands this to be no and backs off.

Hisa started doing this constantly. The problem was, I didn't understand. I'd put my feet up on the table and Hisa would hiss like I'd stepped on his foot. I'd turn and look at him, confused, and then try and nod off. Hisa would contort his body and breathe out really throaty and slowly, as if pulling an arrow from his back like the fucking Japanese Saint Sebastian. I'd raise one eye and look at him concerned. Continually failing to transmit his displeasure, Hisa would up his game again and again, to the point where he looked to be experiencing total organ failure. It was driving me slowly insane. I started to take a lot of breaks off the desk to go to the bathroom and brush my teeth. But there's only so many times a man can brush his teeth.

There was nothing else to do though, so in the end I tried to do what everyone else was doing, perhaps what everyone behind all of those skyscraper windows is still doing today, I got down and pretended to work.

.   .   .

It wasn't good for me. The heart pain got worse. I was losing more weight that I didn't have and I had to register with a private doctor just to get me some more PPIs.

I tried to do some cooking to take my mind off of things. I'd cooked a lot back in London, but in Japan I'd always get everything wrong—when I tried to buy beef, it'd be pork; when I tried to buy pork, it'd be beef. Goddamn why does Japanese beef look so much like pork!

Failing to cook, I would wander the back alleys of Akasaka in the evening, like a hungry ghost looking for food. Akasaka is a fancy area, and there's plenty of restaurants, but none would speak English and there'd never be an English menu. In the end I'd float into a sushi place and just shrug, and they'd sit me down and feed me anyway. It was expensive, but never enough to fill me up. I'd get a Big Mac as I floated home.

I was failing at not sleeping in the office, and it started to affect my sleep at home. I started waking up in a cold sweat at two or three in the morning. When that happened, I'd put my trainers on and I'd run to the Outer Garden and then all the way around the Emperor's Palace. It's about 5K to run all around. After that, I could sleep for maybe an hour. There was a gym on the top floor of my building and if it was open I'd go in there and run 5K on the treadmill. I managed to get my 5K down to nearly 18 minutes. One morning I tried to beat 18 minutes but I had to stop and go back to my room and throw up. I started to get this bleeding in my gums so I went back to the doctor and he told me to stop brushing my teeth so hard.

People were starting to worry about me. I was down to 55 kilograms now. Caleb was worrying and management were worrying. I'm not sure they'd noticed how skinny I'd gotten, but my lack of work ethic was embarrassing for all. Caleb had promised the bosses the kind of kid who carries a hundred burgers in a single lunch break. He'd delivered a kid who was, in most general cases, either sleeping or brushing his teeth.

He invited me over to his house, which was a beautiful place in the Yoyogi area of Tokyo, close to the city's biggest shrine, Meiji Jingu, and its biggest park, Yoyogi Koen. I met the beautiful children and the beautiful wife with whom Caleb had shared the travails of his misplaced thermostat.

They were lovely, they were all really lovely. We had dinner and together we drank.

But something was missing, something important was missing. I was wasting away and nobody noticed. Nobody could see I was gone.

I tried to reach out for something that night, something in Caleb, something important. I reached out, and I tried to search in him, for something there to which I could hold on—something human, something I could feel.

But there was nothing there. He was gone too.

6

A FEW MORE ATTEMPTS WERE MADE TO CHEER ME UP. MOST NOTA-
bly by Florent LeBoeuf.

Florent LeBoeuf had been in my year at LSE and was not in the
slightest doubt that we were old friends. I'd never seen the boy before in
my life.

Chunky and gamely, with terrible posture, Florent had the air of an
unkempt teddy bear. He had moved to Japan with the express ambition
of sleeping with as many women as possible (an ambition not uncom-
mon for *gaijin* in Tokyo) but was plagued by a deep paranoia that Japanese prostitutes were trying to steal his sperm. I quite enjoyed the poetic
symmetry that balanced his dreams and his fears.

Florent was in no doubt regarding what was needed to raise my spirits. He convened the young *gaijin* traders, and they took me out to Roppongi.

Just south of Akasaka, Roppongi is one of several nightlife centers in
Tokyo. A vast, elevated highway arches over it, beneath which hustlers
sell women and kebabs. Overlooking it all, at the end of the road, a
huge, bright orange Eiffel Tower reaches up and pierces the sky.

Roppongi is famous for *gaijin*. Roppongi is where *gaijin* go. Back
when I lived in Tokyo, and even still now, I think, most Japanese were
not comfortable speaking English, and many would, in fact, give foreigners quite a wide berth. But there are thirty-eight million people in
Tokyo, and even if one percent of one percent of those people are young
women with a fetishistic obsession for foreigners, then that is still three
thousand, eight hundred women. All of those women are in Roppongi.

We started off in a small bar that was, bizarrely, decorated from the
inside to look like the carriage of a train. The clientele was the typical

Roppongi fare: foreign-looking bankery types (of which, of course, I was one), dangerous-looking Japanese women.

We'd each drunk one can from a convenience store on the way there (the ubiquitous and appropriately named grapefruit drink: *Strong*), and Florent ordered our second round. While we waited for those, Florent taught me.

"You see those two girls over there? You can get them. Well, one of them. Either one. Which one do you like? Up to you. Anyway. You go there. You say hi. You smile and you bow, just a little. Make eye contact. Introduce yourself. Tell them your name. Ask them if you can buy them drinks. Buy them drinks. Pick one. Talk to her more. Touch her on the arm. Ask her to go with you, over there, to that corner. You take her home. *Bam!*"

I had not requested this lesson, but I appreciated it, even if only for its pointillistic style. After the bar, we went to a nightclub called *Gas Panic* and, as if intentionally designed to undermine Florent's neatly crafted strategy, one of the traders simply walked up to a girl he had never seen before and started making out with her, without saying anything.

I felt a little sick, in my stomach. Maybe it showed on my face. Florent's heavy arm snaked around me.

"Don't worry mate, you don't need to do that. Come on man. We go to strip club."

"Do you think we should do something?"

Now that Kousuke had been brought over to be my junior, a decision had been made to recall Arthur back to Sydney, sadly separating him from his girlfriend. This was to be his second last day on the desk. He was eating sushi from a clear plastic box.

"About what?" He spoke full-mouthed, loudly.

"I dunno . . . you know . . . About the economy."

"We already did something, we bought the green Eurodollars."

"*You* bought the green Eurodollars, I already had them. There's no point buying more at these levels. Besides, that's not what I'm talking about."

"What you talking about then?"

The last of the rice was being shoveled in with chopsticks.

"I'm talking, you know, about the *economy*! Do you think we should *do* something about the *economy*?"

Arthur had finished his sushi, so he snapped his wooden chopsticks in half and dumped them into the plastic container, then sealed it shut.

"I don't know what you mean."

I was getting a kind of a stabbing sensation in my left temple.

"Arthur. I'm talking about the economy. Should we do something? About the economy. What the fuck is there to not understand?"

Arthur chewed that for a bit and he moved his chair closer to mine, and then leaned in as if we were about to do a drug deal.

"So . . . We're not talking about the green Eurodollars here . . . Am I right?"

"For FUCK'S sake Arthur, this is not about *fucking* green Eurodollars! The economy is going to be fucking shit for fucking ever! Do you think we should do something about that!?"

Arthur withdrew his chair about a meter and he balanced me, with his eyes. For a moment, he tried a smile. The smile hesitated and pondered a little. Arthur leaned into the desk with his arms.

"You're fucking serious, aren't you?"

"*Yes*, Arthur, I am fucking serious, do you think we should *fucking* do something about the *fucking* economy!? Fucking hell . . ."

Arthur paused so that he could reload an extra-loud laugh.

"What are you gonna do mate? You gonna become fucking Prime Minister? You gonna save the whole fucking world??"

"Well I don't fucking know, what the fuck do you think we should do? Sit here and do fucking nothing?"

"Ahhhh mate. Things are all right mate. We didn't do fucking *nothing*, we bought the green Eurodollars! And we made a ton of money. You don't need to worry mate, you're gonna be fucking minted. You've got this whole thing figured out!"

"Yeah, but . . ." Yeah, but fucking nothing. It passed through me. I knew he was right. "I dunno . . . I just . . . I don't know mate. It just . . . ? It doesn't feel right."

"You're being ridiculous mate. What the fuck are you talking about? What could you even fucking do anyway?"

"I dunno. I could go back to, back to university . . . Maybe? Try to show the guys there that they're wrong."

I thought about the universities, about the dusty poindexters locked up inside them, inverting matrices in little rooms with no windows, and the idea of them changing the world. Then it was my turn to laugh.

Arthur went back home after that. I'm pretty sure he's still a trader, not yet the leader of the free world. He'll do it though, I reckon, eventually, after ten or fifteen million pounds.

ARTHUR LEFT AND THE WINTER CAME AFTER. IT WAS COLD AND THE
trees were all bare. Tokyo's winter's not like London's winter. It's blue
and all day there's the sun.

With Arthur gone, I only had Kousuke. Kousuke seemed a nice boy:
earnest, honest-looking, hard working. He had that unexceptional but
doggedly determined vibe of protagonists in Japanese teen animes. No
matter how many times he finished that spreadsheet, I was certain he'd
never give up.

I wanted to get to know the guy. He seemed, like, not a maniac,
which was a rarity at that time in my life. The problem was he spoke
very little English. As my Japanese got better, we were able to speak
more and more. One day he told me that he memorized five new English words every single day, and had been doing so for fifteen years. I was
shocked by this, because his English had seemed very poor, and I asked
him to show me his words for that day. The first word on the list was
"notwithstanding." I realized then that his English was actually perfect,
it was just hidden behind his accent.

Once this problem was hurdled, our ability to communicate began to
advance rapidly. I attuned myself to his staccato-Katakana English and
I tried also to speak it myself. This proved a breakthrough not only in my
communication with Kousuke, but also with the whole of Japan.

Now, Japanese people will tell you they don't understand English,
but if you speak Katakana, they do. Katakana is a Japanese phonetic al-
phabet that makes English words sound like Japanese — it's not "black
pepper," it's "bu-rak-ku-pep-paa," it's not "table," it's "te-e-bu-ru." If you
ask your hotel reception for an "iron," they'll look at you baffled; ask for
an "a-i-ro-n," and it'll be in your room.

Being able to talk properly to Kousuke was a real relief. You don't realize how deep a need it is to talk to people who are not crazy until you've not done it for a while. I asked Kousuke to go for dinner.

Kousuke was born and raised on the East Side of Tokyo, the old town, the *shitamachi* as they call it, and he took me there for okonomiyaki. Okonomiyaki is a kind of Japanese savory pancake. It's mostly cabbage, I think. It's big, it's delicious, and it costs about a fiver. In London it's £25.

We turned off the street and went up a tiny, narrow wooden staircase. A sliding wooden door, a jangling of silver bells, a loud, welcoming shout: *"irrashai!"* Bow down, through the fabric, inside.

Inside was all wood and warm lighting, every inch of every wall plastered with old Japanese movie posters, from, I don't know, the fifties? Customers sat beneath low tables bearing huge pancakes, steaming on metal hot plates.

In the office, Kousuke was always quiet and self-possessed. Here, as we sat down, he emitted an ear-piercing scream. A waitress appeared, suddenly, like a cat. "Toriaezu—biiru." First things first, beer.

There was much that I wanted to say. I explained to Kousuke that I had a girlfriend, back at home, that she was coming to Japan but was not there yet. I was pretty sure that I had not hidden this from anyone, and yet there seemed not a man in the Tokyo office unwilling to sprinkle strange women on me. Kousuke drank his beer heartily, and he hummed and hawed at that, thoughtfully.

I told him how I couldn't stand Hisa, constantly twisting and grimacing and observing. Kousuke deeply understood this. Hisa was, as anyone could see, "a man with a very small heart."

I went further, and told him that Caleb had once been a great mentor and idol of mine, that I'd been hoping to rebuild our relationship, and yet, somehow, that he was not there.

I think something might have been a bit lost in translation on that one, but Kousuke conveyed his sympathies, anyway. So earnest and deep were those sympathies, that I felt I should probably move on.

The reason that I'd asked for this meal was that I needed to tell someone, maybe anyone, that I was going to quit. For real this time, I'd really leave. That I would wait until bonus day, in January, and then, when the bonus hit the bank, I would go to Caleb and I'd tell him that I was done,

I was out. That I was going to work for charity, and that, in so doing, I would keep all of my deferred stock. That Caleb had done the same himself, in the past, and as such, then, he'd surely let me.

Often, Japanese people can be hard to read. They don't show their emotions on their face. But Kousuke looked at me, and he struggled for words. I could see he was worried for me.

I had my bicycle by then. It had been flown over all the way from London. Often I'd spend the whole weekend on it.

I'd cycle south to the bright orange Tokyo Tower. Nine meters taller than the Eiffel Tower, right next to my doctor's office, there's a Family Mart convenience store on the first floor. You can go there and buy a carton of milk. A park lies just beneath it, with the old temple, Zojo-ji. A couple times I heard Buddhist monks chanting, in there, and when it comes to the night, and the tower turns its lights on, before the orange the temple glows black.

I'd cycle west, to the huge *torii* gates of Meiji Jingu, or the bustling Takeshita Dori, or the wide-open plaza at the entrance of Yoyogi Koen, where on Sundays, middle-aged men with Elvis haircuts gather round old ghetto blasters and dance battle each other to death.

I'd cycle east to the reclaimed-land, abandoned-skyscraper district of Shiodome, where they took the tops from the mountains and they filled in the sea, and beyond it to Tsukiji Market, where the huge tuna heads pile up in buckets, with their cheeks scraped out, and to Hama-rikyu-teien, where there's a little tea house, and for 500 yen an old Japanese lady will give you beautiful little sweets and green tea.

I'd cycle north to Ueno Koen, with the ponds with the turtles and carp you can feed, or to Senso-Ji temple with its huge, smoking cauldrons of incense, and, if you go past the cauldrons of incense, gray, wizened, curved men and women shake little wooden boxes that tell their fortunes.

Sometimes, I'd go all the way round to Odaiba, the huge fake island in the middle of Tokyo bay, which took a long time, because you can't cycle across the bridge. There's a fake beach there with a sea that you can't swim in, and a fake Statue of Liberty as well, and I'd sit on a little wooden pole by the fake beach and I'd watch the sun go down over the city, and I'd wait for the lights to light up Rainbow Bridge.

At the end of December, for Christmas, I went back to London, and I lived, for two weeks, in a hotel in the Westfield shopping center in Stratford, which is the worst place in the whole world, and Wizard came there, and she held me, and, when she did that, both my legs started to shake.

8

2013 NOW. RECKONING COMES. I KNEW THE DAY WAS CLOSING IN.

The only things I remember about bonus day are that the Frog gave it to me on a big video screen, and that Caleb was also there with me, in the room. They wrote the number in yen so it looked really massive. I don't remember the number itself at all, but I remember my PnL, of course. I'd made 18 million dollars before I stopped trading, so what must I have gotten? Eighteen times point zero seven. One point two six million dollars. Something like that.

That day was in late January, and once that passed it was a count-down till the money hit the bank, sometime in early February. I checked the account every day. The money hit on a Thursday, so the next day was a Friday, and I was supposed to arrange to go and talk to Caleb on that day. But I didn't. What can you say? Coward, I guess.

It was a difficult weekend. I was feeling really shifty. Something shuffled round under my skin. Wizard was in Japan by then, but she wasn't in Tokyo, she had moved to East Osaka, close to Nara, about 300 miles west of me. I'm not quite sure why she did that. I told her I was quitting over a Skype call. She was happy, she'd always wanted me to quit.

Monday. Caleb agreed to meet me in his corner office. Caleb had insisted upon a corner office as one of his conditions for returning to the bank. I know that because he'd told us: me, JB and Billy, that night last summer as we drank by the Thames. I could see for miles in two directions, to the west, and to the south. One sturdy, wooden table, two sturdy, wooden shoulders. Behind them, in the distance, obscured by tall trees, the Emperor's Palace.

There was a watchfulness, a seriousness, about Caleb, which I no-

ticed the moment that I entered the room, and to which I was not accustomed. In hindsight, I suppose that, given the timing, he must have
known what I was going to do, but, for some reason, that never occurred
to me at the time. All I noticed was the tightened control in the eyes and
the mouth. Muscle, caught and held, in mid motion. A chess player; a
poker player; a wolf.

I sat. As we always had done, he looked down and I looked up.

Did he know what I was going to say?

I told him, of course.

I've never been much of a planner, and my speech was not well re-
hearsed. There were a few beats that I needed to hit: that I was leaving;
that I was sorry; that I would go to work for charity (something about
inequality); that in recognition of all he and Citi had done for me, I
would work the rest of the year for no bonus, but that after that I really
would leave. Really, this time. That last addition, about the year with no
bonus, was an artistic flourish: it had been exactly what Caleb had offered the Slug in 2009.

Those were my beats, but I missed them, and often I stumbled and
fell. I lapsed into long spiels about sickness, and I spoke of my stomach
and heart. Things got a mention that definitely weren't supposed to get
a mention: my trainers (why always the trainers?); Gas Panic; Quentin
Benting. I think I may well have seemed mad.

Did Caleb soften as I crumbled before him? Did his eyes glisten
when I said I was sick? The truth is, to be honest, I don't know. It's almost as if I wasn't there. My memory of that speech is hazy, at best—as
obscure as my delivery. I do not remember myself speaking, I'm piecing
the words together.

I remember clearly though, once I had finished, the way he shifted in
his chair. There was a note there, an air of compassion, which I knew,
instantly, wasn't real. Compassion is a thing to hold on to. There was
nothing to grasp in this man.

Caleb was sorry. He was deeply sorry. He knew it was difficult for me.
He had moved, he himself, too, to Tokyo, when he was still just a young
man. He knew what a hard place it could be; how lonely, how cold it
could feel. But the bank didn't want me to leave, though. They valued
my efforts, my work. Take some time. Don't rush. Don't be hasty. Come
back. Speak to me in two weeks.

. . .

I felt like the cartoon man who jumps from a building, only to land on a trampoline and bounce back where he stood. I was back there, once more, on the STIRT desk.

But I wasn't, no, something had changed.

An hourglass had been turned, something had started. At that point, my brain didn't know it, but I knew it though, deep in my bones.

I felt instinctively that something was wrong, but I didn't know quite what it was. I smashed out an email to HR, asking for a meeting. I wanted to make sure Caleb couldn't do anything: cancel my deferred stock, block my route out.

I had to get down to HR secretly. I couldn't reveal my mistrust.

An icicle sat there before me, modeling a chair in a windowless room. Tall, blond, Swiss? Maybe Swedish. Her fingers were slender and long. Unblemished in all aspects of deportment and grooming, she shuffled papers and measured my eyes.

Can management cancel your deferred stock? No of course they can't. Is it possible to leave the bank and work for charity and keep all your deferred stock? I've not heard of that, I'll look into it. But Gary, are you OK? You seem rattled. Tell me, you don't seem quite all there. It's OK, we are here to protect you.

I didn't feel that reassured.

9

THE NEXT TWO WEEKS JUST BLEW ACROSS ME, WITH THE SHARP edge of the winter wind. I took the train out west to Hyotan-yama in Higashi-Osaka, to see Wizard. Off the bullet train at Kyoto Station. Change again at Yamato-Saidaiji.

There's a festival in Nara, near where Wizard was living, called "Yamayaki," which kind of means "burn the mountain." Wizard was working her job as an English teacher in a local middle school that day, so I went out to see it alone. They set the whole of Mount Wakakusa on fire, and then Nara's ancient temples, too, glow black in the orange.

It's impressive; the whole mountain on fire; fireworks; the huge crowds; the smoke. It must be dangerous to set a whole mountain on fire, but the fire engines were all there. They cut all the dry grass around the mountain, to make sure that the fire can't spread.

What about me? Had I cut all my dry grass? Would the fire engines come for me?

Two weeks just passed in an instant, and once more I was back on the desk. It was time, then, for my second meeting.

For some reason, Caleb did not hold this meeting in his office. He must not have wanted the Emperor to see. He took me to a windowless white room, in the guts of the building somewhere.

"So, you've had now your two weeks to think about it. Are you still sure that you want to leave?"

What could change? What could possibly have changed?

"Yes. I am."

"OK. Well . . . I've looked into the details, of leaving the bank to go work for charity. I'm afraid to tell you that the option is only possible with the approval of bank management. Bank management will not be giving approval."

He smiled. Big piano teeth, shining. By that point the bank owed me, I think, more than 1.5 million pounds. It might have been closer to two. I was well past my era of remembering numbers, by then, it was above my threshold for "more than a lot."

It was clear what he was saying. You can leave, but the money stays here.

I didn't like that. No, I didn't like that. That isn't how one robs a bank.

The realization that had been caught in my bones flooded finally into my brain.

It's war, then. It's war that they're wanting.

I said to myself, that's no problem. It's not the first war in your life.

What happened after that was the rapid descent of my entire life into a farce. I entered what I now remember as "the Meeting Period"; the part of my life which was only meetings.

Suddenly, I was called in to three or four meetings every day. It wasn't always exactly three or four, some days may have been two or five, but meetings replaced trades as the building blocks of my life.

All meetings were with senior management, but the combination was quite variable. For example, in the morning, I may have had a one-on-one meeting with Hisa Watanabe: he'd smile and he'd pat me on the back. In the early afternoon, it would be a video call, with Rupert Hob-house and the Frog: they'd orate my decline sternly, in grave tones; I'd stare at my feet and I'd nod. In the evening, it was Caleb in the room, and the Slug on the screen: we believe in you! You can do this!

Between Hisa, Rupert, Caleb, the Frog, the Slug, and the many, many other managers who I'd never met before but were suddenly very keen to be a part of the action, the possible permutations were endless, and there were so many different games we could play. Rupert and the Frog liked an Imparting Of Wisdom and, in general, to Talk Of Them-selves. Hisa and the Slug were keen on Support And Encouragement, and generally were Pretty Nice. Caleb was a surprising fan of The Hair-dryer, and enjoyed a Good Cop/Bad Cop vibe.

My favorite meetings were The Shoutings. The Shoutings were always quite fun. Caleb did a lot of these, shouting and shouting: "We've Been So Good To You!," "How Dare You!" and other things such as that. They were always much better in person, when fingers could be jabbed into faces. They lost a lot of impact on videoconferences, where people could accidentally leave their microphone on mute, so I'd work especially hard to ham those ones up. Yes, I enjoyed The Shoutings, they reminded me of being a kid, and you don't get them much as an adult. I wondered if they were ever effective. It would be strange, to change one's mind, wouldn't it? Simply due to a shouting in one's face. I wonder if anyone ever does it.

The general vibe of the meetings was that I needed to Man Up And Make A Choice. Was I going to Be A Man And Do The Job? Or was I going to Fuck Off And Walk Out?

Tricky choice.

The best ones for this vibe were the Imparting Of Wisdoms, because you got to see a little of how people thought. On a video call from London, the Frog sat me down and told me very matter of factly that, even if I could have been able to keep all the money (which of course, I definitely couldn't), that the amount of money was never enough. How much had I made, after taxes? What was it? Two million pounds? He let out a big laugh at that number. That wouldn't even last me five years! I'd be back on my hands and knees, begging! We both laughed, and I looked at my shoes.

Rupert was fun too. I liked him. He spent a lot of time Talking About His Dad. His Dad Who Used To Be In The Army. He'd once told His Dad he wasn't happy with his bonus, and His Dad had told him to Man Up. I wasn't sure how that was relevant. I guess it meant I should Man Up As Well.

But the best feature of all the meetings, without any doubt, was the phenomenal Inconsistency of Roles. This was not official Citibank strategy, so I probably shouldn't have capitalized it, but it did give me the will to live. Such color! Such drama! Such theater! You never knew who you were going to get! Caleb's Bad Cop act would often be immediately followed by the Slug's Good Cop, and there were a few joyful opportunities where Caleb was lucky enough to be present in both meetings. The dramatic juxtaposition these occasions offered was simply exquisite. Watching Caleb transform, in an instant, from snarling wolf to teddy bear, it really gave you hope for humanity. Nobody cared one bit about these inconsistencies. There are no dishonest moves in chess. The only person who even noticed them was me, so it seemed. And for me? Well, I truly loved them.

In the face of these various strategies, I made up a game of my own. It was called Try To Say Nothing For As Long As Possible, and it's something I really perfected as a child. The aim of the game is pretty much explained by the title—only grunts are allowed. This gave me something to play for, but at times, such as the one-on-ones with the Frog or with Rupert, it was disappointingly easy to win. It was best in Caleb's adversarial meetings, because you had to achieve a lot with your eyebrows.

At no point, in any of these meetings, did I ever engage in any way with the Leave/Stay Dichotomy which was constantly laid at my feet. No way. Fuck them. No way I was leaving and not taking my money. And no way was I working anymore for those fucks. The thing was, the best outcome for me was to be fired. That way I would leave AND get the money I was owed. So what the fuck were they gonna do? Nah, nah, no way. Fuck them.

Fuck them. Fuck them. Fuck them. Fuck them.

Those fuckers could shout me to death.

Eventually, my lack of choice, and possibly my lack of actually saying any words, provoked a Final And Very Big Meeting, in which every single member of senior management was either present or there on the call.

The Slug took precedence at this meeting, which meant that The Meeting Would Be Very Nice.

The Slug lined everyone up and he made his big plea. He said he understood; that he knew I was sick. He believed it. He thought it was true. The bank would throw everything behind me, to help me, to get me better. Medical support, practical support, emotional support, whatever. Whatever I needed, I'd get. All he needed, from me, was commitment. To be there. To trade. To make cash.

Take it easy, he said, just relax, just let go. Don't be stressed. Take The Time That You Need. Don't worry, he said, it is OK. We Will All Of Us Be Here For You.

After that, he went through every single member of senior management, one by one, and they each spoke of their belief in me. It was wonderful. Soul-enriching. Heart-warming. When Caleb spoke he had tears in his eyes.

After that, I decided to try a new game. My trust in the Slug was unblemished and total, and as such, I took him at his word. I Took All The Time That I Needed, to Be Well, to Take Care Of Myself.

I Started Working My Contracted Hours.

My contracted hours were nine to five. I think it's possible that everyone in Japan's contracted hours are nine to five.

Nobody works nine to five.

Having the full and unwavering support of every single member of senior management behind me, I embraced a relaxed and holistic approach to my work. I took an hour off the desk, for a lunch break, every day. Sometimes even an hour and a half! I went on walks, in the winter air of Tokyo, to the Outer Garden to count all the trees. Sometimes I was tired, so I thought I'd Lean Into It. I'd put my hood up and I'd go to sleep.

It was wonderful. It was truly relaxing. It was the most PnL that I ever made in one week in Tokyo. It was the last full week of my career.

The next week, just after 9 a.m. on the Monday, Caleb came up to me and touched me, on the shoulder, quite gently, and he asked me if I'd like to go for dinner with him, in the evening, the following day.

And then, of course, that is when it happened.

10

IT WAS THEN, ON A COLD, DARK TUESDAY EVENING IN THE MIDDLE OF February 2013, in the anonymous sixth-floor ramen restaurant of an anonymous Marunouchi shopping center, that a large, very wealthy and fat-fingered man, with a hatred for ill-positioned thermostats, painted for me a vision of my life.

It was a future of courtrooms and poverty, years of bank robbery gone to waste.

It was brutal, and behind it was power: one of the largest corporations in the world.

What do you think? What do you think when you are twenty-six years old, one of the most profitable traders in the world, for one of the world's biggest banks, having come from nothing, having come from fucking £12 a week paper rounds, and a man who was once your idol sits there, across a table from you, over two bowls of ramen, and looks in your eyes and says to you, "Sometimes bad things happen to good people. We can make life very difficult for you."

As if he's a gangster. As if he's a don.

What do you think?

You know, it was almost exactly ten years before that day that I got expelled from school. I wasn't a drug dealer or nothing, but it was a grammar school so it was kind of a posh school, and the kids there knew I could get drugs.

And I *could* get drugs. They were right. It was true. I could get drugs because there were drug dealers on my street. Quite a few. There were no drug dealers on their streets, but there were drug dealers on my street. That's why posh kids would ask me to get them drugs, and that's why I'm the kid that got expelled.

And you know, those drug dealers, they didn't have the options that I had, or the options those other kids had. They cannot go to LSE. They cannot win investment banking internships in card games. They have no reliable routes out of poverty, and so, then, instead, they sell drugs. Sometimes they do other things too—fraud, burglary. And some of them make money and others of them don't make money. And some of them go to prison and others of them don't go to prison. And sometimes, kids like that, really bad things happen to them. Sometimes they get stabbed. Sometimes they get killed. Sometimes people wait for them outside of nightclubs in cars and they wait for them to cross the road and then they run them over, and then their bodies spasm on the floor.

What I realized then, at that moment, is that we are the same. We are all the same. The drug dealers, the bankers, the traders, me now, me then, Caleb, Saravan, Brathap, Rupert Hobhouse, Jamie, Ibran, JB. We are all the same. The only difference is how rich our dads were. If those drug dealers went to Eton, or St. Paul's, or whatever the fuck boarding school Rupert had gone to, they would be there, with me, on the trading floor, sitting next to Arthur, sitting next to JB. Buying fucking green Eurodollars. And if those traders were born where I was born, in Barking Hospital, in East London, where Bobby Moore was born and where John Terry was born and where a million other little hustlers were born, selling penny sweets on their school breaks, then they'd be there, too, selling drugs on the corners. We are the same. We are all the same. Stupid. Smart. Young. Ambitious. Wanting to *be* something. Not quite sure what. Chasing something, not knowing what we're chasing. Running to it and running away.

It's just the path isn't it, for young hungry hustlers, selling drugs or selling fucking bonds. We're all the same. We ain't no fucking different. It's just sometimes that God shakes the wrong box, in the wrong fucking temple somewhere; and someone like me, or like Billy, falls out backward and lands on our faces, in the wrong game, on the wrong fucking board.

We're the same. You're not better than us. You're not better than us. It's two different games, from the very beginning. From the *very* beginning. Since birth.

But you don't think all that there, in the moment. All that stuff floods through you in your dreams. At the time you just fix on that fat face, and you think,

"Mate. Don't talk like a gangster if you're not a fucking gangster."

And I knew, straight away, I would fight.

It was not a decision, it was never a decision. Sometimes you have to look the devil in the face.

Was it wise? Was it wise to fight Citibank? One of the biggest corporations in the world?

Well, I don't know. Fuck it. I never did claim to be wise.

I didn't sleep that night, not one single second. I went straight home and I threw up. No fucking food in it. Just a weak fucking piss-colored bile. No acid even, because of the pills. Wipe your mouth off and start pacing. Then you pace and you pace and you pace.

I'd fucked it. I'd really fucking fucked it. I had come into this with no plan. What the fuck can you do, now, at this point?

I'd already checked in with HR. The stuff that he'd said was legit. I couldn't go work for charity unless they signed it off.

I wasn't leaving without the fucking cash.

But that wasn't even the game now. There was far more here now to be played. The whole situation had switched round. Now it was my turn to defend.

So, are they gonna sue me now? For what?

He couldn't have had anything on me. If he had a hand he would have showed it. To make it more clear I was fucked.

But did he need a hand? He probably fucking didn't. Just like back in 2009 when the politicians said they were going to tax the banks and they all fucking laughed. They knew who was in charge. They could probably do the same to the courts. This is Citibank we are talking about here. They probably sue whoever they want.

But still. They can't just walk it. They have to have *something*. Was there anything? Could there be anything? Did they have anything to hold over me?

Thank fuck for Billy. Thank fuck for Cover. Your. Arse. I'd been covering mine for a bit. I was clean. I was sure. There was nothing. I'd been playing it clean. From the start.

Hadn't I?

Was there something? There could have been something. How many trades had I done? Fucking hell it must have been fucking millions. How many chat conversations? How many calls with brokers? Every single one of them recorded. Notarized, tabulated, filed. They had every single one of them. All of them. And what did I have? I didn't have shit.

With all that evidence, they could always paint something. FUCK FUCK FUCK FUCK.

What do you do?

It occurred to me that maybe they had overplayed their hand. Maybe they'd thought there was more on me than there was. Maybe that was why nobody in management ever asked me how I made so much money. Maybe they thought there was some dodgy secret behind it all, and they didn't want blood on their hands. Maybe they thought that's the only way dodgy kids like me make fucking money, selling drugs or through some dodgy shit. Maybe that's what *they* do. Maybe that's what their lives are like. Fucking over and shitting on each other all the way up their grease-covered poles.

No. No. Gary. Not productive. You need to have a fucking plan here.

OK. This is it. You need to move first. You need to move now-fucking-quick.

What time does the doctor's office open? The one close to Tokyo Tower. Google it. Nine a.m. OK. As soon as that clock hits 9 a.m. you call that fucking office and you get yourself the first fucking appointment available. You tell them you're going insane. Ham it up a little. You tell them you're not eating, you're not sleeping, you're losing weight. Well, that's not really hamming it up a little, it's all true, but add a little something on top, anything. Most of all *you-get-fucking-sick-leave*, you do not leave that fucking medical office without a sicknote, then you send that email fucking immediately, to everyone: to Caleb, to HR, to the Slug. Hit it up. As soon as you've done that then you've raised that bar up high for them. A fake case is a fake case, but a fake case against someone who has just applied for sick leave for stress is a different ballgame. It will look like punishment for the request. You'll be protected. Disability law or something? What the fuck do you know about disability law? Fucking nothing. Listen don't get mad at me here, what else have you got?

Nothing. I didn't have nothing. This was the plan and it's what we would do.

Should we ask someone for advice? What time is it now? Two a.m. That's still 5 p.m. in London, everyone will be awake. Who could you ask for advice? Billy? Snoop?

Nah, this is my shit. This is my shit and I'll fucking fight it. I'll fucking fight it and I'll win.

I only texted one person, Kousuke, at 2:30 a.m.

"Kousuke, some fucked-up shit happened. Don't tell anyone I text you. Can I meet with you ASAP?"

I decided I would text the bosses at 5 a.m. and tell them I'd been up all night throwing up so I couldn't come in. That gave me three hours to kill. In the deep night I ran round the palace.

I ran fucking fast round that palace, winter air on my fingers and face. I kept getting flashbacks from the dinner. At the end of it, Caleb had wanted to shake my hand, and I had literally no memory of whether I did it or not.

I guess that means I fucking did.

Five a.m. Send the text. No replies. Good.

Lot of time between 5 a.m. and 9 a.m. Can you sleep maybe? Set an alarm. No, you can't sleep. Go run again. When was the last time you ate?

Nine a.m. Call the doctors. It's a special doctor for foreigners; the receptionist speaks English. When's the first appointment? Ten thirty.

Ten twenty, Tokyo Tower. Big and orange beneath the blue sky. Ten twenty-eight, receptionist, sit down. Ten thirty, doctor's office. Punctual. Sit down and look like a madman. OK, you already look like a madman. Can you look more like a madman?

Tell him everything.

"My boss is threatening to kill me."

No. That's too much, wind it back.

"Sorry I mean my boss is threatening to sue me. I'm really scared. I've lost a lot of weight."

He's a tall Japanese man with a bald head and a white coat. He looks at you, for a long time, using just his left eye, as if that's the only good eye that he's got.

Two weeks of anti-anxieties. One month of sick leave. All scrawled down in beautiful blue ballpoint pen on a little white slip of paper. That'll do.

Back home now. Send the email. You went to the doctor, he's worried about you, he's written you anti-anxieties and one month of sick leave. Tell them you need to take the rest of the week off, because you fucking do because you're a mess. Turn off your fucking Blackberry.

Go to sleep now Gary. Go to sleep.

By the time I woke up it was the middle of the night. Well, I didn't know what time it was, to be honest, but it was already black in my room, even though I'd fallen asleep with all my clothes on and the curtains wide open.

I didn't turn my Blackberry on. Na fuck that. I didn't need none of that shit no more. But I looked at my phone. It was like eleven or something and I'd gotten a text back from Kousuke.

"What's happened? What's wrong? I can meet you this evening or tomorrow."

He'd sent it in the middle of the day. Well this evening was probably a lost cause. I asked to meet him the next day.

I met Kousuke back outside the okonomiyaki place. God knows what I looked like. From the look on Kousuke's face when he saw me, probably like a fucking mess.

I think it's quite possible I was shaking a little, as I told Kousuke what had happened over beers.

Kousuke's mouth hung wide open. He couldn't believe it. The thing about Caleb is, he's a fucking nice guy. He is, you know, he really is! If you met him, you would like him. I promise. Everybody does. Everyone did.

Kousuke had nothing to say when I'd finished. He just sat there with his mouth open, catching flies.

Eventually, he realized it was his turn to say something.

"That's illegaru!"

He shouted that, three times.

"Kousuke, I know it's illegal. That doesn't fucking matter mate, no-body cares. This is Citibank, it's the biggest fucking bank in the world. They can just do whatever they want."

"No! They cannot! This is Japan! There are rules! It is not allowed to break any laws."

"Kousuke, I think not breaking laws is a pretty fucking international rule mate, and that hasn't fucking stopped them, has it??"

Kousuke was angry, he was furious. He carried it in a bottled up, in-visible way that's at home in his country and mine.

"You must record it. You have to record it. Buy a recorder. Make him say it again."

And he literally went to Yodobashi Camera and he turned up outside my building on his little blue bicycle late in the next evening, and he handed me a little, tiny handheld voice recorder that he'd bought and he repeated,

"Record everything. Make him say it again."

Well, what can you say about Kousuke?

Good kid.

What did I do the next few days? I drowned. And then Monday, back in the office.

I'd been taken off the yen book, quite wisely. It had been given back to Hisa. Touché. As such, the only reason for me to come into the office was to walk straight into a meeting with Caleb.

This was to be an interesting meeting, for I was planning to debut a new strategy. It was called Make Caleb As Angry As Possible So That He Says Something Mental And You Can Record It. In a strange way, I was looking forward to it. It would be a big switch-up in style.

I'd practiced using the handheld recorder a few times on the week-end. It was a little cylinder of a thing, no longer than four inches, with a little red record button on it. Obviously I couldn't pull it out and press record in the middle of the meeting, so I went to the bathroom first and hit the button and put it in my pocket. I'd trialed that out a few times at home, but still, I was constantly terrified I'd accidentally press the but-ton again with my thigh and switch the thing off.

Onto the trading floor and into the office. Here we go, time for a game.

From the very beginning, Caleb was restrained and placid. His story-telling panache was all gone. What a shame. Such a far cry from the man in the restaurant. I needed the old Caleb back.

Don't give up! Poke him a little. Nothing. It was like getting blood from a stone. Fuck! Why hadn't I thought of this before the dinner in the restaurant? Why hadn't I recorded it then?

Maybe he knows. Maybe your sudden increase in expansiveness has drawn his eyes to the bulge in your pocket.

Never mind that, keep going. Fucking hell, what have you got to lose?

"We're very sorry that things have gone this way. We're very sorry you've made this choice."

"You're not sorry! You never fucking cared about me! You never gave me a fucking chance! From the very beginning you've had Hisa fucking stuck up my arse! How am I supposed to trade with him sitting behind me like that!? Fucking timing my fucking toilet breaks! What were you thinking fucking keeping him on!? Everyone knows that he should have been fired!"

"Oh Come On!" He's shouting now. He's cracking. We've got him! "It was you who never gave it a chance. You've not been serious since the day you got here. You always knew that you wanted to leave! Turning up the day after bonus day and saying you want to quit. That was your plan since the day you arrived! And you didn't even take a moment to think about it, did you? You went from my office straight to HR. Do you know how it makes me look, you coming over to Tokyo and doing absolutely nothing? I moved heaven and earth to get you here! Do you know what this makes me look like!? After everything I did for you!? I hired you! I made you! You were nothing! All that money we paid you!"

I should have let him run, but I didn't.

"Money!? Oh I owe you money, do I!? Listen. For every fucking dollar I made out of Citibank, Citibank made ten out of me. You fucking know it. You *know* that's the truth. And you *never* could have made it without me."

That shut him up, and that sat him down, and for one moment I glowed with pride. Then I remembered the whole plan had been to get him fucking talking and we sat there for a minute in silence.

"So. Am I getting my sick leave then?"

He was right back to the Caleb that had entered the meeting. Cold, professional, aloof. Fuck, I'd fucked it.

"We are not allowed to approve your sick leave. The Company Doctor will decide."

11

SOMEWHAT RIDICULOUSLY, I WAS BACK, ONCE AGAIN, ON THE STIRT desk. Sandwiched between Hisa and Kousuke, with literally no work to do. I pulled out my Japanese textbooks and I started studying kanji.

I was pissed that I hadn't gotten anything good from the meeting. And I was shitting myself about the company doctor. It was obvious from what Caleb had said that he had the whole of HR lined up. He was bound to have the company doctor as well. If the company doctor denied my sick leave, I would be fucked. I'd die if I stayed on the desk.

Wait a minute. Wait wait wait wait. Maybe we've got something here. What did he say? "You went from my office straight to HR." He shouldn't be in cahoots with HR, should he—surely that isn't allowed? He shouldn't know that you went straight to HR after your first meeting with him about leaving. He shouldn't know about that . . . right? That shit should be confidential . . . shouldn't it? Fuck, maybe you've got something here.

Email HR under the pretense of arranging a meeting with the company doctor.

Dear Icicle,

Could I have a meeting regarding my application for sick leave.

Kind regards,
Gary Stevenson

Once more to the windowless room, dear friends. This time make sure you press record.

As always, she's cold and impassive. Her posture impossibly straight. In the face of such prodigious straightness, I felt even more like a rat.

Who cares, there weren't nobody looking. This time, at least, there's a plan.

"Can I ask you a question?"

My opening gambit.

"Of course, Gary, what's the question?"

"Are our meetings confidential?"

She hadn't been expecting that. Did she waver a little? If she did it was less than a blink.

"It depends."

"It depends? What do you mean it depends?"

"It depends."

"Depends on fucking what!?"

She placed both her perfect hands on the back of a perfect Moleskine notebook. You really shouldn't swear to HR.

"Some conversations are confidential, and others are not confidential. So you see Gary, it really depends."

"OK, so," I was getting a little exasperated. "What is confidential and what's not?"

"Well, for example, if you were to suggest anything about hurting yourself, I'd have no choice but to escalate that."

"Oh for fuck's sake I'm not talking about hurting myself. Listen, when I came to talk to you at the beginning of February, to ask you about me leaving and going to work for charity, did you talk to Caleb about that?"

"No, I didn't."

She answered that quickly. Too quickly.

"Are you sure?"

"I did not talk to Caleb about that meeting."

A slight pause. Are we going to do this? Yeah, we're gonna do it.

"OK so why have I just come right now out of a meeting with Caleb, where he has told me that you did?"

A much, much, much longer pause now. I know, in fact, exactly how long it was, because I have listened back to the recording several times. It was forty-seven seconds. That's a long pause in a one-on-one meeting.

Throughout the pause, the Icicle was motionless. Perfectly motionless, like a statue. Her long, slender fingers did not tap once on the back of her notebook. Not the slightest quaver of her mouth. Her eyes did not dart. Was she thinking? I'm pretty sure she didn't even blink.

For my part, I vibrated gently. I wondered to myself as I watched her: does her hair even sway in the wind?

Finally, she spoke:

"I have looked into the details of your deferred compensation, and of you leaving to go work for charity. If you want to do that, no one can stop you. It's beyond the power of the bank."

Well. What can you say about that then? There was still yet some fight in the rat.

After that, I went to the company doctor. He was three floors below, far from the trading floor. In a small, brightly lit office, a middle-aged, salt-and-pepper-haired, friendly-looking Japanese man sat low, arms on his ample stomach, on a small plastic chair. Behind him stood a young, pretty Japanese woman in a nurse's uniform.

The man sat me down. He asked me what was wrong. It felt somehow as if he cared.

Well. I suppose I should tell you what happened. I spoke for a minute, and then I broke down. Those were the only people I could cry to. Two people I'd never even met.

I don't think I had realized, until that moment, quite how fucked I had become. I think I had told myself, at times, that it was all just a strategy, a game. Maybe it wasn't a game though. Maybe it was my life.

He wrote me three months' paid sick leave.

After that, for a moment, I faltered. I wavered and I didn't move.

Once more I found myself at the edge of the atrium. I looked down, but I didn't jump.

I had it now, I had my sick note. But I didn't apply for the leave.

After I came out of the doctor's office, I went back to the trading floor, just to pick up my little string bag, and then I went home.

At some point that day, the cat must have gotten out of the bag, and the situation escaped from the circle of just senior management. I know that because I started getting texts from the guys back in London.

Snoopy texted, "Don't give up! You can beat them! You're smarter than those fuckers!"

Titzy texted, "It will be a shame to see you go man, I thought you were going to run this place one day."

I thought I would get a text from Billy, but I didn't until very late in the evening. It said: "You all right Gal? Management said you're trying to leave, and they keep asking me to get you to stay. They said that you applied for sick leave for stress. What's up Gal? R u OK?"

That was the only message I replied to.

"Don't worry about me boss. I'm always OK."

Probably that was a lie.

So. Why didn't I apply for the sick leave?

What I told myself at the time was that it was risky. I was worried that if I applied for the sick leave, it would trigger legal action from the bank.

Was that real though? Was that danger real? You can't get sued for going on sick leave . . . can you?

I suppose, looking back, it was more than that. I think on some level I knew what it meant. No more PnL, no more Liquidator. No more envious looks from ambitious young men.

I had a meeting with Rupert, for the meetings had still not stopped. There was no one else in this meeting, just Rupert and me. He was on the screen, on the video call, in Caleb's bright room in the sky.

I sat down and I looked at my shoes.

"You know, Gary, nobody believes you. Nobody believes that you're sick. They think that this whole thing's a ploy, for more money, or to get out of the bank with your deferred stock, so you can go and work for Goldman Sachs."

I did nothing, I stared and I nodded. Sometimes I used to do long division in my head.

"But I believe you."

That caught my attention. I looked up and into the screen.

"Gary, where would you want to be right now? If you could be any-where?"

I thought about it for a little, and then I answered him honestly.

"Nowhere. I don't want to be anywhere. To be honest Hobbs, I don't really care."

"How's Harry?"

"How's Harry!? He's fine . . . Yeah, he's fine."

Of course, Rupert had no idea that we'd fallen out, that I'd not spoken to Harry in nearly a year.

"How about playing football with Harry, back on the street where you grew up, in Ilford. Is that a place you'd rather be?"

How old was Harry when we started playing football together? He must have been only five or six. I must have been nine or ten then, in that case. How old was he when he got better than me?

"Yeah. Yeah I suppose so. Yeah, I would."

Those days on the street were a long time ago, and that lamp post and that telegraph pole, and that concave wall on the recycling center, they were all a long, long way away. Often we'd kick the ball over into the recycling center, and we'd have to climb in to get it, round the side. Over the big iron bridge, through the garden of an old man who would shout at you through his window, and then into the recycling center itself, with its huge mounds of old dirty newspapers that must have been twenty feet tall. Then you'd kick the ball over and you'd climb back around, and you'd start playing football again. In the winter we'd keep going until way after the sun went down, until someone's mum came out and shouted it was time for dinner. Sometimes it would be my mum, sometimes it would be Harry's mum. Sometimes we'd eat together, sometimes we'd eat alone.

"You can get there. You can get back to that place."

No I fucking can't, I'm never speaking to that kid again.

"It's OK. Everything's going to be OK. You just need to stay strong and get through this. You will be OK."

Why was he doing this? Why was Rupert doing this?

"Thanks Hobbs. I appreciate that. Thank you."

"That's OK, you're going to be OK."

Call signs off.

I sat there alone in the office, staring out at the Emperor's Palace. I got a text on my personal phone. It was Rupert.

"Apply for the sick leave. The bank can't do anything. They don't have anything on you."

So I did.

12

THREE MONTHS.

Three months isn't a long time. To me it felt like forever.

I hadn't had three months free since I'd been nineteen. I spent most of that time fluffing pillows.

It felt like coming up for air.

The first thing I did was I took the bullet train out to Hyotanyama. Change at Kyoto. Change at Yamato-saidaiji.

Wizard used to live in this tiny little plastic apartment that had been given to her by her school. You slept at the top of a ladder, on a shelf, your nose nearly touching the roof. Lots of young Japanese people live like that, no real kitchen to speak of, windows frosted so no one can see.

The only heating was a little air conditioning unit, and in winter it was always freezing. It was ours though, we didn't have to share.

I went there and I don't think I'd even told her I was coming, so she was surprised but she wasn't surprised.

We'd climb up the ladder and throw the futon to the ground, and I'd spend a lot of time down there, on the floor, and she'd patter round and heat up a cup of ramen, and ask me if I had seen any good films.

It was cold but we'd dress up warm and go to a little local park in Hyotanyama. She'd put down a little picnic blanket she had, and she'd lay on her front, and I'd nestle my head in the small of her back and we'd both just lie there and read books. Or we'd go to the big parks in Nara, see the huge, old, wooden temples. Feed deer.

But around it all still, there were meetings, which hadn't stopped, even though I was on sick leave, only now they were just on my phone. I'd lay the phone down, on speakerphone, on the futon, and I'd lie next to it, on the floor. I'd spread myself out, like a starfish, and then I'd look upward, over my own head, so that I was looking, upside down, through the frosted window, and as management nattered on in the background, I'd watch the distorted blue sky as it slowly turned black.

Sometimes Wizard would come, and sit next to me, and when she did that, she'd pick the phone up and she'd just hang up the call, and she'd say,

"Come on Gary, that's enough of that."

I took a flight home, to see my mum. I'm not sure why, we were never really close. I took her out for a ride, on the little black Vespa that I'd bought with my first bonus, all the way through central London to Regent's Park. We took a walk, through the gardens and round the lake. I asked her why she'd never learned to play guitar.

She looked at me strange. Everyone used to look at me strange back then. Then she asked me,

"Gary, are you OK?"

And I said,

"Yeah yeah yeah. Yeah I'm OK. You know me, I'm always OK."

On the plane back I watched *Cool Hand Luke,* for the first time, with Paul Newman, the most handsome man in the world. He gets sent to prison, I don't know, coz he's messed up, and he ends up on a chain gang.

The leader of the gang is a bit of a bully, and he challenges Paul Newman to a fight. Paul is much smaller, and he doesn't have a chance, and the bully hits him again and again. Each time he goes down he gets up again, a thousand times, till he's beaten black and blue. Eventually the bully gives up.

What a guy, I thought, that Paul Newman. What a wonderfully handsome guy.

I floated for a bit, in this period, and my sleeping and eating were weird. I slept in the day, and then in the night, I wandered and scavenged for food.

But I meant it, I really do mean it, there could not have been a better place.

Tokyo has plenty of food, for the lonely man, and as spring comes, it brings warmth as well.

There was a little ramen place, near my building. They did pork ramen, but chicken ramen too. The broth was clear and fine, and very vinegary. It was delicious. That place is closed down nowadays.

The opening hours of that place were not very long, I usually slept through them, but then there was Yoshinoya. Sweet Yoshinoya, the queen of my nighttimes, your bright orange windows never let me down. Yoshinoya is 24/7 beef on rice. Delicious, always, fast and cheap. Unlimited pickled pink ginger. Sometimes, they even sell eel.

There were things you couldn't find in Japan, like green peas. Sometimes, I would miss them a lot. I finally found them in Saizeriya, the most Japanese Italian restaurant chain in the world. Cheap, generous portions, beloved of students, they'd mix the green peas in with bacon, and serve with a barely cooked egg.

It wasn't always fast food. Sometimes I'd be up at the right time, and I could get something gourmet: steak frites at the French restaurant in Toranomon. Citibank were still paying me, you know.

Not that you really need money, in Tokyo, to eat like a king. The sushi might as well have been free. Sushi Zanmai, Kamiyacho, at least three times a week. Tsukedon, marinated tuna on rice. The large size (*oomori*), the same price. Comes with miso soup and green tea, for only 500 yen. They gave me a little hundred-yen discount voucher every time I went, so then it was only 400 yen. £2.50! I'd sit at the counter and banter with the sushi man.

Do yourself a favor. Go to an Izakaya. Ask for umeboshi ochadzuke. You don't have to thank me. Just enjoy.

Freshness Burger. Miso/shio/shouyu/tonkotsu ramen, in that order. But the karashibi ramen in Kanda is the best. Banh mi from a back alley in Takadanobaba. Cold soba with that brown sauce from 7-Eleven. Tuna mayonnaise onigiri from 7-Eleven. Famichikin. Gyoza from that place in Azabujuban. Tuna on rice, every day, for breakfast (if you've just woken up, then it's defined as a breakfast). Dipping noodles from Fu-u-u-u-unji. Grilled mackerel from Yayoiken.

All of these places were open, and full of alone, lonely men. The ramen places were especially like that, and Yoshinoya deep into the night. Lonely men line up next to one another, and slurp down delicious food, in a line. Their shoulders and elbows rub against one another as they dip their chopsticks into bowls. Then they pay their 600 yen, and they leave.

Where on earth could be better to be depressed?

I woke up in the middle of the day one day, fully clothed, and I checked my phone. It was 12:37 p.m. I had 127 missed calls, all from Harry.

I sat up in bed, and I thought for a little. The previous day had been his birthday.

13

OK, I SUPPOSE IT'S TIME TO MOVE NOW. ONE SHOULD NOT WAIT FOR
vengeance to come.

Yes, yes. I had had enough ramen. It was time to go get lawyered up.

I messaged Sagar Malde. Remember him? The Kenyan boy from
LSE. He'd been at Lehman for two months before they collapsed back
in 2008, and he knew people who'd sued the bank. I needed someone
who knew about that kind of thing, and I asked him to put me in touch.

In the end, I ended up with three lawyers, one in the UK, one in
America, and one in Japan. It was expensive, but Citibank had upped
my salary to £120,000 a year when they moved me to Japan, so in a way,
it was all on them: the lawyers, the sushi, the ramen. I should really be
thankful, I guess.

The lawyers didn't really tell me anything I hadn't already figured out
for myself.

Can the bank sue you for doing fucking nothing?

Well, obviously, legally, they shouldn't. But you definitely wouldn't
be the first.

Can I go to work for charity and keep my deferred stock?

Technically, according to the paperwork, yes. But what's paperwork
against Citibank?

Should I be suing the bank?

You could do, but you'd probably be in court for years, plus they owe
you two million pounds.

Hmm, court forever. What do you think about court forever? Wasn't
that what we were trying to avoid?

But in that case then, what are your options? There's nothing to do really, but wait. You sit out the rest of your three months, you sleep in the daytime. You try to recover some weight. After the three months, you go back, apply for charity (you'll have to find a charity) and hope that it works.

It wasn't really a foolproof plan.

I found a video on the internet about wealth inequality. No one hardly ever talked about wealth inequality back then. It was by a South African professor who was teaching anthropology at LSE. I emailed him and told him I was looking to work for a charity that was looking at wealth inequality. He put me in touch with one, and we had a meeting. They said they would help me to leave.

That was the only piece of work that I had. I waited for my time to run out.

With the lawyers, and the charity, and some weight on my bones, I felt a bit more confident. I had a plan now; I had a game. But it didn't go away though, that pounding sensation in my stomach and heart. I suppose it was fear, what I felt then. I had these dull pains in my thighs.

I used to lie on the floor a lot. Belly down, in the sunlight, by the window. It was exactly like I used to do when I was a kid, when I was expelled and I didn't have no school to go to. Belly down, on the floor, by the window, doing maths homework on a little wooden board.

It doesn't fill me with pride to admit this, but I was terrified about going back. I was terrified of those three months running out, and having to go back to the bank.

Before long, the three months had gone. My first meeting was with the company doctor. I walked in and I told him, truthfully, how scared I was. The terror I had of going back. He looked in my eyes and he nodded, and he wrote me another three months.

By then it was late May, which is a beautiful time to be in Tokyo. Many Japanese don't like it, because it is the beginning of the rainy season. The city becomes very hot, very quickly, and the sun gathers a blazing strength. The air becomes immensely humid, and when you go out, into the world, it feels like a hot towel has been dropped on your shoulders.

I liked it. I really did like it a lot.

The Japanese word for "rainy season" is "tsuyu," and the Chinese characters that they use to write it, "梅雨," translate to English as "plum rain." I'd never seen that rain before, in England; the rain that comes down as hot plums. Heavy, hot rain comes down in thick walls, as if they were waves from the sea.

The rain was so heavy that if I got caught in a rainstorm on my bicycle, I'd be soaked through within ten seconds. I'd carry an entire spare set of clothes, wrapped tight in a plastic bag inside my backpack, and when I arrived anywhere, I'd have to get completely changed. My favorite was when it was raining with a really strong wind; the hot rain driving into your face.

When I got written that second three months, the thought occurred to me, of course: "Could it be this, then, forever?"

Could I live in this way, onward and onward, season after season, just sick? As long as I was sick forever, I'd never have to go back to work. The world would float on, like the seasons, and I'd spend my life cycling through rain.

How would that be? Would that be a good thing? Is that a good game? Is that a good life?

I started to cycle even more in the nighttime, when it wasn't so blindingly hot. My favorite places to cycle were Shinjuku and Shibuya. Those two places were palaces of neon, that would smudge through your eyes in the rain. One time I cycled to Kabukicho, in Shinjuku. There were tiny bars there with drunk Japanese people, the perfect places to practice Japanese.

I parked my bike toward the south end of the area, close to the Prince Hotel and far from the bars. I wanted to walk through the packed, bright neon alleys, to rub my shoulders with more lonely men.

I locked my bicycle to the railings, in the broad plaza that faces the hotel. To the front, a huge road is filled with taxis. They sit, in three lines, and they purr. To the side, the green trains of the Yamanote line trundle over a railway bridge. Everywhere tall tall tall buildings, and everywhere huge neon signs. To the west, to my right, as I stand by the road, the skyscraper district looms in the sky, one black tower draped in white metal cobwebs. Across the road, glowing in orange, Yoshinoya places more beef on rice. Above it, a huge LED screen, the size of five houses, rolls and glows. Kyary-Pamyu Pamyu dances on that screen, enormous red bow on her head.

A hot wind hit my face as another train passed.

I suppose I should make this a home.

After that, I tried to do more. Learn more Japanese, make some friends.

I got myself a lovely, middle-aged Japanese tutor. Her name was Yoko Ueno. She wore a face mask in every season: in summer, it was for the humidity, in autumn, it was cold and flu; in winter it was for the dryness, and in spring to keep out the pollen.

I found out about "English Language Conversation Cafés," which is where insane people in Tokyo go to speak foreign languages. You sit there and drink tea and you talk to nutcases. It was perfect for me, at the time.

My favorite English Language Conversation Café was in Takadan-obaba, a student area just to the north of Shinjuku. I loved watching the students. In the summer, they'd get blind drunk in big groups and fall through the streets, and then someone would drop to the floor. When that happened, their friends would have to pull them up, but they'd lie there and shout, "I'm OK!" The game was to try, with your whole might, just to stay there, to lie on the floor. Normally, your friends manage to raise you. If they don't, you just sleep there all night.

I was getting better. I thought I was getting better. But I'd been away from work for five months.

The more time I spent out of the office, the more impossible it seemed to go back. When I spoke to Wizard about the end of my sick leave, I would sometimes get a little overwhelmed. I started to get these very slight twinges, in the corner of my left eye, and these very slight shakes in my arm.

When that used to happen, Wizard would put her hand on my hand. She would never say anything about how it was shaking, but she would say, "Why do you fight them Gary? You don't need to fight them. You've got enough. Why don't you just leave?"

She was wrong there. It's never enough. And I'd never leave. Not if it meant letting them win.

14

MY SECOND THREE MONTHS OF SICK LEAVE WAS APPROACHING ITS end, and I was pretty sure it would get extended again. I was definitely still good and sick.

But a week before I was due to see the doctor, I got an email from Kyle Zimmerman.

Kyle Zimmerman was an American, and the head of HR in the Tokyo office—the Icicle's boss. He was small and he looked like a rat. That reminded me of me, at that time of my life. I felt that that made things more fair.

His email explained, in great detail, a legal technicality, referring to the money I was owed. It came with an awful lot of paperwork, but the summary was quite clearly made.

A sabbatical from the office, for more than six months, meant the money, in its entirety, would be canceled.

I wouldn't really have called it a sabbatical, but I don't think that anyone cared.

I went in and I spoke to the doctor. He was very clear: I shouldn't go back. I told him it wasn't really up to me. I had to go, I had no choice.

He put his hand on my shoulder then, when he spoke to me, which is a very rare thing for Japanese people to do. He looked at me, for a while, before speaking.

"I suppose, then, that it can't be helped."

Wizard came to Tokyo. I told her that I had to go back.

I could see that she could see that I was scared, and I could also see that she was hurt.

"Don't go," she said. "Just don't do it."

In her green eyes, there, we both could see it. Me not sleeping, me losing more weight.

"It's not about that Wizard, it's not an option. It's something that I have to do."

"You don't *have* to do it, you're *choosing* to do it! You don't have to do any of this! You've got enough! You could leave at any moment! Why are you doing this to yourself!?"

"It doesn't matter. It doesn't matter what I do to myself. This is something that I have to do."

She looked at me and she looked like she was going to cry. But she didn't cry, and she pursed her lips and she didn't say whatever it was that she was going to say. I'll probably always wonder what she would have said.

I broke up with her later that day. A week later I went back to work.

The day before I went back into the office, a strange thing happened. I was eating at a restaurant that was at the top of my building. I didn't live in the sky in the Prudential Tower anymore. By this time, I had moved to another area called Atago, which has a tiny shrine at the top of a hill, up a tall flight of very steep stairs. A samurai rode his horse up the stairs one time, to deliver plum blossoms. It took him forty-five minutes to get down.

In my new building I was no longer on the thirtieth floor. I was on the eighth floor, which is still high, but my new apartment faced up a hill, over a graveyard, which meant that, from my window, I could see the very tops of trees. I liked that a lot.

It was a fancy corporate apartment building that I lived in, and there was a private restaurant on the top floor. The prices were surprisingly reasonable, and I would eat there quite often, if I was awake for its opening hours.

I would always get the same thing: a little salmon, avocado, rice bowl thing they did, that came with an umeboshi, which is the sourest and most delicious circular food in the world. It was so sour that every time I ate it, my face would twist up from the sourness, and there was a Japanese waitress there, in her late twenties or very early thirties, who thought it was very funny.

The day before I went back into the office, late in the evening, after eating in the restaurant, I noticed a little, hand-written letter had been placed under my door. All it said was,

You looked very sad in the restaurant. I hope everything's OK. If you need someone to talk to you can message me at this address. Maki.

The next day I went back to work.

15

BY THIS POINT, SIX MONTHS INTO MY SICK LEAVE, NOBODY CALLED
me anymore. Caleb didn't call me, the Slug didn't call me. There were
no more management meetings.

I had firmly passed into the realm of HR now. Kyle Zimmerman;
HR's super-rat. The Icicle, it seemed, had been removed from the board;
a skillful take, I thought, on my part.

One of the earliest pieces of advice that Billy had given me was that
"Talking to HR is never a good thing." I'd definitely fucked that one up.

Kyle Zimmerman's office was in the corner of the small HR department. I had to walk through the department to get there and I tried to
make eye contact with the Icicle, but she never looked up the whole time.

The office was small, with a window, and orderly. Filing cabinets
spanned the length of one wall. The desk was sparse, with little ornamentation. One notepad, one expensive pen. There was life in Kyle's
eyes as I walked through the door, and he smiled as he welcomed me in.

I was recording everything, of course, and I had considered shouting
and slinging accusations, in the hope of eliciting some sort of admission or
slip, as I had tried doing with Caleb. But I was too curious to know what
their plan was, so I listened. Surely they couldn't put me back on STIRT?

Kyle spoke with a smooth animation. Efficiency paired with élan. He
was glad to see that I'd recovered. That was quite funny, and I quite
nearly laughed. He was delighted to say they'd found me a new role.
That was really quite funny as well. I enjoyed the dark style of Kyle Zimmerman, I wished he'd been in more meetings.

Kyle took me upstairs and led me out onto the trading floor. I can't
lie, my heart skipped a beat. I could see everyone, especially, back there
in the far corner, Caleb's lumbering frame.

The STIRT desk was directly in front of me, but we didn't go there. Instead, Kyle led me right, and then right again. Round a corner, past the printers, and into a nook. That's where I met Gerald Gunt.

Gerald Gunt was, without a doubt, the most boring man that I have ever met, on a trading floor or anywhere else. He was a man who wore glasses more alive than his eyes, with a soul that seemed yearning for death.

Really, I thought, I know I'm not at my best, but really, now . . . *Me* against *him*!? I felt the blood back in my fingers, again. I thought: here's a game I can win.

I was quite a little while without wins by that time, so the thought brought some small cheer to me. I reached out and I took his hand tightly.

"Hello Gerald, my name is Gary."

The decision had been made to move me into "Business Management." Don't ask me what Business Management is; I didn't know then and I still don't know now. All I know is it's Gerald's department. They did spreadsheets. They did paperwork.

Gerald didn't smile. I have never once seen Gerald smile. But he looked to the ground, and he pushed his glasses up the bridge of his nose. He levered himself from his chair slowly, with what seemed to be his very last reserves of willpower. He started to walk, and I followed him, to the most depressing office in the world.

The only light in Gerald Gunt's office came from a single and sickly-blue halogen bulb, which buzzed and sputtered its death throes on the wall. The ceiling light was broken. Weren't we all?

Gerald Gunt spoke in tones that were long and wide-drawn and monotonous. There was a boringness to his voice that was so extreme that it bordered on intensity. It had a mournfulness; deep, like an echo; like the moans of a lost, lonely whale.

He was explaining my job to me. I wasn't listening. I was looking all around the room. This must be the room that you wait in when you're going to hell but there's some sort of administrative delay. It was completely devoid of ornament or decoration, excepting one, single, personal touch. There, on the desk, was a single framed photo, of Gerald, and, presumably, his wife.

His wife looked young in the picture. Maybe in her mid-twenties. She was Japanese, and she was very pretty. She was smiling. He was smiling too. He must have been a similar age himself, in the photo. God, how old must he be now? It was impossible to say. What happened, Gerald? What happened to you Gerald? Where did you go? Did you take a wrong turn?

I don't know how long I sat in that office and looked at that photo, but it must have been a long time, because Gerald was finished. I smiled at him, genuinely and deeply, and I tried my best to crush his hand.

I had gathered not one single thing from Gerald's monologue about the work I was supposed to be doing. I had, in fact, recorded the entire thing, but I never listened to it again in my whole life, due to a great fear of it aging me by several years.

As such, it was, from an administrative perspective at least, something of a relief when Gerald followed up our meeting with an email outlining my work.

It was long, arduous, detailed, spreadsheet work, which made sense entirely, for Gerald was a long, arduous, detailed, spreadsheet man. From my brief scan of his email, the quantity of the work he had assigned me was enormous. It would take several weeks, if not months.

This was it. After all my fear of returning, after all that trepidation, this was all they had. This was all that they fucking had. Putting me in the corner, next to the recycling bins, and trying to get me to write lines on Excel like a permanent fucking detention. And they were paying me one hundred and twenty fucking grand a year for that. Well, fuck that. I've had a lot of detentions in my lifetime, they never once stopped me being a dick.

I opened a new sheet on Microsoft Excel, and did the whole thing in fifteen minutes.

Two weeks later, Gerald called me into his office, and he asked to see my spreadsheet. I had been looking forward to this.

I had emailed it to him, in advance of the meeting.

He opened it, and was completely baffled.

"What is this? Where is it? Is this all that you've done?"

I caught the dull gray of his eyes and I smiled.

"Yes Gerald, that's all that I've done."

"But nothing's here! None of the work's here!"

I furrowed my brow and I scratched my hair. That was, indeed, quite concerning.

"I'm sorry Gerald . . . Are you sure there's a problem? I'm sure that's what you asked me to do!"

One more smile, and Gerald was defeated. The meek shall inherit the earth.

Gerald never once gave me a single piece of work to do after that. Nobody did.

In fact, nobody spoke to me at all, ever. And I had absolutely nothing to do. On very rare occasions, when he was sure nobody was looking, Kousuke would sneak by and leave an onigiri on my desk or something. There was a long corridor between the trading floor and the bathroom, and sometimes I would see Caleb coming toward me in the opposite direction as I went to or returned from brushing my teeth, and he'd always suddenly pretend he'd forgotten his passcard or something and turn back.

Once I felt I knew how the land lay, I emailed Kyle and asked him how many holiday days I had accumulated.

I had not taken a lot of holidays over my career as a trader, really not a lot. And of course, the previous six months had been sick leave with no official holidays. He told me I had over fifty days accumulated, so I posted the next six weeks off work.

It was autumn now, and I traveled. I had already been to Kyoto, many times, with Wizard, so I decided to go further, to Hiroshima, where they put noodles in the okonomiyaki.

I hadn't been expecting the return to the bank to be so easy. In my mind the police would have been there, or something, with lawyers to take me straight to jail. I hadn't expected a well-paid job, with absolutely no work, and with convenient access to the printers. What did it mean?

Did it mean they really didn't have anything on me? Had they looked and found nothing to find?

I went to the English Language Conversation Café in Takadanobaba many times, and I spoke to many, many people. Often I spoke to Japanese people, but the café also served as a hub for miscreants and wandering reprobates from every corner of the earth. One time I found myself drinking tea for several hours with a middle-aged Dutchman with sandy brown hair and a towering nose. He'd met a Japanese girl when he was young; they'd gotten married; they divorced. He had become a priest, and he stayed.

I found myself talking and talking, and the whole of my story spilled out. I'd never told anyone the whole story; I'd never told anyone I was a millionaire. I probably talked for over an hour, while the Dutch priest nodded and sipped a few beers. Eventually, I finished, and I waited, and he said,

"Fock man. That's pretty focked op."

My sister came to visit and, since I had really liked the place, I took her back to Hiroshima, and to the holy island of Miyajima, which is also called Itsukshima, where the huge, red torii gate stands in the sea, and I stripped down and swam through the torii gate, and when the sun went down we fed the deer.

My sister asked how work was going, so I showed her some pictures I'd drawn, on my desk, in the office. One was of John Lennon, one was of Paul McCartney.

I hadn't really explained my work situation to my sister and she squinted at the pictures and then squinted at me, and then she asked me if I was OK. I laughed and said, "Yeah Debz, I'm always OK."

And she laughed, because she knew it was true.

When I went back to the office, in late autumn, early winter, I devoted myself full time to studying Japanese, studying kanji (the little, originally Chinese, pictorial characters from which Japanese is written) and drawing pictures of the Beatles.

My drawing actually got pretty good. At one point, a junior staff member, who presumably did not know the details or history of my extended detention, passed my desk and noticed my work.

"Hey! That's really good! It's Ringo Starr, right?"

"Thank you. Yes it is."

"That's really good! You're really good, man! What is it for?"

"I'm not really sure, to be honest . . . I guess maybe something like . . . Creative development? I'm trying to make it look like this photo."

And I showed him the source photo. He looked a little confused.

"Yes . . . but . . . What's it *for*, you know? How do we use it?"

I didn't say anything. I was also confused by this question, and we shared a brief, intimate, mutual confusion. After a little while, he started to nod and slowly backed away.

After a few weeks of this, I started to realize that, due to having no actual work, I had quite a lot of spare time, and so, after a meeting with all of the people in the office who were speaking to me, which was no one, we unanimously agreed that I should reduce my working hours to one or two hours a day.

I would come in at about ten and start studying or drawing. Sometimes I would have paperwork from my lawyers, which I would print on the printers that were conveniently nearby. At about twelve I would go and get lunch, and then I'd go straight home. My favorite place to get lunch was Kikanbou Karashibi Ramen in Kanda, where white-shirted salarymen would sweat profusely whilst eating insanely spicy ramen in a small, smoky, dimly lit room, which was covered with red demon masks. The spicy ramen would make me really tired, and get me ready for a really good nap.

I did that for another few weeks. In the evenings I would go to the conversation café, and on the weekends I would meet up with this Japanese girl who worked as a waitress in the Beatles Bar in Roppongi. She was cute, and she didn't speak any English, and my Japanese was getting a lot better. She used to come to my big corporate apartment, and sit on the floor instead of the sofa. One day, she turned round and she said to me, "Hey, how do you afford this place when you hardly ever work?"

Gradually, I started to wonder if I might have found the best job in the world.

16

IN DECEMBER OF 2013 KYLE CALLED ME INTO HIS OFFICE. I WAS hoping that I might be fired, which would have been the ultimate victory.

Kyle sat me down in a chair and he did that smile. Such a wonderful smile for a rat.

"How's work going?" he asked.

"Yes, it's wonderful. My work's really wonderful. How's yours?"

"Yes, it's good. Yes, it's good." He stopped smiling. "Why haven't you applied for the charity route?"

"The charity route?"

"Yes, the charity route. The Icicle said that you'd like to apply."

"Oh! The charity route! Yes, that is true. I'd very much like to apply."

"That's very nice, so why have you not applied?"

"Well, you know . . . I've just got so much work . . ."

"What kind of work is it, Gary, that you're doing?"

"I'm not quite sure you'd understand it Kyle . . . You know, it is very creative."

He smiled again and turned to his computer. He sent me the documents to leave.

As you might imagine, I was very pleased with that development. The door was there, I just had to walk through.

But, did I want to leave?

Listen, looking back, in hindsight, I can see that my situation was not particularly healthy. I was not, strictly speaking, a free man, and I was in constant fear of being sued. Senior management would occasionally glare at me, and I, being sensible, had to submit and resist glaring back.

That pained me, but, in a way, really, my quality of life was really quite good. I was kind of getting my first Japanese girlfriend, my Japanese was coming on a storm, I'd made quite a lot of half-friends now from the conversation café, and I had a list of restaurants you wouldn't believe. Plus, you know, Christmas was coming. I decided to give it some time.

The Japanese are not great at Christmas; they confuse Santa with the KFC man. A group of madmen from the conversation café went to karaoke to celebrate.

I still didn't like karaoke. I'm not actually that bad a singer, but I used to get really self-conscious. An old Japanese man named Hiroshi, in his sixties with a proud head of white hair, sat me down after I sang my song.

"You know, in karaoke, it doesn't matter if you sing well or sing badly. What matters is, your guests have a good time."

After that, I enjoyed karaoke much better. Maybe that, too, is a lesson for life.

For New Year's Eve, at midnight, I went with a group of people from the café, to Hanazono Jinja, to pay my respects.

Paying your respects at a shrine at midnight on New Year's Eve is a Japanese tradition, and long, long queues form in the cold and the dark. Some people wear traditional dress.

The old shrine of Hanazono Jinja is in Kabukicho, which is Tokyo's biggest red-light district. The drinking area is there, Shinjuku Golden Gai, with the tiny, tiny bars for professional drunks, and all around, in every direction, is alcohol, sex and great food.

Those bars were really the place where I learned Japanese, especially my favorite one, the shabby, rundown, but always warm and welcoming "Kangaroo Court Decision." When I went there, I would always order shochu with grapefruit. Eventually, they'd run out of grapefruit, so I'd gradually get more and more shochu in my drinks, until they'd run out of grapefruit completely and the owner would have to run to 7-Eleven to buy more.

We queued up for a long time, at Hanazono Jinja, me and my half-friends from the café. Usually, Japanese people spend New Year's Eve with their families, so all of us there, at the Jinja, were the same on that night: cold people with no families.

I got to the front. I threw a little golden five-yen coin into a little wooden box, and it bounced around a few times before it slipped in. Metal on wood. I grabbed the thick, heavy rope, and I shook it, and the bell rang with a tinny, rattling sound. I bowed, twice, I clapped, twice, I waited. Suddenly, there, in that moment, I felt the cold air come into my lungs again. A cold, wet, midnight kind of air. This time, though, it didn't burn me.

"I guess then it's time to go home."

It took me till about the end of January to get my paperwork together. If I'm honest, I didn't rush it. That charity had offered me a job. They were an American charity, but they said I could work from London, writing about inequality. The global economy had continued its slow-motion collapse all of this time; same old no growth, falling living standards, though it was easy to forget that, from Japan. Sometimes I wondered if they'd kept my old trades on, or if they had closed them all out. They really should have kept them, but I guessed that they hadn't. For some reason, the paperwork package to leave and go to charity was enormous. I waded through it all and applied.

I didn't get a reply until a month later, by email.

"Your application has been rejected."

I suppose that you might have reacted to that in the same way I did at the time.

"Why the fuck did they ask me to apply then?"

It's a stupid question, because the answer was obvious. They did it to show me I was trapped.

They did it to show me that, sure, if I wanted, I could eat all the gyoza in fucking Tokyo. I could cycle around the city for months on end, and

I could cavort with local Beatles fans and I could ring bells on New Year's Eve and swim through historical shrines. I could do all of that, if I wanted. But I couldn't leave. I couldn't go home.

How long would it take me to get all the money out? Three more years? I'd be thirty by then. Nah, fuck that. Fuck that man. Fuck 'em. What would have even been the point of the game?

I hit the red button on my recorder, which I had on me at all times, I slipped it back into my pocket, and I stormed right down to Kyle unannounced.

"What the fuck are you doing!?"

Kyle was so happy. It almost made me happy as well.

"Gary! It's so good to see you! Do we have a meeting? Take a seat."

I sat down.

"What the fuck are you doing?"

"What do you mean, Gary? What is this all about?"

"You know what this is fucking about! What the fuck are you doing?"

"I'm sorry Gary, but I don't know what this is about. I don't think this meeting was prearranged. Is there some problem? What's happened?"

"Why did you reject the charity application?"

"Ohhh the *charity* application!" He smiled and leaned into his chair. "I see now, you've come about that. What's the problem?"

"Why did you reject it?"

"Well now let me see."

He turned to his computer, whose screen I of course could not see, and he spent some time looking at it. He was humming a gay tune which I didn't recognize. I wondered if it was Japanese.

"OK, I've got it. Unfortunately, the charity that you've applied for is not an officially registered charity in the US. It doesn't meet the criteria. Unfortunately, you can't work for them. I'm sorry."

We stared and again he was smiling. That wonderful smile for a rat.

"I know what you're fucking doing."

"I'm sorry, I don't know what you mean."

"You lied to me, and the Icicle lied to me, and Caleb lied to me as well. And the Icicle spoke to Caleb about confidential meetings, and that was illegal. What do you think about that?"

"I'm sorry, Gary, I don't know about any of this. What is this that you're talking about?"

"You *fucking* know what I'm talking about, you fucking *know* it! You've been fucking colluding from the *fucking* start and you *know* you've been doing it, what the *fuck* do you think about *that*?"

There was no way. There was no way to catch him. To anger him, to draw him out. He loved it, he absolutely fucking loved it. Like a pig, he delighted in shit.

"I'm sorry Gary, I really am sorry, but I really don't know what you mean."

It really was a beautiful smile he had. I swear that fucker nearly winked.

There was nothing to do. I went back to my desk and I requested, by email, the official Citibank HR definition of whatever the fuck a fucking charity was. They didn't reply for three weeks. I broke up with the Japanese girl that weekend. I wasn't having another fucking girl watch me with tears in her eyes as my life turned to ashes and bone. I started running around the palace again. Get all the fat off, all the fucking fat off. Cut all the fat off that isn't even there. Cut off everything that you don't need.

What would it mean if I couldn't get out? What would I do? Would I sue the fucking bank? Would I just sit around on the trading floor for another three years, like the fucking ghost of Christmas Past? What would I turn into? What would I become? Would I give up? Turn back? Become Caleb? Would I grow old and gray like Gerald Gunt?

My sleep got fucked up almost immediately, and again I was a creature of night. It was the back end of winter then and the nights were still real cold, and I was flying round in that cold and the neon with icy breath, on my bicycle looking for food.

It was round about then that the police stole the bicycle.

No one steals anything in Japan. No one steals fucking anything. You can throw your wallet on the ground and come back three days later and it won't even have lost any cash. But the police will steal your bike so you best fucking watch it. Don't park it in front of the station.

I asked the reception at my building how to get my bicycle back from the police. They gave me an address and I went there. I had to take the fucking train.

When I got there, I had arrived at what surely must have been, with absolute certainty, the biggest bicycle impound in the world. I have never seen, couldn't even imagine, so many bicycles in one fucking place. A world, a universe, made of bicycles. There can surely, in the entirety of history, have never been a more voracious bicycle thief than the Tokyo police. I guess they have to do something with their time.

They took me to my bicycle. How the fuck they knew where it was precisely was a miracle of modern engineering. It took fifteen minutes just to walk there.

The wheel was broken. I'm not quite sure how. I tried to get it fixed but it was a stupid fucking custom size or something and fixing it was impossible. I'd have to get a brand new one custom made. I had, at that point in my life, had that bicycle for longer than I'd ever had a girl-friend. It was the single thing I had flown over from London. It was the closest thing I had to an old friend.

I took the bicycle and I left it outside the station. The same station where I had fucking lost it. There you go Tokyo police, here's some work for you, steal it again. Then I went to an old, second-hand bike store in a quiet, residential area round the back of Yoyogi Park, close to where Caleb used to live. There was a creaky, old, bent-over man in there, and I asked him in Japanese to show me the cheapest bike they had in the shop.

He took me to this tiny, comedy, yellow "mama-chari," with a little basket and a bell. I tried to ring the bell. It was slightly broken. Weren't we all. I asked him how much it was and he said five thousand yen, which at that time was about £30. I gave him the money and I cycled it home. Sometimes in life you lose your old friends.

Spring 2014. Cherry blossom, and the world's slowest battle of emails.

Citibank took three weeks just to tell me what their definition of a charity was. It was a definition which, I was virtually certain, was satis-fied by my charity. I had to get all the little bits of paperwork together to make this absolutely crystal clear, and send them back to Kyle Zimmer-man. He didn't reply to that for a month. Apparently, on that second application, I'd signed one page, page thirty-six or something, in the wrong fucking place.

It was pretty clear what they were doing, and it was clear it could last a long time. I wondered if it would go on forever, and if they would just keep paying me to sit in Gunt's corner. The blossoms then started to fall.

My mental state deteriorated relatively quickly. Ever since that meeting with the Icicle, when she'd told me there'd been nothing to stop me from leaving, I'd felt that I had an escape rope. It was true, sure, that I'd never known quite how sturdy a rope it had been, but I'd always known that it was there. With that assurance, I had felt that, for the first time in a long time, I could breathe a little, away from the wolves. But now I was back, on the trading floor, and it seemed that I couldn't get out.

I started to spend more time in the office, even though there was little to do. I couldn't enjoy the things that I had previously been doing, so in my free time all I did was run. The cherry blossoms were all gone from the trees, and again, rainy season began.

It was then that Citibank made their next move. They canceled my housing.

Since I'd been in Japan, Citi had been paying for my housing. This is pretty normal for banking expats in Japan, and a big housing allowance, combined with the big salary that I was still getting, was supposed to have been one of my big inducements to move.

I liked the apartment that I lived in, with the view of the graveyard from the balcony, and the restaurant with the umeboshis at the top. If I leaned over and craned my head, from the balcony, I could just about see Tokyo Tower, and that restaurant, up on the forty-second floor, was a good place for people-watching. One time I had watched an American banker talk to a Japanese man and his wife for an entire hour about the novel *Moby-Dick* without the Japanese couple saying a single word the entire time. They spent the whole time just humming and nodding. As the banker walked out he had smiled broadly and nodded at me, while behind him, just over his shoulder, the Japanese man had his head in his hands.

In the evenings, the restaurant was usually empty, and, in summer, which was firework season, I'd sometimes watch the fireworks, out in the distance, over Tokyo Bay, from up in the dark restaurant, alone.

No more fireworks, for me, I guessed. The rent was really expensive and if the bank weren't paying for it and I was leaving the industry I could probably only afford to pay it for two months. I knew that I was totally fucked by this point, and probably wouldn't be able to work again for years. I had started to budget on the assumption that I would never be fit and healthy enough to work again, possibly for the rest of my life.

I had a friend, a guy from Romford, in Essex, which is not far from where I grew up, who had moved to Japan with the express purpose of becoming a stuntman for Power Rangers movies. It had been his childhood dream. He rented a shabby room in a shabby apartment in the Korean town of Shin-Okubo, which is the closest thing that central Tokyo has to a ghetto, and was close to our English-language café, where he worked. I texted asking if I could start sleeping on his floor. He said "Yeah, of course man. No problem."

I wondered if Citibank were gonna keep hitting me like this, with stupid random shit till I gave up and walked. Fine, then, I thought, let them hit me. I won't give up. They won't be the first.

17

IT WAS VERY HOT, AND VERY WET, AFTER THAT, AND I STARTED, ONCE more, to go mad.

I was very sick of sitting and waiting, so I decided to try something new.

I started to email people, lots of people, a different person every day. I emailed the CEO, several times, I emailed the Global Head of HR. These strategies were neither suggested nor approved by my lawyers. They were my own little creative touch.

I can't really remember what I said in these emails. Sometimes I'd refer to their recipients by stylish and innovative nicknames I'd made up, or talk vaguely about cryptic things. At times, I would talk specifically, about the things that Caleb and the Icicle and Kyle Zimmerman had done. Sometimes I would hint darkly that those things would look terrible if they appeared in the newspapers. At other times I would try a bright levity, and tell humorous anecdotes, or talk about food. I learned that the Global Head of HR was a Mormon, so I'd intersperse his emails with little woven snippets of Mormon scripture. I thought that was a very nice touch.

After about two weeks of that, at the very hottest peak of the summer, Kyle Zimmerman called me into his office.

I knew that Kyle Zimmerman would be happy to see me. He always was.

Kyle's office was very familiar to me by this point, and I noticed that he had added a family photo to his own desk. I could now see that Kyle's wife, like Gerald's, was also Japanese, and he had three children who, I supposed, must have been half Japanese. Upon entering the office, I bent at the waist and I looked at this photo closely for a very, very, very long time. It was only then that I looked up at Kyle.

Kyle looked different. As always, he was smiling. But not with his mouth—with his eyes.

This was not right: a total inversion. Kyle Zimmerman was upside down.

This captivated me, and I sat down before him, and for a while, we didn't talk, we just looked.

After that, we had a long conversation, and in that conversation, everything changed.

Now, there are times in stories, as in life, where things happen of which we can't speak. We all know them: they've happened to you, as to me.

There are a variety of reasons for which this can happen. Maybe we cannot betray the trust, or the memory of another—a lover, a very close friend. Maybe the emotions are so deep to us, that they cannot be spoken, cannot be named.

At other times, the reasons we cannot speak come not from the heart, but the head. This is why we don't tell our mothers, when we make four hundred thousand pounds.

And other times still, those reasons are not internal, but external. Sometimes society takes our names onto paper, and it takes that paper and it rolls it up into a ball, and then that ball it stuffs into our mouths.

Which of these happened to me? Did any?

The answer to that, I can't tell you. I'm sorry, honestly, I am. I suppose when we cut ropes that bind us, sometimes we also cut our skin.

I will never forget how happy Kyle looked at the end of that meeting. Not fake happy, not make-believe happy. He was really, honestly, genuinely happy. He shook my hand and I saw pride in his face, like a father who was proud of his son.

Fuck you, I thought, you're a fucking rat. A fucking rat, you are, just like me.

And then, that was it, I was free.

18

HOW DID I WIN? HOW DID I WIN THAT BATTLE?

I would like to tell you it's because I was crazy. Because I was smart and because I was brave. Furthermore, because I was original; because I was creative and wild. That I stepped outside the artificial constraints that bound me, and decided to go totally mad.

But I don't know. It probably wasn't that.

A week before I was set free, at exactly the same time that I was sending insane emails to C-level management, the Slug was fired. I'm not sure why. I would like to think that I was at least one of the reasons, but, again, that probably isn't true.

I am reliably informed, from several sources, that after the Slug was fired, he arranged a video call with all of Citibank Global Sales and Trading, and that on that conference call, he thanked everyone with heartfelt emotion, for all of the work that they had done beneath him, and that then, after that, he broke down in tears. Right there on the call. In front of everyone. All of senior management were on that call, and each one of them, every one of whom hated the man, wiped a cold, mournful tear from his eye.

The confluence of these two separate occurrences—the Slug's firing and my personal descent to a new layer of insanity—mean that I have no way of knowing who won my freedom. Was it me? Or was it the Slug?

The Slug had always been the kindly figure in my meetings, and for that reason, I, perhaps somewhat naively, assumed that it had been Caleb, not the Slug, who had been keeping me at the bank, paying me a £120,000 yearly annual salary, plus housing, for no reason other than to publicly humiliate me, and, perhaps, to prevent me from completing, more fully, the escape that had slipped from his hands.

But maybe I was wrong. Perhaps it never was Caleb. Perhaps it really had all been an act. Perhaps it had been the Slug, after all, keeping me there, and once he'd left, Caleb just let me go.

I do not know. I will never know. I will never know how I won the game.

But it's like that, isn't it? You never really know how much is luck and how much is skill, do you? Perhaps if that Russian linesman, who wasn't even really Russian, didn't give that goal that day, in 1966, then England never win the World Cup. Perhaps if John Terry, who was born where I was born, does not slip in the Champions League Final that evening in Moscow, then Avram Grant is the greatest manager in the world. Perhaps if that day, back in October 2002, Ilford County High School had called the police on me, I would have gotten a criminal record, and I would have been one of those boys with no options, selling drugs on street corners, forever, and none of any of this would ever have happened. You never know, do you? How much is luck and how much is skill?

Maybe I did outplay Citibank, maybe I outmaneuvered them. Maybe I really did play a great game. Or maybe I didn't do any of that. Maybe I just kept getting up, like handsome Paul Newman, and kept getting punched in the face. How do we ever know which of our wins, and which of our losses, were from luck, and which ones were from skill?

And trading is like that, too, isn't it? Sure, I made money in 2011, and 2012, by betting on the collapse of the global economy, the slow but constant and certain collapse of living standards for ordinary people, for ordinary families, the descent of hundreds of millions of families across the world into inescapable poverty, and sure that did actually happen, in the real world, but, in the end, does that mean I was right?

And sure, I did continue betting on those things, almost every year, from my sofa, from my bedroom, until now, until 2023, and sure, it did continue to happen, and sure more and more families now fall into ever-worsening poverty every year, and can't pay their mortgages and can't feed their children. But is that skill, or is that just luck?

We don't know, do we? And maybe we'll never know. So what, in that case, do we do? Do we let it happen or do we stop it from happening?

Do we close our eyes and say, it's just a game? Do we tell ourselves that it is just luck?

For after all, the wealthy economists, with their small hearts and smart suits and even smarter accents, are confident that they're right, as well. They are just as confident as I am, when they tell us that things will get better, that our problems are just temporary. And, sure, they have been wrong, every single year, since 2008, and sure, they and their class get richer and richer while they do it, but still, couldn't that be just luck?

There is no way of knowing, ever, is there? Who is right, and who is wrong, or what we should do or whether we should change things. We just have to wait and see, don't we?

And maybe Arthur was right, also, when he said there's nothing we can do. Well, he didn't say there was *nothing* that you could do, did he? We can do something. You can do it too. We can bet on it. We can bet on the end of the world. We can bet that interest rates will always be less than inflation; that the economy will always collapse. That house prices and stock prices and gold prices will go up, making the rich richer while wages stagnate and, in real terms, collapse. We can do that, right? We can all do that. And if we do that, then we can all get rich from it? Can't we? As long as we're lucky enough. We can all of us get rich from the end of the world, but not stop it, just watch it collapse.

You know, I had a friend when I was child. He didn't have a father, he only had a mother, and his family was much poorer than mine. His mother would often skip meals, so that the children could eat, and she thought that my friend, and his sisters, didn't notice. But they did notice. I know. Because he told me.

I don't know, I suppose, games are like that. Sometimes you win and sometimes you lose. And, you know, what's more important than winning? I don't know. I can think of nothing.

19

I TOLD KYLE TO GIVE ME TWO WEEKS.

I don't know why I asked for those two weeks. I suppose I wasn't ready yet. I hadn't known that I would win my freedom that day. I needed a little time to breathe it in.

I went into work every single day, in those two weeks, and I stayed in for the full work hours. Well, my contracted hours, which were nine to five.

Why did I do that? I'm not sure. I think I just wanted to hear the sounds. That Tokyo trading floor was not my trading floor, of course. It was not the trading floor where I made my name. It is not the trading floor I see in my dreams.

But still, though, it was a trading floor. It was a place where men compete with each other, to try to make money, to try to be right, to try to be better than one another and to buy flats without doors but with rotating walls, and where all of their dreams don't come true. A place where young kids can still come from nowhere, and suddenly be the best in the world, though they almost never do, and where old rich men and young rich boys, alike, look across at them, as they walk to the bathroom and think:

"Look at him, with his stupid shirt from Topman. What the fuck has he got that I don't?"

And, you know, as we've said, maybe they're right, maybe the whole thing was really just luck.

Sometimes, you know, I still hope it was luck. God knows if it wasn't, the future's not good.

. . .

And then it came, my final day on the trading floor. I didn't have to say many goodbyes. I went to Florent Leboeuf, and we spoke and laughed a little about his recent womanizing, and he said he'd get in touch next time he passed through London. He never did.

And I went to the lunch connoisseurs, and we spoke a little about what we'd been having for our lunches, and they said, "Oh Gary, your Japanese is so good."

And I went and spoke to Kousuke, lastly, and I thanked him so much for everything, and he smiled and waved his hand right in front of his own nose and he just said in Japanese, "That's OK, that's OK," and after that I never saw him again.

There was no applause when I walked off the trading floor, but this time I did stop to look back, just once.

20

I WENT AND I UNLOCKED MY LITTLE YELLOW BICYCLE. IT WAS chained to a lamp post by the side of the bank. I put my bag down and I unbuttoned my striped white shirt, and I scrunched it up and I put it into the bag. It was very, very hot outside, and I took out a little gray 7-Eleven vest, which had been a gift from Wizard when she had first arrived in Japan, and which always made the staff at 7-Eleven laugh, and I put it on, and I decided, this time, not to cycle home, but instead to walk, one more time, through the Outer Garden of the Palace.

It took a fair while to walk home, and the sun shone down hard on my skin. I walked my little yellow bicycle through the million identical trees, and I tried to count them, but I kept getting distracted.

I wondered what it meant that I was leaving, and I wondered who was right, and who was wrong.

Was the Frog right, that I would run out of money? That eventually I'd come crawling back?

Was Arthur right, that there is nothing to do when the world is collapsing? That we can do nothing but profit and watch?

Was I right? That the economy *would* keep collapsing? That life would just get worse and worse?

And what about the rest of us? Were any of us right? Was Chuck right, to pile up his coins and get lost? Was Caleb right? To leave and come back. What about JB, and Harry, and Snoopy? What were we doing? Were any of us right?

It was too much, and I couldn't count any of the trees, I couldn't number them all up. And I could feel the sun burning the back of my neck and my shoulders, and I thought maybe I should take out my shirt.

But then I thought, no, no, just leave it, because you never know when you'll come back.

So the sun of Japan burnt my shoulders, and I tried to stop thinking at all, and I walked to the sound of cicadas, and I tried to taste the wet heat of the air.

After that, I flew back to London, to try to find a game I couldn't win.

And I thought, I don't care if I win anymore, but I should really stop playing alone.

Play this one with me.

Good Luck.

Postscript

(AS TOLD TO ME MANY YEARS LATER, IN A BEAUTIFUL VILLAGE PUB, IN Harpenden, Hertfordshire, by William Douglas Anthony Gary Thomas, in a lilting and slightly drunk Scouse.)

"You know, the day that you left, there was a conference call. It wasn't for you leaving or anything, it was just the monthly call. It happened to fall on the day that you left. So, everyone was on the call, all the STIRT traders and all the STIRT management, in New York and London and Tokyo and Sydney, as well as Chuck (for Chuck hadn't died, he'd had his tumor removed and been "promoted" to Singapore). Maybe about twenty-six or twenty-seven traders and management, in all.

"And we did the usual stuff, talking about trades, talking about markets, and then at the end, Caleb came in and he just said, 'I would like to let everyone know that today was Gary Stevenson's last day at Citibank.'

"And then nobody said anything and there was just a bit of silence for a bit. And then fucking Chuck came in and he just said, 'So who won then? Gary, or Citibank?'

"And then there was a little fuzz and a click and a crackle, of Caleb unmuting his phone, and then all he said was, 'Gary won.'

"And then no one said anything, but all you heard was about ten or fifteen little clicks as everyone whose phone wasn't on mute muted their phone quickly, and then, once everyone's phone was muted, we all pissed ourselves laughing, even the Frog."

THE END

Acknowledgments

There are a few people without whom this book would probably never have happened. Firstly, my agent, Chris Wellbelove, who was the first person to ever suggest that I write a book, and was politely told to sling it. Secondly Louise Dunnigan, who persuaded me that said book was actually not that bad, when I'd given up on it. Finally my sister, Deborah/Debris Stevenson, who taught me that shape and structure were things that I could manage, and that even mathsboys can write books.

I should thank everyone who read the book as I wrote it, and helped to shape it—my editors Tom Penn and Paul Whitlatch—and all my friends who were in the Google Doc, reading it on their trains on the way to work, especially Anastasia DeRosa and Richard Parasram.

I have to thank the real-life inspirations for Billy, Caleb, Snoopy, Titzy, JB, Rupert, Rodin, Hongo, Chuck, Arthur, Kousuke, Kyle, Gerald, Jamie, the Icicle, the Frog, the Slug, and most of all, Harry and Wizard. You were beautiful, you were terrible, you were wonderful. You gave me no choice but to write.

Finally I would like to thank God, or whoever it was who made it so easy to bet on terrible things, but so hard to stop them. Were it not for you, I'd probably be on a beach somewhere, getting sunburnt and bored out my skull.

ABOUT THE AUTHOR

GARY STEVENSON left his trading career behind, convinced that solving inequality was the only way to repair the world economy. He has since studied for an MPhil at Oxford, worked with economic think tanks, and founded a YouTube channel, GarysEconomics, teaching people about real-world economics. He regularly appears on television and radio and has written for *The Guardian* and Open-Democracy, among others.

YouTube, Twitter, Instagram, Facebook, Tiktok:
@GarysEconomics

thetradinggamebook.com

ABOUT THE TYPE

This book was set in Electra, a typeface designed for Linotype by W. A. Dwiggins, the renowned type designer (1880–1956). Electra is a fluid typeface, avoiding the contrasts of thick and thin strokes that are prevalent in most modern typefaces.